DATE DUE

FEB 1 1 1993	
MAR 2 6 1993	
JAN 3 1 1994	
FEB - 5 1994	
NOV 2 9 1995 MAR 2 1	
APR - 1 1997	
NOV 2 0 2000	
NOV 1 0 2003	

BRODART, INC.   Cat. No. 23-221

MARY GREW

Mary Grew

MARY GREW

Abolitionist and Feminist
(1813–1896)

Ira V. Brown

Selinsgrove: Susquehanna University Press
London and Toronto: Associated University Presses

Associated University Presses
440 Forsgate Drive
Cranbury, NJ 08512

Associated University Presses
25 Sicilian Avenue
London WC1A 2QH, England

Associated University Presses
P.O. Box 39, Clarkson Pstl. Stn.
Mississauga, Ontario,
L5J 3X9 Canada

The paper used in this publication meets the requirements of the American National Standard for Permanence of Paper for Printed Library Materials Z39.48-1984.

Library of Congress Cataloging-in-Publication Data

Brown, Ira V. (Ira Vernon), 1922–
    Mary Grew, abolitionist and feminist, 1813–1896 / Ira V. Brown.
        p.   cm.
    Includes bibliographical references (p.   ) and index.
    ISBN 0-945636-20-2 (alk. paper)
    1. Grew, Mary, 1813–1896.   2. Social reformers—United States—
Biography.   3. Feminists—United States—Biography.
4. Abolitionists—United States—Biography.   I. Title.
HQ1413.G76B76   1991
305.42′092—dc20
[B]   90-50769
                                                       CIP

Contents

Preface

IN many cases, pioneers in the American woman's rights movement served an apprenticeship in the antislavery crusade.[1] Two Pennsylvania women are especially good illustrations of this connection. The best known of these is Lucretia Mott (1793–1880), whose contributions to both movements were substantial and whose name is familiar to historians.[2] Another significant Pennsylvania abolitionist and feminist was Mary Grew (1813–96), the subject of this biography, whose life and work have been neglected by students of these two social reform movements.[3]

Born in Hartford, Connecticut, and educated at Catharine Beecher's Hartford Female Seminary, Mary Grew settled in Philadelphia in 1834 and resided there until her death. Despite considerable illness, she worked steadily in the antislavery crusade from 1834 to 1865, in the Negro suffrage campaign from 1865 to 1870, and in the woman's rights movement from 1848 to 1892, her eightieth year. She was corresponding secretary of the Philadelphia Female Anti-Slavery Society from 1836 to 1870 and wrote its annual printed reports. She was one of the eight women delegates denied seats in the World's Anti-Slavery Convention, which met in London in 1840. Elizabeth Cady Stanton dated the inception of the woman's rights movement from the rejection of the American female delegates to this convention. According to tradition, she and Lucretia Mott made a resolution at that time to hold a woman's rights convention after their return to the United States. This they did at Seneca Falls, New York, in 1848.

In addition to her work for the Philadelphia Female Anti-Slavery Society, including direction of many of its fund-raising bazaars, Mary Grew was a member of the executive committee of the Pennsylvania State Anti-Slavery Society from 1844 to 1865 and served for several years as editor of its newspaper, the *Pennsylvania Freeman*. She followed William Lloyd Garrison after the 1840 schism in the American Anti-Slavery Society. She disagreed with Garrison, however, on the question of continuing the antislavery societies after the passage of the Thirteenth Amendment; she thought it was essential to do this until the freedmen were firmly protected in their right to vote. Beginning in

1848 she labored for married women's property legislation. When the Pennsylvania Woman Suffrage Association, an affiliate of Lucy Stone's American Woman Suffrage Association, was organized in 1869, she was chosen as its president, a position she held until 1892, when she decided at the age of seventy-nine that it was time to retire. She died in 1896 at the age of eighty-three.

This biography is based chiefly on primary sources, and to a large extent Mary Grew is allowed to tell her story in her own words. She wrote extremely well and had unusually legible handwriting. I was able to obtain photocopies of several hundred of her letters from a number of different depositories. Particularly interesting was her correspondence with Wendell and Ann Phillips, in the Crawford Blagden Collection, which was recently acquired by the Houghton Library of Harvard University. Ann Phillips was Mary Grew's cousin. Also very useful were the papers of Sydney Howard Gay and his wife Elizabeth Neall Gay, which are preserved in the manuscripts division of the Columbia University library.

The minute books and correspondence of the Philadelphia Female Anti-Slavery Society and the Pennsylvania Anti-Slavery Society are held by the Historical Society of Pennsylvania and are now available through University Microfilms in the Microform Publication of the Papers of the Pennsylvania Abolition Society at the Historical Society of Pennsylvania. The records of the National American Woman Suffrage Association at the Library of Congress include letters from Mary Grew to Lucy Stone and Henry Blackwell. I am grateful to Dr. Lori D. Ginzberg of the Pennsylvania State University for making copies of these for me. The vast antislavery collections of the Boston Public Library, particularly the papers of William Lloyd Garrison, were very useful. The Sophia Smith Collection at Smith College and the Friends Historical Library of Swarthmore College also kindly supplied me with copies of Mary Grew letters. The Schlesinger Library of Radcliffe College provided me with a typewritten copy of her diary of her trip to London to attend the World's Anti-Slavery Convention. I am deeply indebted to the staffs of these institutions for their generosity in making it possible for me to use this invaluable manuscript material.

Also very useful in my research were the three newspapers that served as organs of reform societies with which Mary Grew was associated: the *Pennsylvania Freeman* (Philadelphia), sponsored by the Pennsylvania Anti-Slavery Society from 1838 to 1854; the *National Anti-Slavery Standard* (New York), vehicle of the American Anti-Slavery Society and outlet for the Pennsylvania society from 1854 to 1870; and the *Woman's Journal* (Boston), which reported on activities of the Pennsylvania Woman Suffrage Association during the period of Mary Grew's presidency, 1869–92.

Other important sources were the proceedings and annual reports of the various reform societies. Especially notable are the reports of the Philadelphia Female Anti-Slavery Society, written by Mary Grew and published in pamphlet form from 1836 to 1870.

I found much of value in *The Letters of William Lloyd Garrison,* edited by Walter M. Merrill and Louis Ruchames, and in the *History of Woman Suffrage,* edited by Elizabeth Cady Stanton and others. William Cohen's master's thesis on the Pennsylvania Anti-Slavery Society (Columbia University, 1960) and his doctoral dissertation on James Miller McKim (New York University, 1968) were of help in my research on Pennsylvania abolitionism.

A gifted writer, Mary Grew was also an able public speaker. She was one of the small band of pioneers who broke the taboo against women addressing mixed assemblies. Though small in stature and plain in appearance, as well as modest and unassuming in manner, she made her influence felt effectively. She worked well in groups. She got along well with people even when she disagreed with them. While her ideas were radical for their time, her manner was conservative.

I have followed a conventional biographical method, for the most part narrative rather than analytical. While my approach to the subject is sympathetic, I have generally let the record speak for itself, avoiding speculation on such intriguing questions as why Mary Grew never married. I have not tried to go beyond the evidence available to me as a historian.

I owe a great debt to the staff of the Pennsylvania State University Libraries, especially the Inter-Library Loan department and the Microforms section. Dr. Charles D. Ameringer, head of the History Department, and Dean Hart Nelsen of the College of the Liberal Arts at Penn State kindly gave me a leave of absence that greatly facilitated my research. Mrs. Sara T. Close did an expert job of typing.

I am indebted to an anonymous reader chosen by the Susquehanna University Press who gave the manuscript a searching critique and made many suggestions for improvement.

Three of my former students were of help to me in producing this book: Mrs. Katherine Y. Armitage, who assisted me in the research I did for my sketch of Mary Grew in *Notable American Women* some years ago; Warren P. Faust, who wrote a paper on Mary Grew for his master's essay at Penn State in 1978; and the Reverend Robert S. Hochreiter, who wrote a history of the *Pennsylvania Freeman* for his doctorate in 1980.

My wife, Helen M. Brown, provided wise counsel and unfailing moral support.

MARY GREW

1
An Antislavery Apprenticeship (1813–1840)

LIKE Lucretia Mott, Mary Grew was a transplanted New Englander. She was born in Hartford, Connecticut, on 1 September 1813.[1] Her grandfather, John Grew (1752–1800), resided in Birmingham, England, where he belonged to the circle of liberals associated with Dr. Joseph Priestley, a distinguished Unitarian clergyman remembered mainly for his discovery of oxygen.[2] Birmingham was noted as a center of religious and political dissent as well as of opposition to the slave trade. Mary's father, the Reverend Henry Grew (1781–1862), was born in Birmingham but came to the United States with his parents in 1795. He lived for a time in Providence, Rhode Island. He was pastor of the First Baptist Church of Hartford from 1807 to 1811.[3] By nature rather contentious, he became involved in a dispute with his congregation over the observance of civilly appointed fasts and thanksgiving days. He also was suspected of holding some unorthodox theological views, and he resigned or was dismissed from his pastorate. He was the author of a number of religious tracts.[4]

Apparently he was a man of independent means. In a letter to Wendell and Ann Phillips, he spoke of expecting daily "another amount of rent from England."[5] In his 1861 will, written a year before his death, he provided a ten thousand dollar trust fund for his wife and gifts not only to his children but also to a dozen different benevolent and social reform agencies, one of which was the Pennsylvania Anti-Slavery Society.[6] He devoted his life mainly to the work of such groups.

Henry Grew was married four times; his first three wives preceded him in death. By them he had six children. Mary Grew's mother was Kate Merrow (1812–45) of East Hartford, the third of Henry's wives. Mary was the fifth of Henry's children, the eldest by this marriage. She was quite close to her half-sister Susan (1804–81), who spent much of her life in Providence, Rhode Island. Susan also became an abolitionist. One of Mary's cousins, Ann Terry Greene, married Wendell Phillips, abolitionism's premier orator. Ann's mother, Henry Grew's sister, was also named Mary, as was Henry's mother. The name Mary carried through three generations.[7]

Mary Grew studied at the Hartford Female Seminary, founded by Catharine Beecher in 1823 and directed by her until 1831.[8] When the school was incorporated in 1827, Henry Grew bought stock in it.[9] In the same year, the school moved into "its own handsome neoclassical building."[10] Mary's name appears in the school's catalogs for 1828 and 1829. At that time the school had a staff of eight teachers and offered a complete classical curriculum comparable to that provided boys in the best academies of the day. Catharine Beecher herself taught a course in moral philosophy. She wanted to prove to the world that the character of individuals could be "made over": "Women would first themselves be made over and then they would reshape the society."[11] She also remarked that "a lady should study, not to shine, but to act."[12] While a pupil at the Hartford Female Seminary, Mary Grew taught a Sunday school class for black children.[13]

In the early 1830s the family moved to Boston. On 10 March 1834 Henry Grew gave a public address in that city's Masonic Temple under the auspices of the New England Anti-Slavery Society.[14] Later that year the family settled in Philadelphia, which remained their home thereafter. Mary Grew and her half-sister Susan soon joined the Philadelphia Female Anti-Slavery Society, which had been organized on 9 December 1833, only a few days after the American Anti-Slavery Society had been founded in Philadelphia, during 4–6 December 1833. In the preamble of their constitution the women declared that slavery and race prejudice were "contrary to the laws of God, and to the principles of our far-famed Declaration of Independence." They deemed it their duty "as professing Christians" to manifest their abhorrence of the "flagrant injustice and deep sin of slavery" and vowed to work toward "its speedy removal" and the restoration to "the people of colour" their "inalienable rights."[15]

Contrary to what one would think, Lucretia Mott, the most prominent of the society's founders, was not chosen president. This honor went to Esther Moore, the wife of Dr. Robert Moore, a Quaker physician. The first recording secretary was Margaretta Forten, daughter of James Forten, a prosperous sail maker who was for some years Philadelphia's leading black. Lucretia Mott was chosen corresponding secretary.[16] Officers were chosen annually. In later years Mrs. Mott occasionally served as president, but throughout most of the society's long history (1833–70) this position was held by Sarah Pugh, a teacher. She and Mary Grew, who became corresponding secretary in 1836 and held the position until the society was dissolved, were its most active members.

On 13 November 1834 the society opened a school for black children, and Mary Grew was put in charge of it. By 2 April 1835 the school had twenty-seven pupils. On 7 May 1835 the society's board of managers expressed their thanks to her for superintending this school.[17] Mary Grew became convinced that black people had an equal intellectual capacity with whites if they were given equal educational opportunities.[18] It is not clear how long she continued in this position. In later years the society supported a school taught by one of its black members, Sarah Mapps Douglass.

The society gave Mary Grew another important assignment on 11 August 1835 in connection with arrangements for a petition to Congress asking for the abolition of slavery in the District of Columbia. She was appointed to a committee charged with responsibility for soliciting signatures. This was an arduous task. Many, probably most, of those contacted refused to sign. However, she wrote later, "We do not regard those visits as lost labor, where our request is denied, or that time wasted which is spent in unsuccessful efforts to convince persons of their duty to comply with it." Often, "the seed then laboriously sown, falls into good ground, and after a little season springs up, bringing forth fruit, some thirty, some sixty, some an hundred fold."[19] Mary Grew was an inveterate optimist.

Early in 1836 Senator Samuel McKean and Congressman James Harper presented the society's petitions in Washington. Both men warned the Philadelphia women that such memorials might do more harm than good. McKean wrote that while he agreed with the ladies on the evils of slavery, he thought that, in the light of "the present excited and exasperated state of public feeling," the petitions might actually add to "the sum of moral evil and human misery" and delay the consummation of "the object we devoutly desire."[20] Harper expressed the opinion that "there never has been, there never can be, a more perplexing question presented to the statesman and philanthropist than the abolition of slavery in the U. States."[21] Before long, the House of Representatives adopted a "gag rule" providing that antislavery petitions would be automatically tabled without debate. The Senate provided for automatic rejection of the prayers of such petitions.[22]

At the annual meeting of the society on 4 January 1836, Mary Grew was chosen corresponding secretary. In this capacity she wrote its annual reports, most of which were published in pamphlet form. On 8 September 1836 she was appointed to a committee to prepare an address to the women of Pennsylvania on the subject of slavery, which was also published. It is probable that Mary Grew wrote this address. In this eight-page pamphlet the society called attention to the complicity of Northerners in maintaining the institution of slavery and appealed to Northern women to sign a petition for the abolition of slavery in the District of Columbia and other federal territories and for the prohibition of the interstate slave trade.[23]

At the same meeting (8 September 1836) Mary Grew was appointed to a committee to make arrangements for a "public sale." Out of this decision came the first of a long series of annual "fairs" or "bazaars" held shortly before Christmas from 1836 through 1861. In addition to raising money, the fairs had a considerable propaganda value. Many of the sale items bore antislavery drawings and mottoes. The most popular of these were the two based on the famous Wedgwood medallion (1787) of a male slave in chains kneeling in a posture of supplication, inscribed with the words "Am I Not a Man and a Brother?" Quite similar, but appearing some years later, was the emblem "Am I Not a Woman and a Sister?" whose history and significance have been brilliantly analyzed in a recent book by Professor Jean Fagan Yellin.[24]

On 4 August 1836 Maria Weston Chapman, on behalf of the Boston Female Anti-Slavery Society, addressed a letter to Mary Grew proposing the formation of a national executive committee to coordinate the work of the female societies, especially as it related to the petitions with which these groups were bombarding Congress. On behalf of the Philadelphia society, Mary Grew replied that the proposal was "expedient and desirable," though some of their members would much prefer a recognition of female members and delegates in the American Anti-Slavery Society, still a citadel of men. The Philadelphia women went on to suggest that a convention be held in New York City during the second week of May 1837.[25]

"Do not despair of Pennsylvania," Mary Grew wrote the Boston women on 18 November 1836. "She will do her part of the work yet. The mantles which have fallen from Penn, Woolman, Benezet, and a host of kindred spirits, are being gathered up, and the spirit of the fathers shall live again in the sons."[26] On 25 February 1837 Benjamin Lundy's Philadelphia paper, the *National Enquirer and Constitutional Advocate of Universal Liberty,* published an editorial endorsing the proposed female antislavery convention to be held in New York:

The Grimkés, the Motts, the Grews, the Chapmans, the Clarks with hundreds of noble kindred spirits, it is to be hoped, will there assemble, and, by a concentration of moral power and influence, give a new spring to active energy—a fresh and irresistible impetus to the ball of reformation.[27]

Other female antislavery societies were notified and asked to send representatives to this convention, which assembled in New York on Tuesday, 9 May 1837, at 4:00 P.M. Seventy-one delegates, including a number of blacks, were present for this unprecedented national convention of women. Massachusetts and Pennsylvania sent the largest contingents, 22 each. New York sent 19, Rhode Island, 3, New Hampshire and Ohio, 2 each, and New Jersey, 1. Sarah and Angelina Grimké were listed among 103 "corresponding members," but they were present and participated actively. Lucretia Mott served as temporary chairman, but Mary S. Parker of Boston was chosen president. Mary Grew was selected as one of four secretaries. She was also appointed to a committee to prepare a "Letter to the Women of Great Britain" and another to revise Angelina Grimké's "Appeal to the Women of the *nominally* Free States." The convention adopted a great variety of antislavery resolutions: declaring that the antislavery cause was "the cause of God"; asserting that slaveholding was wrong in principle, not just because slaves were mistreated; censuring the American Colonization Society; condemning Northern complicity in the preservation of slavery; and denouncing race prejudice.[28]

The chief controversy in the convention grew out of a resolution proposed by Angelina Grimké declaring that the time had come for woman to move out of the constricted sphere to which "corrupt custom and a perverted application of Scripture" had confined her and to do all that she could "by her voice, and her pen, and her purse, and the influence of her example, to overthrow the horrible system of American slavery."[29] Several amendments were proposed, including one by Mary Grew (not specified in the *Proceedings*), but the resolution was finally adopted without change, though not unanimously. Twelve women were listed as objecting to "some parts of it." On the final day of the convention, Friday, 12 May, Mary Grew moved that it be adjourned to meet in Philadelphia during the third week of May 1838.

The Anti-Slavery Convention of American Women recommended a plan for circulating petitions in each county of the free states, asking Congress to abolish slavery in the District of Columbia and other federal territories and to prohibit the interstate slave trade. The Philadelphia women soon thereafter appointed a committee to arrange for the printing and circulation of such petitions. They assigned each of the eastern and central counties of Pennsylvania to one of their members for this purpose. Mary Grew was made responsible for

sending petitions to Lehigh and Tioga Counties. She was also instructed to write to the female antislavery society of Pittsburgh, asking
that its officers arrange for the circulation of petitions in the counties
west of the mountains.[30] Within a few weeks two thousand petitions
were printed and ready for signatures. A circular from the Anti-
Slavery Convention of American Women suggested that "when all the
maids and matrons of the land knock at the door of Congress, our
Statesmen must legislate."[31] On 12 October 1837 the Philadelphia
society resolved to circulate petitions opposing the annexation of
Texas.[32]

Professor Gerda Lerner has analyzed 402 petitions against the
annexation of Texas sent to the Twenty-fifth Congress in 1837–38
and found that women predominated among the signers. She concluded that the petitioning activities of antislavery women in the
1830s and 1840s were "of far greater significance to the building of
the antislavery movement than has been previously recognized." She
also suggested that these activities "contributed directly to the development of a contingent of local and regional women leaders, many
of whom were to transfer their political concerns to feminist activities
after 1848."[33] Their work in the antislavery movement gave them
political experience that they were able to put to good use in fighting
later for the rights of women.

In the fourth annual report of the Philadelphia society, the first one
to be printed, Mary Grew noted that the number of signatures to
petitions obtained in the city during 1837 had exceeded those of 1836
by about one thousand.[34] She further reported that more than forty
new members had joined the society during the year.[35] In this document she also commented on the death of Elijah P. Lovejoy on 7
November 1837 at the hands of an antiabolitionist mob. "The murderous blow which has bereaved us of a beloved brother and valiant
coadjutor" had been leveled not at him alone but at "the foundation of
civil and religious liberty; at the inalienable right of free discussion,
and, therefore, at every Anti-Slavery Society in the land." Nevertheless, she regretted that he had used force to defend his press. She
wished that he had perished girded only with the "whole armor of
God," having his "feet shod with the preparation of the *gospel of
peace.*"[36] On 14 December 1837 the society had instructed its corresponding secretary to transmit to Lovejoy's widow such funds as
could be raised for her "with the assurance of our heartfelt sympathy
in her deep affliction."[37]

On 8 February 1838, acting in behalf of the Philadelphia Female
Anti-Slavery Society, Mary Grew addressed a circular to other similar
groups throughout the North announcing that a second Anti-Slavery

Convention of American Women would meet in Philadelphia on the third Tuesday in May. She expressed the hope that the meeting would "convince our friends and enemies that we intend to promote this cause of God by spiritual weapons alone." The Philadelphia women would be happy to extend to their "respected coadjutors, the hospitalities of the land of Penn."[38] As it turned out, the Quaker City proved a good deal less than hospitable to the antislavery women.

Mary Grew was appointed to the local arrangements committee for the convention, which met on 15 May 1838 in a handsome new building called Pennsylvania Hall, erected at Sixth and Haines Street with funds collected largely from abolitionists and dedicated to the principle of "free discussion," not only of slavery but of other political and social issues.[39] Abolitionists had been experiencing difficulty in finding quarters in which to hold their meetings and had determined to construct a building of their own. Stock had been sold in shares of twenty dollars each in order to raise the forty thousand dollars needed for this purpose. Many of the subscribers were women. Henry Grew chaired the session that organized the Pennsylvania Hall Association and served on its board of managers.[40] This group raised the funds and supervised the construction of the building, which contained four stores, two committee rooms, a lecture hall on the first floor, and a large auditorium with galleries on the second floor.[41] It was officially opened for use on Monday, 14 May 1838.

Because no space was available in Pennsylvania Hall on Wednesday, 16 May, the women's convention met in Temperance Hall for their second session. At that time, Mary Grew offered a resolution declaring that it was "our duty to keep ourselves separate from those churches which receive to their pulpits and their communion tables, those who buy, or sell, or hold as property, the image of the living God."[42] A lengthy and animated discussion ensued. Six delegates spoke in favor of the resolution and five against it. The dissenters argued that they could do more for the antislavery cause by working within their churches instead of withdrawing from them. The resolution was adopted by a divided vote.[43]

That evening William Lloyd Garrison and several women, including Lucretia Mott and Angelina Grimké Weld, spoke at a public meeting in the large auditorium of Pennsylvania Hall, which was packed to capacity by a mixed audience of three thousand men and women, white and black. This was not an official session of the Anti-Slavery Convention of American Women; indeed, many of its members considered it improper for women to address audiences consisting of both sexes. A mob gathered outside the hall and began throwing rocks at the windows. The glass was smashed, but no one in the auditorium was injured, because shutters *inside* the windows were securely fastened. Considerably shaken but unharmed, the women returned to their lodgings for the night. They held another official session in the small lecture room of the building on Thursday morning. Again a mob gathered, and the managers of the hall appealed for police protection. Instead of providing this, the mayor of the city came to the hall, ordered the building closed and locked, appealed to the crowd to disperse, and then left. The mob remained, forced open the doors of the hall, and set it afire. It was soon left a smoking ruin. It had been open for "free discussion" only four days.[44]

Most Northern newspapers condemned the violence but took pains to say that the abolitionists had brought it on themselves by mixing the races and sexes in public assembly. Newspapers all over the country carried reports that white female delegates to the antislavery conventions had been seen walking arm-in-arm with black male delegates.[45] Some even went so far as to suggest that interracial meetings were but a prelude to interracial marriage. A Saint Louis paper said that Pennsylvania Hall should not have been called a "Temple of Freedom" but a "Temple of Amalgamation," that is, miscegenation.[46] The New York *Commercial Advertiser* said that those "females who so far forget the province of their sex as to perambulate the country" in order to attend antislavery meetings should be sent to insane asylums.[47]

Undaunted by the threat of further mob action, members of the Anti-Slavery Convention of American Women converged for the next meeting on Temperance Hall, where they had previously agreed to meet on Friday. They found the door closed against them, the building's owners fearing that it would meet the same fate as Pennsylvania Hall. Sarah Pugh, president of the Philadelphia female organization, offered the use of her schoolroom as a place for the convention's closing session. At that time the members adopted a resolution proposed by Sarah Grimké that it was the duty of abolitionists to combat race prejudice by sitting with black people in their churches, "by appearing with them in our streets, by giving them our countenance in steam-boats and stages, by visiting them at their homes, and encouraging them to visit us, receiving them as we do our white fellow citizens."[48] This motion was passed by a divided vote. Finally, the convention decided to hold another meeting in Philadelphia in May 1839.[49]

At its next meeting the Philadelphia Female Anti-Slavery Society passed a resolution declaring that the burning of Pennsylvania Hall "because the principles of the Declaration of Independence were there advocated and maintained" demanded from its members "redoubled efforts to awaken the public mind to a sense of the ruin in which the enslavement of a part of our countrymen threatens to involve the liberties of all."[50] In the society's next annual report Mary Grew wrote that "though the flames of a thousand temples, dedicated to liberty or religion" were to rise on "the midnight air" and though "the dwelling of every lover of truth be levelled with the dust," the truth would still exist, "immutable, eternal." "The citadel of slavery" would be "stormed, and taken, and destroyed, for the promise is certain, and the fulfillment sure."[51]

Writing to Anne Warren Weston of Boston on Christmas Day 1838, Mary Grew expressed the hope that "our New England friends" had not repented of their decision to hold another meeting in the "City of Brotherly Love" next May. "We will endeavor to give you a better reception, and accommodations, than you met with last spring." The cause was prospering in Philadelphia, she wrote with characteristic optimism, "and public opinion is improving."[52] However, there was difficulty finding a suitable place for the convention to meet. The women finally settled on the hall of the Pennsylvania Riding School, where 102 delegates assembled on Wednesday, 1 May 1839. Mary Grew had served on the local arrangements committee, had called the convention to order, was appointed to the business committee, and served as one of its four secretaries.[53] This meeting was undisturbed. The women adopted resolutions and issued circulars similar to those emanating from the two previous gatherings. They agreed to meet in Boston the following year. That meeting was never held, because by that time women had been fully integrated into the work of the American Anti-Slavery Society.

The significance of these three trailblazing women's conventions is twofold. In the first place, they enabled women who had previously known each other only through correspondence to become personally acquainted and inspired to greater zeal in a difficult undertaking. In the second place, they gave women such as Lucretia Mott and Mary Grew political experience that they were able to put to good use in their ensuing campaign for woman's rights. Elizabeth Cady Stanton considered these conventions to have been the prelude to the organized campaign for woman suffrage that began at Seneca Falls, New York, ten years later.[54] Dr. Keith E. Melder, one of the first historians to study female abolitionism, has written, "Most women who attended them agreed that these conventions of women combined exhilaration and liberation, with a strong sense of sisterhood, and an awareness of braving the prejudice of the world outside."[55]

Among other subjects discussed at the 1839 convention was the question of duties owed by abolitionists to the free black population of the North. In accordance with the spirit of a resolution passed at that convention, the Philadelphia women divided their city into sections, appointing two visitors for each section whose responsibility it would be to get acquainted with all the black residents therein and offer them such instruction and assistance as they could. They also continued to support Sarah M. Douglass's school for colored girls.[56]

In addition to procuring signatures asking Congress to abolish slavery in the District of Columbia and in Florida and to prohibit the interstate slave trade, in 1839 they circulated a petition to the General Assembly of Pennsylvania, praying them to grant a jury trial to persons claimed as fugitive slaves.[57]

On 10 October 1839 and for some years thereafter, Mary Grew was chosen as a delegate to annual conventions of the American Free Produce Association, the first of which met in Philadelphia on 15 and 16 October of that year, with more than one hundred persons in attendance.[58] In her annual report for 1839 she urged the duty of abstinence from the use of the products of slave labor. She also denounced the complicity of American churches in the institution of slavery and assailed "that stern and cruel prejudice" against blacks that she thought was "deeply rooted, and warmly cherished in the breasts of Americans."[59] Finally, she took note of the death of Benjamin Lundy, remarking on his "generous and self-sacrificing consecration" to the antislavery cause.[60]

Dispute over the role of women in the antislavery movement precipitated a schism in the American Anti-Slavery Society in 1840. It is true there were other sources of discord, such as the question of whether abolitionists should organize a third party, but the "woman question" was the last straw. In 1839, a few days after the final session of the Anti-Slavery Convention of American Women in Philadelphia, the American Anti-Slavery Society met in New York and, following Garrison's lead, granted women the right to take part in its proceedings.[61] In May 1840 Garrison packed the national convention with his followers, and the society voted to permit the election of women as officers. By a vote of 557 to 451, the convention approved the appointment of Abby Kelley to its business committee. Lucretia Mott, Lydia Maria Child, and Maria Weston Chapman were named to the executive committee for the ensuing year.[62] Those men opposed to women serving as officers promptly withdrew and formed the American and Foreign Anti-Slavery Society under the leadership of Arthur and Lewis Tappan, Henry B. Stanton, and James G. Birney.[63] This group, which became known as "the New Organization," contributed to the formation of the Liberty Party, which ran Birney for the presidency of the United States in 1840. Members of the Pennsylvania

Anti-Slavery Society generally remained loyal to "the Old Organization." They followed Garrison, favored equal rights for women, and were opposed to political parties. The Pennsylvania state society, which had been organized early in 1837, had admitted women to membership in October 1838 and chose Sarah Pugh to its executive committee in May 1841.[64]

In her annual report for 1840 Mary Grew commented on the "melancholy fact that division has entered our ranks, once so closely linked together. . . . While we view these events with deeply painful feelings, we do not consider them cause for despondency." Refusing to analyze the origins and nature of the dispute, she preferred to express the gratitude of her Philadelphia cohorts that the quarrel had not been "permitted to interrupt the harmony of our own association." (The Boston Female Anti-Slavery Society had been practically destroyed by the divisions in the national organization.) She preferred to look on the bright side.

> *Our cause is prospering,* amid all its difficulties, the evidences of its progress are all around us, and our opponents may see them if they choose. It prospers and will ultimately triumph, because it is a righteous cause.[65]

Only one month after the split in the American Anti-Slavery Society over "the woman question," Mary Grew and others of her female associates faced another crisis. They were excluded from membership in the World's Anti-Slavery Convention, held in London in June 1840. A total of 409 abolitionists participated in this unprecedented international gathering. About 40 were Americans, 6 or 7 French, and the rest from Great Britain and her colonies.[66] The meeting had been suggested by the *New York Emancipator,* organ of the American Anti-Slavery Society, on 28 March 1839. The newly formed British and Foreign Anti-Slavery Society, under the leadership of an English Quaker, Joseph Sturge, in June 1839 had issued invitations to "friends of the Slave of every nation and of every clime" to attend an international conference that would meet in London on 12 June 1840.[67] When the sponsors learned that several American societies were planning to send female delegates, they changed the invitation to include only "gentlemen."[68]

Despite the revised invitation from the London committee that was arranging for the convention, several American antislavery societies went ahead with their plans to send women delegates. From the Philadelphia Female Anti-Slavery Society came Lucretia Mott, Sarah Pugh, Abby Kimber, Elizabeth Neall, and Mary Grew. Lucretia Mott also represented the American Anti-Slavery Society, the Pennsylvania

Anti-Slavery Society, the American Free Produce Society, and the Association of Friends for Promoting the Abolition of Slavery. The Massachusetts Anti-Slavery Society named Abby Southwick, Emily Winslow, and Ann Greene Phillips, along with a number of other women who for one reason or another did not go. Prominent American male delegates included James G. Birney, Wendell Phillips, and Henry B. Stanton.[69] Also present, but not a delegate, was the latter's bride, Elizabeth Cady Stanton, destined to become the founder of the American woman's rights movement. The trip was their honeymoon.

Both Lucretia Mott and Mary Grew kept diaries of the trip, and those documents survive. Mary and her father sailed from New York on the ship *Roscoe* on 7 May 1840. There were thirty-two cabin passengers and twenty-one in steerage. Among those traveling first-class were a group of Garrisonian abolitionists including James and Lucretia Mott, the other Philadelphia women, Emily Winslow, and her father, Isaac, Abby Southwick, and George Bradburn, who had been a Unitarian minister at Nantucket and a member of the Massachusetts legislature.[70] The Phillipses were already traveling in Europe. Mrs. Mott observed that Elizabeth Neall was "the life of our company—a favorite with the Captain & the darling of the passengers." She also noted that "Father Grew" read and preached on the Sabbath and that Mary Grew and George Bradburn became "quite intimate."[71]

"The sea! the open sea!" Mary Grew wrote in her diary, "I am upon it! For the first time in my life, with the broad blue sky above me spread and the mighty ocean round me."[72] The Atlantic crossing took three weeks. On the first day of the voyage the cry "a whale! a whale!" brought passengers to the deck. Within the first five days they experienced two severe storms. On 15 May, however, they were "almost becalmed." Mary Grew was impressed with the beauty of the sunrise and sunset on that day. She also enjoyed the moon "shining brightly on the untroubled waters."

> They had "a pleasant party," she wrote, "consisting of clever persons, whose philosophical and theological diversities are sufficient to produce animated and interesting discussions, which pleasantly employ our time and our thoughts. We roam at will over the wide fields of theology, each earnestly contending for his, or her, own faith; or, if purer metaphysics tempt us, there are materialism,—immaterialism and phrenology—the latter of which has, among us, as zealous a defender as a science was ever blessed with. Or in more *practical* moods, non-resistance,—temperance— and woman's rights, exercise our *combativeness, veneration, conscientiousness,* or *self-esteem,* as the case may be."[73]

She added, "When weary of reading, we talk, and when weary of talking, we are silent." Nothing was done regularly but eating and sleeping, "and scarcely the latter. . . . We rise whenever it suits us, breakfast at nine o'clock, lunch at 12, dine at 4. Take tea at eight." In the evening they usually sang. Women were banished from the dining room after "a moderate quantity of wine" had been consumed by the men, so the latter could talk without restraint.[74]

On 27 May she wrote, "Here we are at last; anchored in the river Mersey, at Liverpool."[75] The passengers went onshore early on the morning of the twenty-eighth and spent the day touring the city. "The houses are strongly built," she observed, "and very black with the dust and smoke of bituminous coal."[76]

Mary Grew and her companions traveled for ten days before going to London for the antislavery convention. They had "a delightful ride" by stagecoach from Liverpool to Chester. She was thrilled by the beauty of the scenery, especially the ever-present green hedges. They passed "fine estates," some old churches, and "fairy cottages." They visited Eaton Hall and the "venerable cathedral" at Chester.[77] On 30 May they arrived in Manchester, which she found "more dirty and smoky than Liverpool or Chester." They visited silk and cotton mills, where she noted that the workers "generally looked healthier and happier than we expected to find them; particularly the children in the silk factory. They attended church services at "an Independent chapel" and heard "an excellent sermon."[78] She wrote,

> It was good again to lift up the voice of thanksgiving and praise, in the courts of the Lord's house. And to join with an English congregation in singing the very hymns and tunes which I have heard from childhood, and feel the strong bond of Christian union with those whose faces I never before saw, and shall never see again.[79]

She also visited two Sunday schools, attended chiefly by children working in the factories.

On 2 June they went by train from Manchester to Birmingham— "my father's birthplace (to me the most interesting of all England's towns and villages)." What attracted her the most were the places where "my dear father played in his boyhood." She thought Birmingham "decidedly the handsomest, *cleanest* town that we have yet seen in England."[80] From there they took excursions to the Norman castle at Warwick, the ruins of Kenilworth, Stratford-on-Avon, and Blenheim Palace. On their way to London they stopped at Oxford, where they visited the Bodleian Library.

On Saturday, 6 June, they arrived in London. Mary Grew thought the Tower one of the most fascinating places in the capital city. On Monday the eighth she visited Elizabeth Pease, a prominent English abolitionist. That evening, at a party held in the London Anti-Slavery Office, she met with "surprise and pleasure" Wendell Phillips, who had been married to her cousin Ann Terry Greene in 1837. Mary Grew was "quite delighted" with Wendell, she wrote, and "every succeeding interview" had increased her love and respect for "his noble intellect and heart."[81] The next morning she spent "a delightful hour or two" with Ann Phillips, "talking of old times and departed friends."[82] In the afternoon she toured the zoological gardens, Westminster Abbey, and the National Gallery.

The Philadelphia delegation found comfortable lodgings at Mark Moore's, No. 6 Queen Street Place, Southwark Bridge, Cheapside. There they met many other abolitionists, including James G. Birney, Henry B. Stanton, and "his nice Elizabeth."[83] On Saturday, 6 June, Joseph Sturge, who had masterminded the convention, breakfasted with the Pennsylvania women and begged them not to contest the decision of the London Committee denying them membership in the convention. "We endeavored to shew him the inconsistency of excluding Women Delegates," Lucretia Mott wrote—"but soon found he had prejudged & made up his mind to act with our New Organization; therefore all reasoning was lost upon him, and our appeals made in vain."[84] On Tuesday, 9 June, they received official notice that women were to be rejected. On Thursday the eleventh, the day before the convention was to begin, Sarah Pugh, on behalf of the Pennsylvania women, drew up and presented a formal protest against their exclusion.[85]

"The first meeting of the Convention, held on the 12th inst.," Mary Grew wrote, "was full of interest, as all concerned had anticipated. The presence of the venerable and beloved Clarkson, the renowned and noble-hearted O'Connell, and many others of the *truly great* of earth, made it a memorable occasion to us."[86] The question of seating women delegates was the first item of business on the convention's agenda. The women entrusted their case to Wendell Phillips, whose wife is supposed to have said to him, "Don't shilly-shally, Wendell!"[87] Phillips proposed the appointment of a committee to prepare an approved list of members of the convention, "with instructions to include in such list all persons bearing credentials from any Anti-Slavery body."[88] An extended debate followed. Several English delegates argued that mixed assemblies of this sort were against "the custom of the country" and that it had never occurred to members of the London committee that they were including women in the invitation to "the friends of the slaves." Many American delegates felt the same way. Indeed, Henry Grew asserted that the admission of women would be not only a violation of British custom but also of "the ordinance of Almighty God!"[89] (It would be interesting to know what Mary Grew thought of her father's position, but surviving documents do not supply this information.) Phillips replied, "We think it right for women to sit by our side [in America], and we think it right for them to do the same here."[90] When the vote was taken on the following day, the male members of the convention decided by an overwhelming majority to deny seats to the female delegates.[91]

The women were allowed to observe the proceedings from the gallery but not to take any part in debates or votes. William Lloyd Garrison, arriving several days later, refused to take his seat in the convention and joined the ladies in the balcony to show his sympathy for woman's rights.[92] The rejected delegates received a great deal of attention in London's social circles. Lucretia Mott became known as "the Lioness of the Convention."[93] "Our delegation is regarded as quite a phenomenon, which every one is anxious to see," Mary Grew wrote in her diary. "We are, almost every day, introduced to numbers of persons who request this *privilege,* and who look upon us with countenances of mingled astonishment and respect."[94] The exclusion of the female delegates produced an unexpected but momentous side effect. Lucretia Mott formed an enduring friendship with Elizabeth Cady Stanton and, according to tradition, they resolved to hold a woman's rights convention when they returned to America.[95] Such a convention was held in Seneca Falls, New York, in 1848, thus inaugurating the woman's rights movement in the United States.

"Well! the Convention has closed," Mary Grew wrote on 23 June. "Its last meeting was held to-day. It has been full of interest, and we trust that great good will result to the cause of freedom from it."[96] Before leaving London she toured the British Museum and Saint Paul's Cathedral, the latter in company with the notorious abolitionist George Thompson, who had been hounded out of the United States by mobs. On Monday the twenty-ninth she joined the whole American contingent for a visit to the home of Samuel Gurney, the wealthy owner of a handsome estate. There she met Thomas Fowell Buxton. From London she and her father went to Leicester for a relatively quiet two weeks. Thence they went again to Birmingham. "Yesterday bade adieu to my father's birthplace," she wrote on 28 July, "probably to see it no more. It will ever be among my most pleasant and dear reminiscences of England."[97] After that they went on a tour of Wales. Returning to Liverpool, they left England on 8 August aboard the packet ship *England.* Mary Grew, suffering from a severe cold, celebrated her twenty-seventh birthday at sea on 1 September 1840. The ship's captain and some of her fellow passengers drank champagne to her health, but she refused to partake; she was a teetotaler. She thought that America had advanced far beyond Great Britain in temperance reform. On 12 September, after more than a month at sea, they reached Sandy Hook, New Jersey. "Dear America!" she wrote in her diary. "I love it better for my short absence from its shores." In her opinion, America was not in any way inferior to England. "If her scenery is exquisitely beautiful, ours is majestically grand." While England was strong in military power and "resplendent with the paraphernalia of royalty," America was "strengthened and beautified with the simplicity of republicanism. . . . Could I for a moment forget *one* foul spot upon my country's banner, how would my heart exult." She was confident that this spot—slavery—would be eliminated and, "dishonored by it no longer, republicanism, illustrated in America, shall excite the admiration and imitation of the world." In conclusion, she noted that she loved England better also for having visited its "pleasant and honored shores." It was her hope that the sword would never again be lifted between the two countries and that they would "combine their moral and intellectual power, to bless the world."[98]

By 1840 Mary Grew had served a six-year apprenticeship in the antislavery crusade. The basic features of her work as an abolitionist had been established. She had also been introduced to the question of woman's rights. In the next decade she was to see broadening fields of service in the cause of reform.

2

Broadening Fields of Service
(1840–1850)

UPON their return from London, three members of the Philadelphia female delegation to the World's Anti-Slavery Convention wrote a statement on their experience that was printed in the annual report of the society for 1840. These women were Lucretia Mott, Sarah Pugh, and Mary Grew. They wrote that on their arrival at London, a few days previous to 12 June 1840, the opening date of the convention, they had received information from members of the executive committee of the British and Foreign Anti-Slavery Society and other English abolitionists that the presentation of their credentials would "probably be a signal for dissension and strife" and "injurious to the cause of emancipation." Three reasons were given for this conclusion: (1) the admission of women to male antislavery societies was contrary to English custom; (2) their inclusion would "offend the prejudices" of one portion of the British community and "shock the religious sensibilities of another"; and (3) it would never be permitted by such an assembly as was about to convene.[1]

In deference to these pleas, the Philadelphia women had resolved not to present their credentials until the convention had made a decision on the subject of female claim to membership. The convention had refused membership to women. There were some in the convention, however, who felt that "the anti-slavery platform was large enough to admit the lovers of truth and freedom, of every nation, or sect, or sex, or color." The Philadelphia women expressed their gratitude to those delegates (Wendell Phillips, for example) who had "eloquently sustained" the women's cause despite "storms of tumultuous opposition" and "at a sacrifice of popularity and influence in the convention." The Pennsylvania trio also expressed their gratitude to various English friends who had extended "tokens of kindness" to them outside the convention. In conclusion, they declared that although the convention had not accomplished all that friends of the slave hoped, enough had been done to excite their gratitude to

29

"Him in whose cause they labor, and who aids their toil." Although it was not "in truth, a *World's Convention*," yet it was a convention that would bless the world.[2]

Having served a six-year apprenticeship in the Philadelphia Female Anti-Slavery Society, including four years as corresponding secretary and author of its annual reports, in 1840 Mary Grew was ready to enlarge her sphere of activity to include the Pennsylvania State Anti-Slavery Society. This was one of the last of the state organizations founded. Statewide groups auxiliary to the American Anti-Slavery Society had already been established in all of the New England states except Connecticut and in New York and Ohio. Early in 1837 Pennsylvania fell into line. A call signed by approximately twelve hundred men invited all those who believed in "immediate emancipation" to assemble at Aller's Hotel in Harrisburg on Tuesday, 31 January 1837, to organize a state society. About three hundred persons, including several blacks but no women, took part in the convention. Dr. Bartholomew Fussell of Chester County called the convention to order. Dr. F. Julius LeMoyne of Washington County was chosen president. Among the delegates were James Mott, Henry Grew, and James Forten, Philadelphia's richest black. The latter's daughters had worked with Mary Grew in the Female Anti-Slavery Society. The patriarch of American abolitionism, Benjamin Lundy (who died in 1839), was present, as were two youngsters who were to become lifelong abolitionists and pillars of the state organization—James Miller McKim and Robert Purvis. They were both born in 1810 and were only twenty-six years old when the Pennsylvania organization was formed.[3]

The chief work of the convention consisted of the framing and adoption of a constitution. Article 1 declared that the name of the organization would be the *"Pennsylvania State Anti-Slavery Society"* and that it would be auxiliary to the American Anti-Slavery Society, after whose constitution this one was modeled. Article 2 stated the object of the society as the abolition of slavery in the United States and "throughout the world." While admitting the right of states to maintain slavery within their own borders, members of the organization would aim to "convince all our fellow Citizens, by arguments addressed to their understandings and consciences" that slaveholding was "a heinous sin in the sight of God" and that "the duty, safety, and best interests of all concerned, require its immediate abandonment, without expatriation." The society would also endeavor " in a constitutional way" to influence Congress to put an end to the domestic slave trade and to abolish slavery in all those portions of the country that came under its exclusive jurisdiction—that is, the District of Columbia and federal territories in the West and South not yet admitted as states. They would also try to prevent the extension of slavery to any state that might hereafter be admitted to the Union. In article 3 the framers expressed their aim to elevate "the character and condition of the people of color, by encouraging their intellectual, moral, and religious improvement, and by removing public prejudice, that thus they may, according to their intellectual and moral worth, share with [whites], an equality of civil rights and religious privileges." It is not clear whether they considered voting a "civil right"; probably many of them did not. They also warned blacks that they would never countenance the use of "physical force" in efforts by "the oppressed to vindicate their rights."[4]

The constitution provided for the election of the usual officers of such organizations, including a board of managers, that would, in turn, annually elect two executive committees, one in Pittsburgh to act in behalf of the western counties, the other in Philadelphia to represent the eastern counties.[5] It also provided for local auxiliaries to be affiliated with the state society. Dr. F. Julius LeMoyne of Washington, Pennsylvania, was chosen president, and James Mott served on the board of managers. The eastern and western branches of the society soon went their separate ways. Antislavery sentiment was not widespread in the wilderness regions of central and northern Pennsylvania, and within a few years antislavery people in the western counties affiliated with the Ohio organization known as the Western Anti-Slavery Society. The eastern branch later took the name Pennsylvania Anti-Slavery Society, though it always drew its support almost entirely from Philadelphia and the adjacent counties along the bend of the Delaware River.[6] Mary Grew worked faithfully in this organization for thirty years, from 1841 until its disbandment in 1871. Both the Pennsylvania Anti-Slavery Society and the Philadelphia Female Anti-Slavery Society soon came under the control of Garrisonian abolitionists. They were opposed to a third political party, and they believed in equal rights for women.

Women began participating in the work of the Pennsylvania Anti-Slavery Society in 1838, and Lucretia Mott was appointed as one of its delegates to the London Convention of 1840. On 8 April 1841 Mary Grew and several other members of the Philadelphia Female Anti-Slavery Society were appointed as delegates to the state convention.[7] It met on 6 May in the Associate Reformed Presbyterian Church, on Cherry Street below Eleventh, Philadelphia, with Robert Purvis, a rapidly rising young black, in the chair. Sarah Pugh and Mary Grew were appointed to the committee to nominate officers, and Sarah Pugh was also appointed to the business committee. It was resolved that "all friends of the cause from Eastern Pennsylvania" be recognized as members; those from other regions were invited to take seats as "corresponding members." Henry Grew and Mary's sister Susan were among those present. One hundred ninety-six persons attended, including William Lloyd Garrison.[8]

Debate in the convention centered largely about statements that had been made in the annual report of the executive committee concerning the schism in the American Anti-Slavery Society in 1840. The original report included a statement referring to the secession from the organization of "a large number of its members, because the majority, faithful to their understanding of the letter and spirit of the constitution and the requisitions of common justice, refused to exclude women from co-operation with them, or to decide on the abstract question of woman's rights, by denying her competency to participate with men in transacting the business of a benevolent association." Thomas Earle, leader of the "New Organization" faction in Pennsylvania, who had run for vice president on the Liberty party ticket with James G. Birney in 1840, moved that this part of the executive committee's report be deleted and replaced with a reference to "the formation of a new society, occasioned by an apparently irreconcilable difference of opinion among the members of the entire body." Earle's amendment was discussed by Henry Grew, C. C. Burleigh, William Lloyd Garrison, and Oliver Johnson, among others, as well as by Earle himself. It was adopted. The report as thus amended was then accepted.[9] "Regretting that the feeling which induced this separation should have existed among us," the report stated, "we are yet of opinion that, since it did exist, the division was on the whole for the best, and will tend more to the advancement of the enterprise which both parties desire to promote, than a longer continuation of both in one society, but without unity and harmony."[10]

The 1841 report of the Pennsylvania Anti-Slavery Society also dealt with the exclusion of women from the World's Anti-Slavery Convention in London the year before: "Though our expectations in regard to it were not fully realized, and though its proceedings were marred at the outset by a violation of the rights of some of its regularly constituted members, in their exclusion from the seats to which they were entitled, yet on the whole we have reason to rejoice that it was convened, and to believe that much good has resulted and will result from its deliberations."[11] The Pennsylvanians expressed their special satisfaction with the resolution passed by the World's Convention calling on "all Christian Churches of every sect and creed, to refuse Christian fellowship to those, who after due admonition, continue to hold human beings as goods and chattels." Mary Grew, it will be recalled, had sponsored a similar resolution, passed by a divided vote, at the second annual Anti-Slavery Convention of American Women, in May 1838.[12]

Mary Grew continued her activities in the Philadelphia Female Anti-Slavery Society. While the state society met only annually, the women's group met monthly. On 3 May 1841, both the president and the vice president were absent, and she served as president pro tem. At this meeting the women adopted a petition to Congress asking that the Constitution of the United States be amended in such a way that "the inhabitants of this State shall not be required to interfere in establishing, maintaining, or preserving the existence of Slavery in any other State or Country."[13] On 10 June 1841 they adopted a petition to the state legislature calling for legislation requiring that trial by jury be provided for persons claimed as fugitive slaves.[14] At that meeting Mary Grew offered a resolution declaring that while meetings of the society would not be held during the summer months, "the toil of the slave will not be remitted." Therefore, they resolved that they would not suspend their labors on the slave's behalf, but would "faithfully speak, write, or act for him until we meet again." The resolution was adopted and ordered printed in the *Pennsylvania Freeman*.[15]

The first item of business taken up by the Philadelphia Female Anti-Slavery Society when its meetings resumed in September 1841 was the matter of what support it could give to the Philadelphia Vigilance Committee. This organization had been founded by Robert Purvis and other Philadelphia blacks in 1837 for the purpose of assisting fugitive slaves, who were coming through the city in large numbers in search of freedom. Purvis was president of the group in 1839. During a six-month period in that year the committee dealt with more than fifty cases and was successful in sending forty-six fugitives farther north to freedom. Most of them came from Maryland and Virginia, and most of them were bound for Canada.[16] On 13 January 1842 the Philadelphia Female Anti-Slavery Society appropriated fifty dollars to assist the work of this committee.

Between 1840 and 1845 there was frequent and intense debate within both the Philadelphia Female Anti-Slavery Society and the Pennsylvania Anti-Slavery Society concerning William Lloyd Garrison's attacks on the Liberty party, on abolitionist voting, on the Constitution, and on the American Union itself. On 19 April 1842 Mary Grew introduced two resolutions concerning these matters at a meeting of the Philadelphia Female Anti-Slavery Society.

Whereas the measures of abolitionists have recently been denounced by some of the public press as illegal & traitorous & their motives impugned & misrepresented, therefore:

Resolved, that in the work of abolishing slavery, we rely not on physical force, or political parties, but on moral power, on the use of those weapons, which operate on the heart & on the conscience.

Resolved, that while we acknowledge no allegiance to any national compact or legislative enactment which sanctions slavery or contravenes any principle of right, the dissolution of the American Union is not among the objects which as an Anti-slavery Association we advocate or seek.

The first resolution, after some discussion, was unanimously adopted. Lucretia Mott then moved to amend the second one by omitting the word "while" and all words after "right." The amendment was agreed to and the resolution adopted as amended. Thus it read simply, "we acknowledge no allegiance to any national compact or legislative enactment which sanctions slavery or contravenes any principle of right."

Then someone (the minutes do not give the sponsor's name) offered a resolution that "the dissolution of the American Union is not among the objects which as an Anti-Slavery Association we advocate or seek." After much discussion, this resolution was tabled.[17]

While denouncing the American political process, the Philadelphia women continued, somewhat inconsistently, to bombard Congress with antislavery petitions. On 8 September 1842 Mary Grew was appointed to a committee to prepare such petitions. At the 13 October meeting she presented forms for petitions to Congress to abolish slavery and the slave trade in the District of Columbia and to deny Florida and Texas admission to the Union. She also wrote a petition calling on Congress to "take measures for effecting such alteration in the laws of the U.S. as will relieve the citizens of the Free States from the responsibility of supporting & perpetuating the system of slavery which now exists in our country." The Pennsylvania legislature was to be asked to repeal the law that permitted slaveholders to bring their chattels into the state and retain them in slavery for six months. All of these petitions were approved, and a committee was appointed to arrange to circulate them for signatures.[18] On 9 February 1843 Mary Grew reported that 900 signatures had been obtained to the petition to the state regarding the six-months law and 740 to the petition to Congress to abolish slavery in the District of Columbia.[19] John Quincy Adams had not yet won his victory over the "gag rule" that forbade the discussion of such petitions to Congress. That victory came on 2 December 1844.

On 8 December 1842 she presented another petition (approved by the society) "respectfully" asking Congress "as far as you have constitutional power" to endeavor to "abolish every thing in the Constitution or laws of the United States which in any manner sanctions or sustains slavery."[20]

While Mary Grew was not prepared to advocate secession from the South, she still felt there was much merit in abstention from the products of slave labor. On 13 October 1842 the Philadelphia Female Society named her as a delegate to the meeting of the Free Produce Society. On 10 November she reported on this convention and made "some impressive remarks on the duty of abolitionists & particularly the members of this Society in regard to the use of the products of slave labor, urging the inconsistency of their participation in the gain of oppression."

The highlight in the Grews' life for 1843 was their participation in the Decennial Meeting of the American Anti-Slavery Society, which met in Philadelphia to celebrate the society's founding ten years earlier. "I am among the numerous friends of the oppressed in this city," Henry Grew wrote to Wendell and Ann Phillips on 15 November 1843, "who ardently desire to see you here next month, to celebrate with us the formation of a Society, constituted for the relief of suffering humanity. . . . Do you not feel that you owe it to the cause to come? . . . Our arrangements at our boarding house No. 72 South 4th St. are such that we can accommodate our friends without additional expense to them or us. Please come direct to our place where you will receive a cordial welcome from the entire family."[21]

In a postscript Mary echoed her father's invitation: "The weather here is very fine, and much milder [than] that of Boston, usually, at this season." She thought that Ann Phillips's health might benefit from the change of scene. Wendell's wife was ill through most of her married life. Ann could be as quiet and retired "in our snug little parlor," or in her own room, as she wished, and could receive as few visitors as she cared to. Mary Grew reminded Wendell that he had never permitted Pennsylvania to hear his voice and that "Pennsylvania abolitionists are anxiously desiring to hear it, for their own sakes, and still more for the sake of the cause we so much love."[22] Probably on account of Ann's illness, Wendell Phillips did not attend the meeting.

The convention was held in the meetinghouse of the Second Independent Universalist Church in Philadelphia on 4–7 December 1843. In the absence of the president of the American Anti-Slavery Society, William Lloyd Garrison, vice president Robert Purvis took the chair. After the death of James Forten, Sr., in 1842, Purvis became the most distinguished of Philadelphia's black leaders.[23] Mary Grew served as one of four secretaries for the meeting. Henry Grew took an active part in the deliberations, which centered mainly about the issue of political action. The business committee proposed a resolution that the society "reiterates the doctrine put forth at its last annual meeting, that a total separation from pro-slavery parties and sects, is essential to the speedy triumph of our cause." It was tabled until the next day, when it was hoped there would be a larger attendance at the meeting. It was then amended to read "withdrawal of support" instead of "a total separation," and passed in that form. The convention also adopted a resolution asking that abolitionists give "no support, directly, or indirectly," to any candidates for public office unless they would "publicly avow themselves favorable to the repeal of all laws and constitutional provisions which required the aid of public officers or private citizens for the retaining of human beings in a state of slavery."[24]

Henry Grew introduced a strong free-produce resolution. It would have declared that those abolitionists who refused to abstain from using the products of slave labor were "partakers in this abominable system of unrighteousness and oppression and are actually and effectually building up what they are laboring to destroy." Mary Grew was one of the few persons who spoke in favor of it. The resolution was tabled.[25]

A committee was appointed to correspond with members of Congress on amending the Constitution "so that it shall not require the government or the people to support slavery, or aid in slaveholding" or, at the very least, to repeal the Fugitive Slave Law of 1793. The convention also adopted a resolution reaffirming the members' faith in moral suasion rather than in political action as the best means of abolishing slavery. They took a stand against the annexation of Texas on the grounds that it would increase the territory open to slaveholding and that it would be "unjust and perfidious to Mexico."[26] At the end of the convention Thomas Earle presented a lengthy series of resolutions condemning the record of John Quincy Adams on questions involving slavery. A committee was appointed to study them and report at a future meeting of the society.[27]

"We had a good meeting," Mary Grew wrote to Wendell Phillips on 14 December, "but you were sadly missed. May God bless you both."[28]

Because 1844 was the year of a presidential election and because the Liberty party had nominated James G. Birney for a second time, the issue of abolitionist participation in the American political process became more acute than it had been at any time since the schism of 1840. Meeting in Norristown in August, 1844, the Pennsylvania Anti-Slavery Society devoted its time chiefly to this issue. J. Miller McKim, who had been appointed "publishing agent" of the society in 1840 but who actually served as its paid executive secretary until 1862, introduced a resolution "declaring the proslavery character of the Constitution, and the duty of non-voting under it."[29] Professor C. D. Cleveland of Philadelphia, a Liberty party man, introduced counterresolutions declaring that since the words *slaves, slaveholder,* and *slavery* did not appear in the Constitution, and since the Constitution was created for the purpose of "securing the blessings of liberty," it could not possibly be construed as a proslavery document. Furthermore, the Constitution guaranteed a republican form of government to each of the states and declared that no person was to be deprived of his liberty without due process of law. Cleveland argued that abolitionists had a duty to vote and carry out at the ballot box "the true intent of the instrument."[30] Cleveland's resolutions were defeated and McKim's were tabled. So the issue carried over until the 1845 meeting, when the Pennsylvania society settled it once and for all, in Garrison's favor. Henry Grew opened the 1844 meeting with prayer and took an active part in the debate. Mary Grew was chosen corresponding secretary of the society at this time.[31]

The Philadelphia Female Anti-Slavery Society took up the political issue at its meeting on 12 September 1844, when it adopted a resolution

> That this Society heartily co-operates with the American Anti-Slavery Society, in its present measures for the promotion of our cause, and that our influences shall be exerted in support of the doctrine that abolitionists can consistently have no union with slaveholders, by voting for officers, who must swear to support the constitution of the United States.[32]

"As we look for the accomplishment of our object, only through the renovation of public sentiment," Mary Grew wrote in her annual report for 1844, "we deem that it would be worse than useless to expend our time and energies in propelling the machinery of political parties, for we are well aware that until the public mind is rectified, political parties can do little for us, and when it is rectified, they will be, as now, but its exponents."[33] The statistics would seem to bear out her dim view of antislavery political parties. The Liberty party ticket received less than 7,000 votes in 1840, with only 343 in Pennsylvania, despite the fact that a Pennsylvanian, Thomas Earle, ran for vice president with James G. Birney. The record in 1844 was better, but the figures were infinitesimal as compared with the national election returns. In that year Birney, running with Thomas Morris of Ohio, received slightly over 62,000 votes nationwide, including 3,123 from Pennsylvania.[34]

In November 1844 Mary Grew was again urging Wendell Phillips to come to Philadelphia for an antislavery convention. You have never been here," she wrote. "For many years, Pennsylvania abolitionists have earnestly desired to see and hear you, and have not been gratified. It would refresh and strengthen them. . . . The constitutional question needs to be discussed, and many, many minds and consciences, need to be revised and set right, respecting it." The Liberty party people had made "a desperate struggle" in Philadelphia, she continued, but she thought their zeal had subsided somewhat since the November elections. "You could greatly assist in our efforts," she wrote, to extend and deepen the conviction that moral is greater than political power and that reform might be carried on by better agencies than the ballot box. "The constitutional question" had been settled in her mind "years ago," and she had never met with a satisfactory reply to the question that she often put to Liberty party men: "How can you assist to place a man in a situation where he is bound to swear to do that which you acknowledge to be wrong?"—that is, for example, to cooperate in the return of fugitive slaves.[35]

Looking back on the year 1844, Mary Grew saw "cheering evidence of the progress of our cause, fully proving that they who have labored for its promotion, have not spent their strength in vain."[36] She thought it was especially significant that the nation's large ecclesiastical bodies were beginning to take up the slavery question. American Methodism had split into Northern and Southern branches as a result of disagreement over the appointment of a slaveholder as a bishop, and the Baptists were to divide in 1845 over the issue of appointing a slaveholder as a missionary to Africa. She saw some evidence of the growth of antislavery sentiment in the Congress. Antislavery petitions could now be presented in the House of Representatives. "We rejoice," she wrote, "that the country is agitated with the discussion of slavery in its many bearings on our civil and religious interests." The days of slavery were numbered. "To a few more years of arduous toil, to peril or suffering, if it await us, we gladly devote ourselves, with the firm and cheering hope that, over its fall and utter ruin, we shall soon hear the glad shout of the exulting earth, and the rejoicing song of heaven."[37]

The dispute over political action, which had caused such controversy and disharmony in the state society since 1840, was finally settled in the annual meeting that convened in the Friends Meeting House at Kennett Square on 11 August 1845. James Miller McKim presented five resolutions on the subject, and all were adopted:

1. The United States Constitution was "an unholy league with oppression."
2. Its fugitive slave clause was not "morally or legally binding."
3. Voting under the Constitution implied support for it.

4. Efforts to amend the Constitution implied a promise to support the remainder of the document as it then stood.

5. It was "inconsistent for those who hold the doctrine of the immorality of slaveholding, to take any office which requires an oath to support the Constitution, or to vote under it, so long as its pro-slavery features remain."[38]

Thomas Earle, the Liberty party veteran, led the opposition to these resolutions. William Lloyd Garrison, who came from Massachusetts to be present for this showdown, C. C. Burleigh, a veteran antislavery lecturer well known for his long hair, flowing robe, and sandals, Henry Grew, and Mary Grew were among those speaking in favor of the resolutions. They passed by a vote of 442–188. Thus, the Pennsylvania Anti-Slavery Society came under the control of William Lloyd Garrison.

Officers chosen at this convention included Robert Purvis as president, Mary Grew as corresponding secretary, Sarah Pugh as treasurer, and Lucretia Mott as a member of the executive committee.

In October 1845 Mary Grew joined C. C. Burleigh, J. Miller McKim, and his wife, Sarah A. McKim, on a tour of the Pennsylvania counties that bordered on slave states (Delaware, Maryland, and Virginia) to win new converts to the antislavery cause, to reinvigorate old ones, to cement bonds of union among abolitionists, to circulate antislavery newspapers, tracts, and books, to promote the annual fair, and to advance the antislavery movement any way they could. At its conclusion, they reported that the tour had been very successful.[39]

In November 1845 Edward M. Davis (son-in-law of the Motts), J. Miller McKim, and Mary Grew, representing the Pennsylvania Anti-Slavery Society, issued an invitation to three leaders of the Liberty party in Philadelphia to choose one of their members to engage in a public debate with one of the Anti-Slavery Society's representatives over the issues dividing them. The Liberty men turned down the offer, suggesting that such a debate would turn into a free-for-all. It would not be possible, they said, to exclude from the audience disruptive persons who would engage in a verbal brawl. They could not control the conduct of others who might want to participate, and in any case, abolitionists "should not be found contriving to abridge the liberties of free speech." Besides, the Liberty representative would have to defend himself not only against abolitionists with whom they disagreed but also against supporters of the Whig party.[40]

Mary Grew suffered two severe losses in 1845. Her mother died in July, and one of her best friends married and moved to New York later that year. Writing to Wendell Phillips, Henry Grew spoke of "our affecting bereavement in the departure of my beloved wife [Kate Merrow] who has been the companion of my pilgrimage 33 years, [1812–45]. . . . Blessed be God for the consolation of his word & spirit and for the hope of meeting in the everlasting kingdom. . . ." In November Elizabeth Neall, who had been a close associate of Mary Grew's in the Philadelphia Female Anti-Slavery Society, was married to Sydney Howard Gay, editor of the *National Anti-Slavery Standard,* the organ of Garrisonian abolitionists in New York City. "How shall we miss the light of thy presence among us," Mary Grew wrote to her, "and how often pause amid our toils for freedom's holy cause, to mourn the absence of a beloved and faithful fellow laborer!" In "this bright dawning of wedded love," Mary begged her not to forget the slaves, "whose conjugal bliss hangs on a tyrant's word." The affectionate wishes of many hearts would go with her to her new home. Among these, Mary Grew would mingle hers for "unutterable blessings for thee, and for him whose destinies will henceforth be so closely linked with thine."[42]

Several of the state antislavery societies, Pennsylvania among them, supported their own newspapers. The Pennsylvania Anti-Slavery Society in March 1837, only a month after its founding, adopted as its organ the *National Enquirer and Constitutional Advocate of Universal Liberty,* which Benjamin Lundy had established in Philadelphia on 3 August 1836. Most generally remembered in connection with the *Genius of Universal Emancipation,* one of the earliest of antislavery newspapers, which had been published in several different communities, Lundy was the pioneer on this newspaper in Baltimore in the late 1820s and had been imprisoned for libeling a slave trader during that time. The *National Enquirer* was begun with the special purpose of exposing "the grand conspiracy of slaveholders and land speculators," which Lundy and others thought had been organized to wrest "by violence, the territory of Texas from the Republic of Mexico."[43] It carried on the front page of every issue the famous quotation from the Declaration of Independence: "We hold these truths to be self-evident: that all men are created equal, and endowed by their Creator with certain unalienable rights, that among these are life, liberty, and the pursuit of happiness." In March of 1838 Lundy retired from the editorship on account of poor health. He was succeeded by John Greenleaf Whittier, who also served only two years. The name of the paper was changed to the *Pennsylvania Freeman* in 1838. Under this title and a succession of editors, the paper continued until 1854, when it merged with the *National Anti-Slavery Standard* in New York.[44]

In November 1845 Mary Grew was chosen by the executive committee of the Pennsylvania Anti-Slavery Society to serve with James

Miller McKim and Cyrus M. Burleigh as members of the editorial board of the *Pennsylvania Freeman*.[45] She retired from this position on 9 May 1850. During part of the four and a half years of her service, she had the sole management of the paper. Since the editorials were generally unsigned, it is impossible to say for sure which ones Mary Grew wrote. However, the editors were generally in agreement, all served on the board of managers of the Pennsylvania Anti-Slavery Society, and all reflected its principles.

The *Pennsylvania Freeman* after 1845 almost invariably followed the Garrisonian party line when it came to matters involving slavery. It upheld Garrison's slogan, "No Union with Slaveholders!" and was opposed to voting and officeholding or any other participation in the American political process. It regarded the Constitution as "a covenant with death, and an agreement with hell." While the official position of the paper was that the Constitution was a proslavery document, Mary Grew read and was favorably impressed by Lysander Spooner's book *The Unconstitutionality of Slavery* (1845), which argued that slavery was contrary to natural law and natural justice. She thought Spooner's argument was "highly ingenious" and "iron-linked."[46]

The *Freeman* advocated separation from churches whose membership included slaveholders. It went beyond Garrison in its endorsement of the free produce movement, which Garrison thought was of no practical value. It emphasized moral suasion rather than political action as the best antislavery weapon. Nevertheless, it supported petitions to Congress for the abolition of slavery in the District of Columbia and in federal territories not yet organized as states. It advocated repeal of the Fugitive Slave Act of 1793.[47]

The *Freeman* supported the passage of the Pennsylvania "personal liberty law" of 1847. One of the most stringent of Northern laws designed to subvert the fugitive slave clause of the Constitution, this act forbade any state official to aid in the recapture of alleged fugitives and required that all such persons be brought before a judge. It also forbade the use of county jails and state penitentiaries to detain escaped slaves and forbade anyone to use force in recapturing runaways.[48] In effect, it nullified the federal fugitive slave legislation.

Though unwilling themselves to vote, the editors of the *Freeman* fought for the restoration of the suffrage to Pennsylvania blacks, who had lost the right to vote under the state constitution of 1838.[49] In this effort they were unsuccessful. Blacks had to wait for the passage and ratification of the Fifteenth Amendment to the United States Constitution in 1870 before they regained the right to vote they had enjoyed prior to 1838.

The *Freeman* during the time of Mary Grew's service on the edi-

torial board also stood for international peace. It deplored the possibility of war between Great Britain and the United States over the
Oregon question and mercilessly assailed American policy in the
Mexican War.[50] In May 1846 Mary Grew went to Boston to attend an
antislavery convention and the annual meeting of the American Peace
Society. The war against Mexico, she reported, was "the exciting,
absorbing topic of thought and conversation here." The antislavery
convention was "indeed a glorious meeting; sublime in its manifesta-
tions of moral might, of lofty faith, and dauntless courage." It was
"soul-cheering to see the evidences, which the Convention afforded,
that there are noble spirits here who are prepared to dare all, and
suffer all the consequences of a firm refusal, to aid or countenance, in
any manner, the base, unconstitutional, unchristian, and inhuman
policy of the United States toward Mexico." Near the end of the
convention, "a solemn pledge" to abstain from giving any aid to the
war was circulated for signatures.[51]

Mary Grew thought that the members of the convention of the
American Peace Society were too timid in their condemnation of the
Mexican War. The efforts made by "a few true-hearted friends of
peace, to obtain from the Society a hearty condemnation of the *present
existing* war, were utterly vain." The Peace Society did not have "moral
courage enough to speak out boldly on this specific case."[52]

In her annual report of the Philadelphia Female Anti-Slavery Society for 1846, she blasted the Mexican War as the product of a
conspiracy by Southern slaveholders—"the Slave Power." This group
had always had "a powerful ally in our Federal Constitution," she
wrote. "It has long since summoned a very large portion of the church
to its aid, and now . . . has plunged the country into a war of invasion
for the purpose of strengthening itself." She thought "every true-
hearted friend of God and man" should mourn over the war, which
was "all for the sake of furnishing facilities to men to enslave their
brethren!"[53]

The *Pennsylvania Freeman* in Mary Grew's time gave its support to
other reform movements besides abolitionism and the peace movement. Prison reform, the abolition of capital punishment, woman's
rights, sailors' welfare, and the redemption of fallen women also
attracted the newspaper's attention. So did hydropathy, mesmerism,
and "phonography" (shorthand).[54] In 1847 Mary Grew suffered a
severe illness and herself went to a hydropathic treatment center.[55] In
January 1847 a company of Philadelphia ladies met in "a private
parlor" to prepare a petition to the state legislature for the abolition of
capital punishment. A public meeting attended by about five hundred
women soon followed. A thousand copies of a public address on

behalf of the cause were circulated. Almost twelve thousand signed the petition, and a committee was appointed to prepare it for the legislature. At the last meeting of the committee one of the ladies suggested the formation of a society to open a house for "the reformation, employment, and instruction of females who had led immoral lives." This proposal met with an enthusiastic response and was followed by the opening of "a house of industry" supported by the Rosine Association, whose main purpose was the rescue of fallen women. Mary Grew was a member of the association and Henry Grew was one of its benefactors, leaving it five hundred dollars in his will.[56]

Mary Grew and the *Pennsylvania Freeman* also took a keen interest in the incipient woman's rights movement. Lucretia Mott and Elizabeth Cady Stanton had held their long-deferred woman's rights convention in Seneca Falls, New York, in July 1848, and the *Freeman* reprinted its Declaration of Sentiments and Resolutions. The paper publicized significant achievements by individual women like Elizabeth Blackwell, the first female graduate from a United States medical school, and Dorothea Dix, who conducted a nationwide campaign for better treatment of the mentally ill.[57] Mary Grew herself made a significant contribution to the woman's rights movement in 1848 when she circulated petitions to the General Assembly of Pennsylvania for legislation protecting the property rights of married women. Both New York and Pennsylvania passed such legislation in 1848.[58]

Surprisingly, considering their hostility to political action, the Pennsylvania Garrisonians supported the development of the Free-Soil movement. They welcomed David Wilmot's 1846 proviso that would have forbidden slavery in all territory acquired as a result of the Mexican War. They printed the names of Pennsylvania representatives who opposed it.[59] It passed the House of Representatives but not the Senate. They avidly followed the proceedings of the convention, which founded the Free-Soil party in 1848. They rejoiced at the prospect of a "great breach" in the two major parties, "the Sodom and Gomorrah of Whiggery and Democracy," while exhorting the Free-Soilers to take higher ground than mere opposition to the extension of slavery.[60]

On 15 November 1849 Mary Grew assumed complete and sole responsibility for editorial care of the *Pennsylvania Freeman*. Her salutatory editorial reflected what was perhaps her main concern in her abolition work—the church and slavery. It was an attack on the two branches of the Presbyterian church, which did not hesitate to condemn sins such as sabbath breaking and dancing but refused to lift up their voices against the "giant sin" of slavery. While here and there a solitary minister, or church, or presbytery uttered a word of warning, the two national bodies put them down with clamor, declaring that the "peace of Zion" and "the unity of the Church" should not be disturbed. If Presbyterianism were to prosper, it must lend its support to the biblical injunction, "LET THE OPPRESSED GO FREE."[61]

She took advantage of Thanksgiving Day to call attention to those who were suffering "the anguish of sundered human ties, broken not by the gentle hand of the death angel, but by the cruel violence of a brother man."[62] The forcible separation of families was one of the aspects of slavery most fiercely condemned by the abolitionists. Shortly before Christmas she appealed to readers to buy their holiday gifts at the Anti-Slavery Fair:

> Will it not increase the joy of this festival season, to know that the money which you expend in the purchase of your holiday gifts, is also an offering to the cause of Freedom; a Christmas gift to the slave?[63]

On 20 December she published an editorial entitled "Critics of Reform." She charged that there was "a class of persons in the community who seem to think that their especial mission in this world is to carp and cavil at all the reformatory movements of their age." They were fond of saying, "We approve your principles, but we don't like your measures." Such persons, she said, had an obligation to point out some better way than moral suasion through which slavery could be abolished.[64]

On 7 February 1850 Mary Grew attacked "Henry Clay's Compromise." She noted that Clay eminently deserved the title of Prince of Compromisers. His entire life had centered around "one long effort to effect a compromise between right and wrong, justice and injustice, liberty and slavery." Mary Grew believed that it was wrong to admit California to statehood without a specific prohibition of slavery. She believed that the principle of noninterference with slavery in the remainder of the territory acquired through the Mexican War was wrong. She believed that the abolition of the slave trade but not slavery itself in the District of Columbia was wrong. Finally, she believed that the new Fugitive Slave Law was wrong. Clay's compromise measures involved yielding "nearly the whole of the question at issue." She believed that Clay would probably end his public life as he had begun it, "in efforts to reconcile professions of love of liberty with acts of devotion to slavery, and to effect compromises between righteousness and sin, truth and error, Jesus Christ and the Prince of Darkness."[65] Commenting the following week on a speech that Clay had given in support of the measures which became the Compromise of 1850, she accused him of "a want of moral principle." He recognized no higher law than the Constitution, was ruled by the principle of expediency, and denied "manhood and brotherhood" to the slave.[66]

Mary Grew also blasted Daniel Webster's "Seventh of March" speech. She thought his defense of the new Fugitive Slave Law, "coming from a Northern man, a man who has breathed the free air of New England," was "truly *infamous*."[67] The following week she attacked Webster for his argument that slavery had been excluded by nature from California and New Mexico: "Cannot slaves dig gold there as profitably as they can raise cotton elsewhere? What climate or soil has ever been found, where slavery could not exist?"[68]

On 9 May 1850 Mary Grew gave up the editorship of the *Pennsylvania Freeman*, probably on account of poor health. She was succeeded by Cyrus M. Burleigh. In her valedictory, she remarked that conducting a journal of reform, while an arduous task, was "a joyous one, whose ample reward is in itself." It had been "a glorious privilege" to join hands with other "brave and true souls" who were battling "Falsehood and Wrong." She was hopeful for success. There was "a mighty influence" bearing the world on to the Millennium. The Jubilee was coming. "With the expression of an earnest hope that each of us may, by self-denying labor, by unwearied perseverance, and all-conquering faith, perform our full share of the work which remains to be done, we affectionately bid our readers farewell."[69]

3

Toward Civil War (1850–1861)

TAKING stock of the antislavery movement at midcentury, Mary Grew called attention in the *Sixteenth Annual Report of the Philadelphia Female Anti-Slavery Society* (1850) to the revolutions that had swept Europe in 1848 and thereafter. She saw a "desperate and deadly conflict" between two mighty principles struggling for mastery in both the Old World and the New—the principles of "Despotism and Freedom." There was a longing for freedom both in Europe and in America. That "stupendous system of despotism, American slavery" could not wholly escape the moral influence of the European uprisings. She observed that "resistance to tyrants" was "obedience to God" in both hemispheres.

She believed that much had been accomplished for the cause of freedom in the United States during the preceding year. Abolitionists could now speak freely of the evils of American slavery. The "whole nation" was aroused over the issue:

> It is a topic of earnest conversation and discussion in the social circle and by the wayside, in the school and the lyceum, and the church; it agitates the legislatures of our free and our slaveholding states; it has taken entire possession of Congress.

There had been "a mighty change" in public sentiment. It had been effected "simply by the dissemination of anti-slavery truth."[1]

Two antislavery fairs had been conducted in Philadelphia in 1849, the regular one sponsored by the Female Anti-Slavery Society and a special one, apparently put on by black women, for the benefit of Frederick Douglass's paper, the *North Star*. Both had been very successful financially and in terms of moral influence. The Female Society had sponsored Lucy Stone as a traveling lecturer on behalf of the cause in southeastern Pennsylvania. Mary Grew noted in her report that the year 1849 had seen the termination of the Liberty party, which she saw as proof that slavery could not be abolished through "a political organization based upon the Constitution of the United States" but only through moral suasion.[2] Mary Grew vowed that the Philadelphia women would continue their crusade

> Until IMMORTAL MIND,
>   Unshackled, walks abroad,
> And chains no longer bind
>   *The image of our God.*
> Until no captive one
>   Murmurs on land or wave;
> And, in his course, the sun
>   Looks down upon no SLAVE![3]

On 14 March 1850 the Philadelphia Female Anti-Slavery Society appointed Mary Grew, Sidney Ann Lewis, and Margaret Jones to send in the name of the society petitions to Congress against the extension of slavery to new areas, in favor of abolition in the District of Columbia, and asking that the free states be released from supporting slavery, as through the fugitive slave legislation. In addition, they were to prepare a petition to the state legislature against efforts to repeal Pennsylvania's Personal Liberty Law of 1847. Mary Grew was also appointed to prepare a protest against the existing union between free and slave states.[4]

On 13 June the committee that had been appointed to prepare a protest against the Union presented the following resolutions:

> Whereas, The American Union is based on a Constitution which protects the institution of slavery, by providing for the surrender of all fugitives from labor or service according to the laws of the respective states from which they escape and
>
> Whereas, Natural Justice, the fundamental principle of common law, forbids us to aid directly or indirectly, in the enslavement of any human being, therefore
>
> Resolved, That we protest in the name of Humanity and of God, against a Union thus founded and cemented, and that we repudiate all allegiance to such constitutional provisions and to all laws which have been or may be enacted to sustain the system of American Slavery.[5]

These resolutions were to be offered for publication in the *Pennsylvania Freeman*.

On 25 September 1850 she wrote her friend Elizabeth Neall Gay, apologizing for the long lapse of time since her last letter on the grounds that she was "by no means strong enough to write or work for any long period, without frequent intervals of rest." She also wrote that immediately after her return from a summer spent out of town she had become deeply involved in antislavery work, especially with preparations for the annual December fair.[6] On 22 October 1850 she gave up the position of corresponding secretary of the Pennsylvania Anti-Slavery Society and was replaced by Miller McKim. She remained on the executive committee, however. Soon after that, she prepared a circular to the clergymen of Pennsylvania on the question of slavery for printing and circulation by the state society. And on 26 November 1850 she resumed editorial charge of the *Pennsylvania Freeman,* a position she held until 18 February 1851.[7]

During the decade of the 1850s, in the wake of the Fugitive Slave Act of 1850, the attention of abolitionists came to focus largely on cases involving escaped slaves. On 13 March 1851 Mary Grew prepared a resolution for the Philadelphia Female Anti-Slavery Society condemning the recent surrender of a fugitive husband and wife by Philadelphia authorities. By this action the city had been "deeply disgraced, the inalienable rights of man outraged, and the law of God violated."[8] Copies were sent to the *Public Ledger* and the *New York Tribune.*

In April 1851 the case of Thomas Sims attracted nationwide attention. Sims was a fugitive slave who had escaped from Georgia to Boston, where he was captured and brought before a United States commissioner, who ordered him returned to his owner. Plans to rescue him failed. President Fillmore wrote to Daniel Webster, "I congratulate you and the country upon a triumph of law in Boston. She has done nobly." She had freed herself from "the reproach of nullification."[9] Mary Grew, of course, saw the matter differently. Writing to Wendell Phillips on 19 May 1851, she remarked upon the election of Charles Sumner to a seat in the United States Senate: "Does Massachusetts offer it as an atonement for her cowardly and shameful conduct in the Simms [*sic*] case? I believe the South is disposed to regard it thus. I did not believe that Massachusetts would elect Sumner, so it was, to me, a joyful surprise."[10] In October she wrote Phillips again, enclosing a letter to Charles Sumner asking him to speak at the Philadelphia antislavery fair in December and asking Phillips to use his influence with Sumner to persuade him to accept the invitation.[11]

Christiana, Pennsylvania, a small community located near Lancaster, was the scene of the single most violent episode in the history of the Fugitive Slave Law. It took place on 11 September 1851. Edward Gorsuch, a Maryland planter, armed with all the proper legal documents and accompanied by a son, a nephew, and several others, went to Christiana in search of several fugitive slaves who were reported to be hiding in the area. A United States marshal led them to the home of William Parker, one of the alleged fugitives. Free Negroes of the area were summoned with a horn blown by Parker's wife. Armed with guns, knives, and scythes, they surrounded Gorsuch and his party. A riot ensued in which Gorsuch was killed and his son was seriously injured. Though Parker escaped to Canada, a large number of blacks and several Quakers were arrested and charged with treason. Thaddeus Stevens was the best known of the several defense lawyers who secured their release. The Christiana Riot generated great political furor not only in Pennsylvania but throughout the nation.[12]

Public opinion, in the North as well as in the South, blamed the riot on the abolitionists. The executive committee of the Pennsylvania Anti-Slavery Society, with Mary Grew in attendance, devoted most of its attention to this episode at its meeting on 30 September. We do not have a record of what was said, but presumably most of them agreed with the editorial that appeared in the *Pennsylvania Freeman* on 18 September: "The Tragedy; Its Causes; Our Duty." According to the *Freeman*, the riot had grown "legitimately—necessarily—from the passage, and the attempt to enforce, a statute which tramples on Justice, outrages all true reverence for Law, assails the dearest rights and the holiest instincts of men, which virtually outlaws a large class of our population, and sets at defiance the law of God." This, of course, was the Fugitive Slave Act included in the Compromise of 1850. "Such fruits of that act," the editorial continued, "the abolitionists have apprehended, and labored to avert, from the hour that the North yielded to the mad folly of the slave power, and enacted its cruel and disgraceful provisions into National law."[13]

A young Hicksite Quaker named Castner Hanway was one of the bystanders who were prosecuted for not helping Gorsuch and the marshal capture William Parker. He was the first to be tried for treason and was acquitted, after which charges against the other defendants were dropped. On behalf of the Philadelphia Female Anti-Slavery Society, Mary Grew wrote him a letter of sympathy while he was in prison awaiting trial.[14] The *Pennsylvania Freeman* remarked that his acquittal had "diffused a general feeling of joy throughout the city [Philadelphia] and among all classes, save the open partizans of Slavery." His trial would "contribute essentially to the triumph of Liberty over Slavery in the great struggle now impending."[15]

In February 1852 Mary Grew, on behalf of the Philadelphia Female Anti-Slavery Society, sent petitions to the Pennsylvania General Assembly remonstrating against the movement to repeal the Personal Liberty Law or "Anti-Kidnapping Act" of 1847. William A. Crabb, a state senator, replied that he felt obligated by his constituents to vote for the repeal of the sixth section, which made it illegal to use local jails for detention of suspected fugitives.[16] Beginning in 1851, bills were introduced in the state legislature calling for repeal of this section and for the prohibition of all black migration into the state. Both bills failed in 1851 and 1852, but the repeal of section six was adopted two years later, despite abolitionist objections.[17]

In the fall of 1852 Mary Grew opened a correspondence between the Philadelphia Female Anti-Slavery Society and the Bristol and Clifton (England) Ladies' Anti-Slavery Society. The English group had been organized in 1840 as an auxiliary to the British and Foreign Anti-Slavery Society but had broken its connection with this society on account of the latter's hostility to Garrison's control of the American Anti-Slavery Society. Referring to fugitive slaves, she wrote:

> As our fathers fled from British tyranny, to the freedom of America, so are these wretched fugitives from American bondage, continually coming northward, "as the flying come, in silence and in fear," and not until they have passed our northermost border, and their travel-worn feet touch British soil, do they dare to raise "the anthem of the free."[18]

"With such continually renewed incentives to zeal and action," the abolitionists would be "highly culpable were we to falter or grow weary of our work." That the work was arduous and its difficulties great, they well knew, but they had the assurance that "Right is more potent than Wrong" and would eventually prevail. Mary Grew implored the English women to make sure that British churches held no fellowship with the slaveholding and proslavery churches of the United States and that they abstained from the purchase and use of the products of slave labor.[19]

During 1852 the Female Society began devoting a portion of its funds to the publication of antislavery articles in Philadelphia's daily papers, hoping in that way to reach the masses of people who did not read antislavery journals. Mary Grew lamented the fact that not one of the numerous papers published in the city would open its columns to free discussion of the slavery issue and that antislavery articles could be published only as advertisements.[20]

The year 1852 was noted for the publication of Harriet Beecher Stowe's influential book, *Uncle Tom's Cabin*. Philadelphia abolitionists were distressed that portions of the book seemed to give support to the program of the American Colonization Society. On 28 December 1852 the executive committee of the Pennsylvania Anti-Slavery Society appointed Robert Purvis and Mary Grew to seek an interview with Mrs. Stowe "to impart right views to her upon this subject."[21] Two weeks later they decided to give a copy of the book to every person who obtained one new subscriber to the *Pennsylvania Freeman*.

Despite ill health, Mary Grew served as chairman of the female society's fair committee in 1852, as she so often did. Writing to Elizabeth Neall Gay in the spring of 1852, she remarked that she had been "so miserable since you were here, so utterly good-for-nothing that I have been compelled to live in almost entire idleness."[22] In August she spoke of her "extreme physical debility" and remarked that she and her friend Margaret Jones had been to the shore, hoping that the sea air would help restore her health.[23] In November she wrote that the labor of preparation for the fair, which was held just before Christmas, had "nearly overwhelmed" her, but that the benefit she had derived from her long stay at the seashore during the summer had remained with her and that she was "much stronger and better" than she had been for two or three years.[24] She had resolved not to become so engrossed with the fair, on account of the precarious state of her health, but Sarah Pugh's absence (in England) made it necessary for her to take charge.

This was the seventeenth annual fair sponsored by the Philadelphia Female Anti-Slavery Society. It was held in the Grand Saloon of the Assembly Buildings on Tuesday, Wednesday, Thursday, and Friday, the 14, 15, 16, and 17 of December. Mary Grew thought it "a highly successful one, affording great encouragement for future efforts." The hall was crowded with visitors and the tables were thronged with purchasers. On the third evening an address was delivered by the Reverend William H. Furness, minister of Philadelphia's First Unitarian Church. Contributions to the sale came from many communities in southeastern Pennsylvania and from such distant places as Boston, Pawtucket, and New London, and from Birmingham and Bristol, England. The tables were surmounted with "light and graceful Iron Arches covered with Evergreens." The receipts from the fair came to $1,816.60; expenses were $415.55, leaving a net profit of $1,401.05. In January 1853 the female society made a donation of $1,200 to the Pennsylvania Anti-Slavery Society, of which it was a major supporter.[25]

The fair was scarcely over before Mary Grew had to face the task of writing the society's annual report, which was published early in January. In this report she hailed the release of Rachel and Elizabeth Parker, two freeborn black girls who had been kidnapped in Chester County in 1851 and who had been put on trial in Baltimore. She also noted with favor the election of the abolitionist Gerrit Smith to Congress but again expressed her conviction that a moral reform could not be accomplished through a political party. She expressed her regret that Hungarian patriot Louis Kossuth, who had been touring the United States, had left without condemning American Negro slavery. She expressed her sorrow at the death of the well-known abolitionist Isaac T. Hopper. In conclusion, she expressed her faith that "before the influences of truth and righteousness, error and sin are destined to pass away, and the true brotherhood of Man to be universally felt and acknowledged."[26]

In May 1853 Mary Grew made an address to the Female Anti-Slavery Society, alluding to the past labors and trials of the abolitionists during the previous twenty years and the progress of the cause during that time. She went on to point out the vast work that still lay ahead of them and the pressing need for increased labor on the part of all persons regardless of their position or profession. She saw a "sacred obligation of humanity and Christianity to help the deliverance of the slave."[27] Lucretia Mott and Sojourner Truth spoke at the same meeting.

Sarah Pugh returned to her position as president of the female society in 1853 after an absence of seventeen months, which were spent in part giving antislavery lectures in England. On 22 March 1853 the executive committee of the Pennsylvania Anti-Slavery Society asked Robert Purvis, Miller McKim, and Mary Grew to go on a mission to England. Purvis and Mary Grew declined, but McKim decided to go, and Mary Grew helped to draft a letter "accrediting him to the people of England" as a representative of the state antislavery society.[28] It appears from the private correspondence that Mary Grew was not well enough to undertake a foreign mission. "I try to make the most of the comparatively cool hours of the early morning," she wrote to Elizabeth Neall Gay in June, "when I have a little of the breath of life in me, but somehow, I get very little accomplished."[29] "Your very kind letter," she wrote a few weeks later, "found me in the country, whither I had escaped from the heat of the city."[30] She spent the rest of the summer at Long Branch, New Jersey. In October she wrote, "I am suffering from a shocking cold, and am miserable."[31]

In November 1853 there was a flurry of excitement in the Philadelphia Female Anti-Slavery Society when one of its members, Hannah Stickney, suggested that the word *female* be stricken from the society's name. This came in connection with a proposal by Thomas Curtis to form a Philadelphia City Anti-Slavery Society including both men and women. The Female Society would be merged with it. Mary Grew expressed herself as decidedly opposed to any plan that would "materially change the character of our society," which had "ever been true to the highest form of anti-slavery principle professed by American abolitionists."[32] The proposal was not accepted.

The highlight of the year 1853 for Mary Grew and her father was the convention of the American Anti-Slavery Society in commemoration of its Second Decade, which met in Philadelphia on 3–5 December. Wendell Phillips was among those attending and speaking. Henry Grew opened the proceedings with prayer, offered "in a fervent spirit."[33] Mary Grew served on the business committee, which proposed resolutions of thanks to "the many faithful friends of the Anti-Slavery cause, across the Atlantic" and to James Miller McKim and Sarah Pugh for their work in vindicating the American Anti-Slavery Society against its foreign detractors.[34] The convention also adopted a resolution denouncing the American Colonization Society. There was some controversy at the convention over whether emanicipation of the slaves was to be accomplished through human effort or by supernatural intervention. Henry Grew stood on the side of God: "after all the use of the means, the employment of the faculties which God has given us, the powers by which he has distinguished Humanity, we are still dependent on his own Divine blessing."[35]

Philadelphia abolitionists were greatly disturbed when they learned early in 1854 that Senator Stephen A. Douglas of Illinois had introduced in Congress a bill providing for the organization of two new federal territories in the West—Kansas and Nebraska—and giving the white settlers the right to decide whether to permit slavery in those territories. This measure would, in effect, repeal the Missouri Compromise of 1820, which had forbidden slavery in Western territory north of the line of 36°30'. The executive committee of the Pennsylvania Anti-Slavery Society discussed this issue on 7 February and decided that petitions should be circulated and public meetings held to protest the bill.[36] The Philadelphia Female Anti-Slavery Society took up the topic on 9 February, when it adopted a resolution proposed by Mary Grew to send a remonstrance to Congress on behalf of the society against the adoption of the Nebraska Bill. The members also resolved to send a petition to the General Assembly requesting that body to instruct Pennsylvania senators and congressmen to vote against the bill.[37] On 21 February the state society executive board adopted a resolution offered by Mary Grew declaring: "We protest against [the bill], chiefly, and most earnestly, because it will extend the area of Slavery, and doom to the worst form of bondage, successive generations of human beings."[38]

In May the antislavery women became greatly exercised by the use of the full power and purse of the federal government to return to slavery the fugitive Anthony Burns, who had escaped from Virginia to Boston. They adopted another resolution, proposed by Mary Grew, as follows:

That the Society witness with regret the alarming evidences of national depravity exhibited in the violation of the Missouri Compromise and in the recent terrible execution of the Fugitive Slave Law in Boston; and that we regard them as incentives to more energetic labor in behalf of the cause of Freedom; and that we do hereby pledge ourselves never to relax our efforts to abolish American Slavery, until our work is accomplished or until death shall close our labors.[39]

In the spring of 1854 negotiations were undertaken for a merger of the *Pennsylvania Freeman* with the *National Anti-Slavery Standard* of New York, the organ of the American Anti-Slavery Society. The executive board of the Pennsylvania Anti-Slavery Society, sponsor of the *Freeman,* delegated Mary Grew to write an editorial for the Philadelphia paper presenting objections against union with the *Standard.* Her argument appeared in the *Freeman* on 8 June 1854. She presented five reasons why the paper should not merge. One was that the *Freeman* presented local news and advertisements that would not be of interest to readers of the *Standard.* A second was that it was needed to combat the proslavery stance of other Philadelphia papers. A third was that it was a rallying point for eastern Pennsylvanians who loved freedom. A fourth was that it was needed to combat "the alarming advance of the slave power, the terrible execution of the Fugitive Slave law, the heartless apathy of the Church." Finally, Mary Grew thought it was unwise to centralize the money and power of the antislavery forces: "Any moral enterprise is safer while the money and the journals which promote it, are in the hands of several independent societies, than when they are consolidated under one controlling power."[40] The majority of the society apparently found these arguments unconvincing. A meeting open to the entire membership, held on 13 June 1854, voted to merge the *Freeman* with the *Standard.*

Mary Grew was complaining of illness again in September. "I have been very miserable since my return home," she wrote, "and am not, now, good for much. I hope to be able to do something for the Fair."[41] She turned the chairmanship of the fair committee over to the society's president, Sarah Pugh.

By January, however, she was able to produce the society's annual report, its twenty-first. In this document she remarked that the Kansas-Nebraska Act, which had repealed the Missouri Compromise, had produced "a strong reaction in favor of freedom, throughout the North." The Northern press, "even the northern pulpit," had protested "in words and tones of manly indignation, against this shameless violation of faith."[42] Mary Grew also saw signs of moral progress in the reaction of the people of Boston to the efforts of the federal government to return Anthony Burns to slavery. So determined was their opposition to these efforts that "large forces of the Artillery and

Infantry of the United States" and a hundred deputy marshals, "armed with cutlasses and revolvers, were required to carry one poor fugitive slave, from the soil of Massachusetts into slavery." To accomplish "this disgraceful deed," the United States government expended thirteen thousand dollars. "Not from Massachusetts alone, but from almost every northern State, have been heard the threats of earnest men, never known as abolitionists, that the Compromises of 1850 shall be repealed by the people, though they may remain on the nation's statute books."[43]

In this report Mary Grew also denounced the bulk of Northern politicians, whom she saw as tools of "the Slave Power," and Northern clergymen, whom she thought "false to the name of Christian."[44] She saw no hope in antislavery political parties; they had "yielded one principle after another" and finally merged into one of the major parties.[45] With few exceptions, American churchmen uttered no protests against "an institution which robs millions of men of their dearest rights, which violates every command of the Decalogue, and every principle of Christianity."[46] Slaveholders were freely admitted to Northern communion tables and pulpits, while black men were assigned to separate pews or benches. The best hope for the abolition of slavery, she thought, lay in dissolution of the Union.[47] She also dealt in her report with several fugitive slave cases that had arisen in Pennsylvania. One involved a man named Bright, who had remained in Lancaster after his escape from slavery instead of securing his freedom by flight to Canada. He had been captured and returned to slavery. "While we mourn over these infamous deeds," she wrote, "we rejoice in the fact that they have become very unfrequent in our city; while the number of fugitives who pass through it, on their way to a land of liberty, is rapidly increasing."[48] Finally, she expressed her confidence in "the eternal principles which are the foundation of our enterprise. . . . We are not discouraged, though the oppressor seems to triumph for a season." Despite the opening of new territory to slavery and the return of fugitives to slavery, "God is stronger than human governments; and He will, yet, be exalted in the earth."[49]

A landmark in Mary Grew's career, foreshadowing its second phase, took place when she attended the Fifth National Woman's Rights Convention, which met in Sansom Street Hall, Philadelphia, on 18 October 1854. She was appointed to the business committee. Ernestine L. Rose was president of the convention, and Lucretia Mott was one of the vice presidents. One of the most interesting features of this gathering was a debate provoked by the Reverend Henry Grew, who asked for the floor and announced that he was "sorry to differ from the general tone of the speakers present," but that his view of woman's rights was based on Scripture. He quoted numerous Bible texts to show that "it was clearly the will of God that man should be superior in power and authority to woman." He asserted that no lesson was "more plainly and frequently taught in the Bible, than woman's subjection."[50] Among those replying to him was Lucretia Mott, who asserted; "It is not Christianity, but priestcraft that has subjected woman as we find her."[51] William Lloyd Garrison asked, "Why go to the Bible to settle this question? . . . What question was ever settled by the Bible?"[52] Furthermore, he suggested, "Would Mr. Grew say that woman can not preach, in the face of such a preacher as LUCRETIA MOTT?" At this point, Mrs. Mott "begged leave to substitute friend Grew's own daughter, Mary Grew, who had already spoken on this platform!!"[53] She also pointed out that, in opposition to the teachings of Paul, Henry Grew had married a second time; therefore he did not really believe "that the Scriptures were entirely inspired."[54] After protracted discussion, the convention passed a resolution proposed by Garrison stating

> That whatever any book may teach, the rights of no human being are dependent upon or modified thereby, but are equal, absolute, essential, inalienable in the person of every member of the human family, without regard to sex, race, or clime.[55]

Late in 1854 one of Mary Grew's best friends, Margaret Jones, became engaged to Cyrus M. Burleigh, who had served with Mary Grew as coeditor of the *Pennsylvania Freeman*. Normally this would have been a cause for rejoicing, but Burleigh was seriously ill. Writing to her friends Sydney and Elizabeth Gay, Mary Grew said of the engagement, "What it has cost me, I could not tell, if I would, and if I could. I would not pain and worry you with it. *For myself* I have ceased to feel anxious, about it, and, now, all my anxieties, and fears are for Margaret, who, I think, will put her health and life in great peril, if she marries a man who is in the *later* stages of consumption, and who has no *rational* prospect of living six months longer." Burleigh thought that the danger existed chiefly in Mary Grew's own "anxious fancy." "Such things must take their own course," she wrote with resignation. "For my own part, I have learned to submit to the inevitable, and, more than this, I have the comfort of believing that, on the whole, & ultimately, every thing is for the best."[56] The marriage took place on 3 February 1855. On 7 March Burleigh died. Soon thereafter Margaret Burleigh moved in with the Grews and remained with Mary Grew until her own death in 1892. The executive committee of the Pennsylvania Anti-Slavery Society passed a resolution of regret on Burleigh's death. On his deathbed he had dictated to Mary Grew a farewell message to this committee, which was incorporated in its minutes.[57]

In the summer of 1855 Mary Grew and Margaret Burleigh visited William Lloyd Garrison and his family at their "hospitable home" in Boston. Mary became particularly fond of the Garrison children and corresponded with them in subsequent years. From Boston they went to Plainfield and Brooklyn, Connecticut, and to Staten Island, New York. After returning to Philadelphia for about a week in the middle of July, when the weather was very hot, they went on to Salem, Ohio, to visit Benjamin and Elizabeth Jones. Salem was the home of the *Anti-Slavery Bugle,* a well-known abolitionist newspaper, which Jones had founded in 1845. There the Philadelphia women found "a thoroughly anti-slavery atmosphere." Salem, they were told, had "the honor to be a place especially feared and hated by the South, as one from which it is useless to attempt the recovery of a fugitive slave." They looked forward to attending the meeting of the Western Anti-Slavery Society in Salem "if our health permits." "At present," they wrote, "the strength of neither of us is Herculean, but we hope for invigoration from pure air, & the rest and quiet which we are enjoying."[58]

In the fall of 1855 Mary Grew became deeply concerned with the case of Passmore Williamson, a Philadelphia Quaker who was imprisoned for his part in helping a female slave and her two sons, from Virginia, secure their freedom while traveling through Philadelphia with their owner, John H. Wheeler. Wheeler was the United States minister to Nicaragua and was on his way to New York City, where he planned to embark on a voyage to resume his duties in Central America. The slave was Jane Johnson and her sons were named Daniel and Isaiah. While stopping over at a hotel in Philadelphia on 18 July 1855, prior to taking a boat to New York, Jane, disregarding her master's instructions that she was to talk to no one, twice informed passing blacks that she was a slave and desirous of her freedom. She was able to do this while Wheeler was eating dinner. After dinner Wheeler took his slaves and boarded the *Washington,* a boat upon which they were scheduled to sail at 5:00 P.M.[59]

At 4:30 P.M. William Still, a Philadelphia black, clerk in the office of the Pennsylvania Anti-Slavery Society, and a member of the Philadelphia Vigilance Committee, received a note informing him of the plight of the Wheeler slaves. Still immediately sent a message to Passmore Williamson, an officer of the Pennsylvania Abolition Society and also a member of the vigilance committee. Williamson and Still, followed by a group of blacks, hastened to the *Washington,* located Jane Johnson and her sons, and informed her that under Pennsylvania law (the "Personal Liberty law" of 1847), they were free. With the assistance of the blacks, they were escorted off the ship, despite Wheeler's efforts to detain them. Wheeler decided to appeal to Judge John K. Kane of the United States District Court of Eastern Pennsylvania for a writ of habeas corpus compelling Williamson to produce the slaves and bring them to Kane's court. Williamson could not or would not do this. On 27 July Judge Kane committed him to jail on a charge of contempt of court. He spent the next three months in Moyamensing Prison.[60]

The executive committee of the Pennsylvania Anti-Slavery Society commissioned Mary Grew to prepare a pamphlet on this case for public circulation.[61] It was published by the society under the title *Narrative of Facts in the Case of Passmore Williamson* (1855). It was not just a narrative of facts but also an impassioned attack on Judge Kane's handling of the case.

> Citizens of Pennsylvania! What shall be the end of these things? An officer of the Federal Government has usurped authority in a case wholly beyond his jurisdiction, and without law, or the shadow of law, has immured in one of your prisons, a citizen of Pennsylvania.[62]

"The Slave power of this nation," she went on, "which has been long and steadily encroaching upon the rights of the North, emboldened by success, has evidently resolved to re-establish slavery on your soil, by asserting and maintaining, in defiance of your laws, the right to carry and hold their slaves wherever they choose to go, under the Constitution of the United States."[63]

At the meeting of the Philadelphia Female Anti-Slavery Society on 13 September 1855, Mary Grew presented a letter addressed to Passmore Williamson and his wife, expressing "the warmest sympathy of this Society with him in the sacrifice and suffering he is now enduring for the Anti-Slavery cause."[64] She also proposed resolutions regarding the case, which the society adopted and sent to the *National Anti-Slavery Standard* and to the Philadelphia city papers. One declared that "our State, and our nation have been deeply disgraced by the illegal imprisonment of Passmore Williamson, by Judge Kane, on a charge of contempt of Court." The case was one where he had no jurisdiction and where "the only offence of the prisoner was the exercise of his right, and the performance of his duty, in informing a free woman, once a slave, that, by the laws of Pennsylvania, she was made free."[65] A second resolution declared that Judge Kane's action represented "a tyrannical usurpation of power, a bold defiance of the laws of Pennsylvania, an alarming invasion of State Rights, a precedent dangerous to the personal liberty of every citizen of the State, and a contemptible prostration of a Northern freeman before the altar of Southern Slavery."[66]

William Still and the five other blacks who had assisted Jane Johnson and her sons to escape from Wheeler were prosecuted for highway robbery, inciting to riot, riot, and assault and battery.[67] Their trial took place in the Philadelphia county court, Judge William D. Kelley presiding. Jane Johnson, who had left Pennsylvania for New York and Massachusetts, reappeared in Philadelphia to help defend those who had assisted her. She was given aid and comfort by Mary Grew and other members of the Female Anti-Slavery Society, who sat with her in the courtroom as she observed the proceedings. She testified that she had desired her freedom, that it was Wheeler who had restrained her, and that she had not been forced off the ship. At the completion of her testimony, she was safely escorted from the courtroom. Judge Kelley reminded the jury that "when Col. Wheeler and his servants crossed the border of Pennsylvania, Jane Johnson and her two sons became as free as he."[68] The jury exonerated all the defendants of the riot charge and declared only two guilty of assault and battery. These two were sentenced to a week in jail and fined ten dollars and court costs. William Still was not convicted.[69]

On 3 November Williamson appeared in the United States District Court and testified that he had not intended contempt of court and that he had not produced the slaves in court because they had fled. The court accepted his statement and released him from the charge of contempt and from jail.[70] Jane Johnson and her children remained free. Wheeler went on to Nicaragua.

"The ordeal of Passmore Williamson," Professor Ralph Eckert has written, "served further to polarize sectional beliefs, and acted as yet another controversial wedge in the splitting of the Union."[71]

The House of Representatives in Washington was deadlocked during the winter of 1855–56 over the choice of a Speaker. There were 108 Republicans, 83 Democrats, and 43 Know-Nothings, and no group was able to produce a majority. Finally, after nearly two months and countless votes, a rule to elect the Speaker by plurality vote passed, whereupon Nathaniel P. Banks of Massachusetts, the Republican candidate, was chosen by 103 votes to 100 for the Democratic candidate, a South Carolinian.[72] Mary Grew followed this maneuvering with keen interest and wrote about it in her annual report for the Philadelphia Female Anti-Slavery Society:

> During the last two months, the novel spectacle has been presented to the world, of a nation unable to organize its government, because, divided

against itself, it could not decide whether that government should be the support and defense of the Freedom of the people, or of the tyranny of an oligarchy.

The American people had reason to give thanks when the long contest for the Speakership ended with the prize won "for Freedom."[73]

On 10 April 1856 the Philadelphia Female Anti-Slavery Society discussed the fugitive slave issue. Mary Grew said she "rejoiced in the escape of every fugitive, in as much as every slave fleeing from his master lessened the value of slave property, by proving it insecure, thus preparing the way for the emancipation of all."[74]

On 12 June the society took up the case of Preston Brooks's attack on Charles Sumner in the United States Senate chamber. Mary Grew proposed resolutions that were unanimously adopted and sent to Sumner declaring that the recent assault upon him was "another illustration of the despotism of the Slave Power of this nation; another evidence of its base determination to subjugate free speech, free thought, and a free press; and another exhibition of its unalterable meanness in the choice of measures by which to accomplish its designs."[75] In transmitting these resolutions to Sumner, Mary Grew attached a postscript declaring that they "very imperfectly" expressed the women's indignation at "the outrage which has disgraced the Senate of the United States, our sympathy with your suffering, or our joy in your fidelity to the Right." In times like the present, "which, verily, try men's souls," it was cheering to know that there were "men in our legislative Halls who will dare, at all hazards to themselves, to speak the truth which the hour demands." Sumner's "service and suffering in the cause of human freedom" authorized "all true-hearted men and women in this nation to hail [him] champion and friend."[76]

The newly organized Republican party met in Philadelphia on 17 June 1856 and unanimously nominated Colonel John C. Frémont for President. Writing to Wendell Phillips on 23 June, Mary Grew asked, "Do you imagine that Frémont *can* be elected? Do you know anything of Mr. Sumner's condition, which the papers do not tell us?"[77]

Writing to Elizabeth Neall Gay on 11 September, she remarked that Frémont's prospects in Philadelphia were good and that Charles Sumner was in the city, visiting the Reverend William Henry Furness, Unitarian clergyman and abolitionist.[78]

Mary Grew spent the summer of 1856 in Cayuga County, New York. While she was there, "an orthodox Congregationalist minister" invited her to lecture in his pulpit. "Wasn't that a step toward women's rights," she remarked, "for a clergyman to take?"[79]

Writing to Phillips after the presidential election of 1856, Mary

Grew commented that now that the election was over "& things here have settled in their old quiescence (as things easily do here) we abolitionists must cultivate the ground which Republicanism ploughed up. . . . We must, if possible, reach the consciences & hearts of these stupid people who have made Buchanan President, not knowing what they did." She looked to the annual December fair as "an efficient instrumentality in our work." It was usually a time of revival for "the lukewarm." She begged Phillips to come and speak at the fair. "We intend to spare no pains," she wrote, "in the work of regenerating this depraved community."[80]

In the same letter, Mary Grew commended to Phillips's attention the recently published *Autobiography of a Female Slave*, by Martha (Griffith) Browne of Kentucky, who was spending some time in Philadelphia. This was actually the *biography* of a slave written by a Southern white woman, the daughter of a deceased slaveholder. She freed her father's slaves, came North, settling in Massachusetts in 1860, and in 1867 married Albert G. Browne, who had been private secretary to Governor John A. Andrew. She died in 1906. Mary Grew thought her book was "the most terrible & heart-rending narration that I ever read." It was "not fiction, but a collection of facts which have come within the writer's knowledge, & which she has woven into one story. . . . If you are in correspondence with Mr. Furness, you may have heard of this young lady," she wrote, "for he is deeply interested in her, as, indeed, we all are." In this letter, Mary Grew also commented on Harriet Beecher Stowe's new book, *Dred.* "Yes," she told Phillips, "I think you may venture to read it. I finished it the other day. You won't cry over it." It did not "stir the soul" as *Uncle Tom* did, "& neither of them moved & sickened me, as Miss Griffith's book does, though as literary productions they are far superior."[81]

Much of Mary Grew's ongoing correspondence with Wendell Phillips concerned Charles Greene, brother of Phillips's wife, Ann Terry Greene, and cousin of Mary Grew. Charles Greene and his wife lived in Philadelphia in somewhat straitened circumstances, and it appears that he was somewhat less than fully competent. Phillips funneled money to them through the hands of Mary Grew. Late in 1856 Greene opened a small apothecary shop. "Perhaps he may earn something in this way," Mary Grew reported to Phillips. "I see him frequently, & Mrs. Greene occasionally. They both seem in better health than formerly." She assured Phillips that the way in which he was sending money for the Greenes was "perfectly satisfactory. . ;. . There is no difficulty in getting the cheques cashed."[82]

Reviewing the events of the preceding year in the twenty-third annual report of the Philadelphia Female Anti-Slavery Society, Mary

Grew saw "many indications of the progress of our enterprise." It was true that a senator from Massachusetts, "for words spoken in the United States Senate Chamber, in behalf of freedom," had been stricken down "by a murderous hand." It was true that Kansas, "bleeding at every vein," was still "in the grasp of the Slave Power." It was true that in three recent presidential elections "the hosts of Slavery were triumphant." Notwithstanding all this, she declared, "we can clearly perceive that the anti-slavery cause is advancing." The assault on Sumner had aroused "in the heart of Massachusets indignation which will not be appeased" and was leading many of its people to question the value of a Union "which cannot secure, to a sovereign State, freedom of speech in the councils of the nation." The aggressions of the "Border Ruffians" in Kansas had awakened throughout the North a spirit of resistance "such as the Slave Power has never before aroused." The Republican party, with its opposition to the extension of slavery, had suggested to many minds the question: "Should a system, the extension of which would be fraught with such unutterable evil, be suffered to exist at all, in this republic?"[83]

"Among the cheering events of the last year," she wrote, "we may record the safe escape of a large number of fugitives from slavery," many of whom passed through Philadelphia.[84]

In conclusion, she expressed her confidence that "the cause of liberty will ultimately triumph." Whether that triumph was to be won through "the destruction of this boasting and guilty nation" or "by timely repentance" and "a bloodless victory of right over wrong," none could foretell.[85]

Mary Grew was a Garrisonian and accepted Garrison's principles of disunionism and no-voting. Writing to Wendell Phillips early in 1857, she observed that she considered a recent Disunion Convention "remarkable & important" due to the mere fact that it had been safely held despite opposition from the press and the public. "Think of an attempt to hold such a Convention fifteen years ago! . . . Have you any agents to spare to us?" she asked. "Good lecturers, sound in our faith of disunion? Pennsylvania is suffering for want of them." She went on to express her opinion that the Republican party movement "has done our cause much harm, here."[86]

Writing to Wendell and Ann Phillips in April, Mary Grew reported that she was "very slowly recovering from two successive attacks of sickness, the latter being measles." Illness had kept her idle "for about two months." Her friend Margaret Burleigh was talking of attending the annual meeting of the American Anti-Slavery Society in New York in May, but she herself did not feel well enough to go. In the same letter she expressed her regret that James and Lucretia Mott had moved to the country; "we feel the loss very much."[87]

William Lloyd Garrison and Oliver Johnson visited Philadelphia in May 1857 and paid a call on Mary Grew and Margaret Burleigh. "Mary is slowly recovering from her long and severe indisposition," Garrison reported, "but she looks very frail." Henry Grew was "too unwell to see us."[88]

Forwarding some of Charles Greene's bills to Wendell and Ann Phillips in July, she reported that Charles was "constantly expecting the second advent of Christ. . . . I was quite startled, not long ago, by Mrs. Greene telling me that Charles expected to leave her, in about a month, but I soon discovered that she referred to this expected advent." In the same letter she noted that Abby Kelley Foster was in Philadelphia and exclaimed, "What an earnest good soul she is!"[89] By this time Mary Grew was well enough to go to Hartford to attend the wedding of a niece. On her return, however, she was complaining of extreme fatigue. She was planning to spend the rest of the summer at the seashore.[90]

She returned to Philadelphia still feeling poorly. She hoped that "rest and comparative quietness, for some months to come, may restore me to working condition." She found it difficult and painful "to be idle in our cause, at such a time as this."[91] "Our approaching Fair must do without me," she wrote.[92] Speaking of the problems accompanying the Panic of 1857, she observed: "At present, there is little talked about here, excepting the times, which all mercantile men agree in pronouncing awful—the worst ever known, some of them say."[93] In October she wrote William Lloyd Garrison of her deep concern that he might have to renege on his commitment to address the coming convention of the Pennsylvania Anti-Slavery Society in West Chester on the twenty-third and twenty-fourth, begging him to send Wendell Phillips in his place. Actually, neither Garrison nor Phillips attended, but Mary Grew did, served on the business committee, and gave an address.[94] Phillips gave two lectures in Philadelphia a little later, which Mary Grew heard and very much enjoyed. In December she took a trip to Providence to attend the wedding of another niece.[95]

In March 1858 she was again complaining of her "feeble condition"—"very weak and good for nothing, since my return home." She felt unable to write the annual report of the Philadelphia Anti-Slavery Society for 1857, and "as no one else was willing to write one, the Society is left unreported for the last year. . . . No great calamity, I imagine," she concluded philosophically. She used all her strength to

a meeting of the "Old Female" and found the experience
ting.[96] In May, however, she was well enough to speak at an
very meeting in Clarkson Hall, Philadelphia.[97] Neither she nor
her father felt able to attend the annual meeting of the American Anti-
Slavery Society in New York that year.[98]

With reference to the religious revival that swept the country in
1857–58, she confided that she had "much less confidence in its
genuineness, and its power of promoting Christianity, than my father
has. . . . "Notwithstanding his Calvinistic theories of human nature,
which are very sound, he has more confidence in men, more trust in
their devotional utterance & professions of piety, then I possibly can
have." She had no doubt that many individuals found spiritual benefit
in the revival, but she greatly feared that it would strengthen "an
already strong pro-slavery church."[99]

She begged Wendell Phillips to come again to Philadelphia to
lecture in 1858. There was "far too little anti-slavery labor bestowed
on Pennsylvania," which she considered to be "morally and intellec-
tually, in a very stupid condition," out of which it was coming "very
slowly."[100]

In October 1858 she spoke along with Lucretia Mott and several
men at an antislavery meeting in West Chester.[101] In November she
presented a petition to the executive committee of the Pennsylvania
Anti-Slavery Society, asking the members of the state legislature to
pass a law "prohibiting the surrender of any human being claimed as a
Slave upon the soil of Pennsylvania."[102] It was ordered to be printed
and circulated for signatures.

Another fugitive slave case attracted Mary Grew's attention early in
1859, that of Daniel Dangerfield, sometimes referred to as Daniel
Webster. Like many slaves escaping from the South, Dangerfield did
not try to reach Canada but took a job on a farm near Harrisburg,
where he was seized and brought into a Philadelphia court for trial as
a runaway. Lucretia Mott, Sarah Pugh, Mary Grew, and Mary Earle
came to this trial and remained throughout the night, as the trial went
on. Shortly after daybreak Dangerfield was released on the grounds
that the warrant for his return did not correctly specify his height.[103]
Writing of this case in the *Twenty-Sixth Annual Report of the Philadelphia Female Anti-Slavery Society,* Mary Grew observed:

We hailed this triumph of Freedom, partial though it was, as a proof of a
great change wrought in popular feeling; in which change we saw the
result of twenty-five years of earnest effort to impress upon the heart of
this community anti-slavery doctrines and sentiments. For this we thanked
God; from this we took courage to pursue our work with unabated vigor,

and with renewed hope that Pennsylvania will yet become worthy of the name of a free Commonwealth.[104]

She proposed resolutions that the Female Anti-Slavery Society adopted on 14 April 1859, declaring that "Our City and Commonwealth have been again disgraced by the trial of a man on the charge of being a fugitive slave" and resolving that "we earnestly protest against this insult to Pennsylvania, this outrage on humanity, this heinous sin against God." While they rejoiced in the alleged fugitive's release, they regretted that the reason for his discharge was not simply that he was a man but only because of the failure of the claimant to identify him correctly. They expressed their determination to secure the repeal of the Fugitive Slave Act and the passage by the Pennsylvania Assembly of a law to prevent the commonwealth from being any longer "a hunting-ground for slave-catchers."[105]

Mary Grew continued to press for passage by Pennsylvania's General Assembly of a new and stronger Personal Liberty Law. "Our election, just over," she wrote to Wendell Phillips in October, "puts a large Republican force into that body, but whether these Republicans would aid or strangle such a bill, Heaven only knows." She had precious little faith in them or any political party. Her object was to move "the *people*."[106]

On 16 October 1859 the nation was shocked to learn that the abolitionist fanatic John Brown, with a party of eighteen men, had attacked the federal arsenal at Harpers Ferry, Virginia, intending to arm the slaves for insurrection. The attempt was speedily put down by a detachment of United States Marines commanded by Captain Robert E. Lee. Brown was put on trial by the state of Virginia for murder, treason, and insurrection. He was promptly convicted and sentenced to be hanged on 2 December.[107] Reviled throughout the South, he became a martyr in the North. Philadelphia abolitionists organized a public meeting in his memory held on the day of his execution. Mary Grew was among the speakers.

In response to a call from "the Friends of Impartial Freedom," the meeting was held in National Hall at 11:30 A.M. The hall was not opened until a few minutes before that time. A huge crowd gathered in the streets. All seats were filled, many with blacks. Numerous people had to stand. James Mott called the meeting to order amid cries of "sit down" and "hats off in front." The tide of sentiment in the streets was against John Brown. Dr. William Henry Furness, pastor of Philadelphia's First Unitarian Church, opened the meeting with prayer and then gave a speech. Next came Theodore Tilton, editor of the *New York Independent,* a liberal Congregationalist paper. Then

Mary Grew spoke. She was not there to eulogize Brown, she said, but to point out lessons from his experience. "One lesson of this awful hour," she declared, "is an unswerving loyalty to right." Another was that of "self-sacrifice for the good of humanity." A third was "the great brotherhood of man, the great fundamental principles of Democracy and Christianity." The instrument by which reform was effected was the "sword of the Spirit, not the sword of carnal warfare." Lucretia Mott and Robert Purvis also spoke. The *Public Ledger* noted that Mary Grew was the only speaker not interrupted by catcalls from the audience, which included a large pro-Southern element.[108]

A study of *Pioneer Women Orators* (1956) by Lillian O'Connor, a speech scholar who examined five of Mary Grew's antebellum addresses, concluded that she was an effective speaker and was acquainted with the standard rhetorical theory of the day, as exemplified in Hugh Blair's *Lectures on Rhetoric and Belles-letters* (Philadelphia, 1848). She was one of the small group of daring pioneers who broke traditional taboos against women speaking in public.

In her annual report for 1859, Mary Grew remarked that this was the largest meeting ever assembled in Philadelphia for an antislavery purpose. She also reported that "a riotous attempt" was made to prevent the meeting's being held, but that the rioters had been put down by the city authorities—"another triumph of freedom of speech over despotism." A large meeting was assembled "for the purpose of making a peace-offering to Southern slaveholders. . . . "The contempt with which these overtures were received by the Southern press, was a fitting rebuke of such cringing servility to tyranny," she observed.[109]

In the same report she wrote that the "martyrdom of JOHN BROWN was the great event of the year in "the contest between Freedom and Slavery." In later years, she predicted, this event would stand out, "in its true proportions, revealing the grandeur and beauty of the human soul in its hours of self-sacrifice." John Brown would be remembered as "one who freely and deliberately gave his life for the ransom of the American slave."[110] The Philadelphia Female Anti-Slavery Society had adopted resolutions hailing John Brown as "a martyr in the glorious cause of human liberty" but at the same time deploring use of "the weapons of physical warfare" in the crusade against slavery.[111] These resolutions were published in the *National Anti-Slavery Standard* and in several of Philadelphia's daily papers.[112]

For twenty-four consecutive years, Mary Grew wrote in her report for 1859, the annual fair sponsored by the Female Anti-Slavery Society had been held in Philadelphia without disturbance. It had always been conducted "with order and dignity, and with careful fidelity to just principles of traffic." It had been considered an important department of the antislavery enterprise, both account of its financial contributions, which had amounted to more than thirty thousand dollars, and for the moral influence it had exerted. Until 1859 it had never been interrupted by proslavery animosity. It had never been the object of mob violence such as the burning of Pennsylvania Hall. The fair was opened in Concert Hall on the twelfth of December, "with its usual prospects of success." As usual, its flag was suspended over Chestnut Street, displaying a picture of the revered Liberty Bell. Visitors came in throngs, and the fair proceeded without interruption until the fourth day, when "the High Constable" entered and, in the name of the mayor, requested of one of the fair's managers that their flag should be taken down. The manager replied, in protest, that many other exhibitions in the city were allowed the privilege of displaying banners. The officer agreed but stated that "popular commotion" rendered the removal of their flag necessary. The manager then said that they would take the flag down only if it were ordered by the mayor, not merely requested by the constable. The officer said the mayor did order this, and the manager gave directions for its removal.[113]

A few hours later, the sheriff came into the hall, took possession of the building, closed the doors, and informed the fair's managers that their goods must be removed within three hours. The ladies then learned that plans had been developing for several days for their dispossession. An effort had been made to persuade the owners of the building to cancel their lease, which was for a week. The ladies were able to arrange removal to the Assembly Buildings, where the fair continued until the end of the week. Despite the unusual opposition arrayed against it, including that from some of the city's newspapers, the fair from a pecuniary point of view was "very successful," taking in more than two thousand dollars.[114]

In reviewing the events of 1859, Mary Grew concluded that the members of the Philadelphia Female Anti-Slavery Society were confirmed in their confidence in the principles they advocated and in the measures they used for their propagation. "We address ourselves to the work of another year," she wrote in conclusion, "with reverent gratitude for the posts assigned to us in the great moral conflict of the age, and with joyous faith that the God of the oppressed is leading their cause onward to victory."[115]

In January 1860 Mary Grew conducted antislavery meetings at Tullytown and Yardleyville, Pennsylvania, on behalf of the state society—"attendance was good."[116] In February she noted that abolitionism had aroused a good deal of opposition in Philadelphia, but that the civil authorities had protected the reformers' right of free speech.[117] In April she reported that her father had been very sick, and that "for a few days we were doubtful of his recovery," but that he was now well and able to go out.[118]

While maintaining her primary commitment to abolitionism, Mary Grew turned her attention again to woman's rights in 1860, the cause that was to occupy her during the second half of her long career as a reformer. She attended the Tenth National Woman's Rights Convention at Cooper Institute, New York City, on 10–11 May 1860. She served on the business committee and gave the closing address.[119] "The word I would impress upon you all, as you go hence, is this—it is always safe to do right," she told her audience.[120] She was convinced that equality for women was a matter of fundamental, God-given rights. While in New York she visited Sydney and Elizabeth Gay. Since her return to Philadelphia, she wrote, she had spent a great deal of time in "seeking rest from the excitement and fatigue of that most delightful visit."[121]

On 16 May 1860 the burgeoning Republican party held its national convention in Chicago and nominated Abraham Lincoln for president, after William H. Seward had led on the first two ballots. "I regretted Seward's defeat," Mary Grew wrote, "because I thought him more heartily opposed to slavery than any of the proposed nominees." But from all that she was hearing of Lincoln, she was beginning to think that he might be as much opposed to slavery as Seward; "and he is, probably, a more truthful man."[122]

In the fall of 1860 she was in correspondence with Wendell Phillips concerning financial assistance for a movement in Pennsylvania for securing to married women "a right,—no—they have the right—power to control their own earnings, & also a just guardianship of their children." Pennsylvania had passed a law in 1848 protecting married women's rights to hold property "excepting what they earn, the very point where they most need protection." She thought it might be possible to get the statute amended and desired to "put measures in train for it."[123] She had talked with Susan B. Anthony about the matter when she was in New York the previous May, and the latter had sent her a box of tracts relating to it. She wondered whether Phillips could make available to her some proceeds of a fund left by Charles F. Hovey for antislavery and woman's rights work for use in this connection. "I know that some other person than I ought to undertake the management of this affair," she wrote, "but then I don't see that other person." She did know some people who were willing to help. She had no intention of doing this instead of any portion of her antislavery work; she felt "neither inclination nor liberty to do so." But she wanted to try, "without any great expenditure of time or strength, to set the thing in motion, & get other persons to do the main part of the work. Now that's what I call Yankee economy."[124]

Money would be needed, she thought, to print petitions, to help pay for their circulation, to organize meetings and obtain speakers, to publish articles in the newspapers, and to send advocates of the cause to Harrisburg. She asked Phillips to let her know what amount he would deem appropriate to contribute. She had been in correspondence with two members of the legislature, one in each house, and there was a friend of hers, a lawyer, who would help her in this matter and who was well acquainted with the state's newly elected governor, "so I should not be entirely without resources in Harrisburg." She did not know that she could get enough work done to produce "any great results," but she would like to try. She asked Phillips for his advice and suggestions. She noted that the "invigorating air" she had breathed during six weeks in the Catskills had given her a degree of strength that "though to many persons it would seem weakness, I greatly value. . . . Thanks be to God for the mountains!"[125]

Phillips responded promptly and offered financial help. He asked her to "take charge of Pennsylvania," which she felt was "a rather formidable responsibility," especially so because she could not foresee the result. "Such a work as we need here, must be continued, if begun, else the expense of the beginning," she said, "is, in great measure, lost." Still she thought she should attempt it, providing she could find coadjutors. Before asking him to forward money, she would consult persons upon whose judgment she could rely, both in and out of the legislature, as to the likelihood of success. She would not like to assume, alone, the responsibility of so important a movement, but she believed "the thing can be done."[126]

Mary Grew took advantage of opportunities offered by preparation for the annual antislavery fair to formulate some of her plans relative to the legal protection of women in their earnings. In December she asked Phillips to send her fifty dollars in support of the work, promising to "use it wisely." She did not want more until she knew exactly what the need would be. She was in correspondence with "Mr. Irish, one of our State Senators," who promised to advise and aid her. He would present and advocate such a bill as she wanted. She thought she could obtain similar support from several other members of the assembly. She had talked with "a large number of persons, of various professions," on this subject within the past few months and had found all of them assenting to "the justice of the claim which I propose to make." She would be glad to have any suggestions from Phillips as to how to go about the work. In the same letter she noted that she had been attending antislavery meetings "in the country" and exclaimed, "Isn't this a glorious time to live in; and oughtn't we to be thankful that we are abolitionists?"[127]

On 18 December she reported that the Philadelphia women had held their antislavery fair "successfully & *triumphantly* . . . in spite of advice, warnings, and threats." The mayor, "finding we *would* exercise our rights, said he *would* protect us, at any peril to himself, & he did protect us," despite the fact that he was "no abolitionist." He did better than to put down a riot; he prevented one. His forces were stationed throughout the neighborhood of the fair, most of them out of sight, with "just enough show of strength inside & outside of the Hall, to suggest more."[128] The fair yielded proceeds of $963, but its "chief success," Mary Grew thought, was in the maintenance of the abolitionists' right to assemble.[129]

Beginning with South Carolina on 20 December 1860, the Southern states seceded. "The revolution through which this nation has been passing during the last twenty-five years," Mary Grew wrote in her annual report for 1860, "has culminated in the dissolution of the American Union." This was no surprise to the abolitionists. They had predicted that nothing but the abolition of slavery could prevent disruption of the Union. At the time of her writing, around the end of January 1861, six states had withdrawn. The events of the preceding year, she believed, had shown a steady growth in the determination of the North not to surrender to "the Slave Power." The progress of antislavery sentiment was reflected in the election of Abraham Lincoln as president on a platform of preventing the further spread of slavery in federal territories. This was but a prelude to total abolition, which she thought was bound to come. However, "the final victory of Freedom" could not be won "without stern conflict." The work of abolitionists was not yet done. They must continue to reiterate the principle that "the absolute right is always to be obeyed." "Very hopefully, she concluded, "we commence the labor of another year."[130]

4
"The Day of Jubilee" (1861–1865)

THE executive committee of the Pennsylvania Anti-Slavery Society met on 2 January 1861 to discuss the state of the Union. Those in attendance included Margaret Burleigh, Mary Grew, Abby Kimber, Miller McKim, and Sarah Pugh. South Carolina had seceded, and the other Deep South states were to follow shortly. The committee agreed that "recent events give cause for rejoicing inasmuch as they indicate on the part of the Northern people an increased disposition to adhere to principle, rather than to submit to degrading compromise."[1]

The following week Mary Grew attended a meeeting of the Philadelphia Female Anti-Slavery Society (10 January 1861). There she presented still another petition to be sent to the state General Assembly asking its members "for the sake of the honor of Pennsylvania, to prevent the recurrence of the disgraceful scenes which have been, again and again, enacted in the towns and cities of this Commonwealth, when human beings have been seized and forcibly carried to Southern plantations or Southern markets, to be worked or sold as beasts of burden, in order to satisfy the cupidity of their fellow men."[2] The proposal was adopted, and the Female Society sent yet another memorial to the legislature demanding a stronger and more effective Personal Liberty Law.

"To my usual anti-slavery labor," Mary Grew wrote to Mrs. William Lloyd Garrison on 13 January 1861, "I added this winter, (I know not whether discreetly or not) an effort to obtain from our legislature, a law to secure to married women their right to their earnings, and to the equal guardianship, with the husband, of the children."[3] In the same letter she expressed her concern about Garrison's health (he had been confined to bed with illness) and paid tribute to his thirty years of antislavery labor: "Verily he has fought a good fight." "How do you feel about our country?" she asked Helen Garrison. "Through all the storm & strife, I think I see, not very far distant, the salvation of the slave." Paradoxically, her trust was in the South rather than in the North: "I am not sure that the North will not make disgraceful

71

concessions of principle, but I am tolerably confident that the South will not accept them."[4]

Writing to Garrison himself a little later, she extended her congratulations to him on his entrance upon the fourth decade of his labor as editor of the *Liberator,* and "leader of our anti-slavery hosts." She added,

> The memories of the past come crowding so thickly in my soul, this morning; memories of all its toil, of all its strife, of all its victories; the memory of the first time I saw you, the first words I heard from you, and of the effect of those words upon my own soul; the memory, running through all the interval from that time to this, of all the strength and help and joy which God had sent to me through you; mingled with the memory of your unwearied labor for the slave, for your country, for mankind, that I cannot repress the impulse to utter some of them in words to you.[5]

Looking back over the past thirty years, she noted that her strongest feeling was one of "reverent thankfulness that I have been permitted to live through all this glorious period of the world's history."[6]

In March Mary Grew wrote to Wendell Phillips, explaining how busy she had been since the end of the preceding year, so busy that she had not taken time to collect and send Charles Greene's bills. First there had been her normal activities—the antislavery fair in December, writing the annual report in January, and the usual round of antislavery meetings. In addition, she had been occupied with efforts to get "that women's rights bill" introduced in the state legislature. She was glad to report some progress in this matter. "A very satisfactory bill, touching the subject of earnings, has been reported to our Senate, by the Judiciary Committee." Several members of the state Senate and the House had expressed their willingness to aid in carrying such a measure, "indeed, no one of them, to whom I or my friends have written respecting the matter, have declined to aid it." She was confident that the law would be passed, "though perhaps not until next winter." The legislature had been quite engrossed with other important matters, and there had been "a great deal of party strife among them." Despite this, she had a letter from a member of the House who was willing to "move on the matter at once." Thus far, she had spent very little of the money Philips had sent her, having succeeded in getting most of the work done for nothing. She would extend her operations next fall, however, unless the bill should be passed this session, "which is not probable." She thought that, thus far, the results had amply repaid the expenditure of both money and labor.[7]

In the same letter Mary Grew expressed her reservations about the advisability of using the brilliant young orator, Anna Dickinson of Philadelphia, in the cause of woman's rights. Born of Quaker parentage in 1842 and educated in Friends' schools, the latter began her public speaking before she was eighteen years old. She addressed the twenty-third annual meeting of the Pennsylvania Anti-Slavery Society at Kennett Square in 1860. Introduced by Lucretia Mott, she lectured to a large crowd in Philadelphia's Concert Hall in 1861 on "The Rights and Wrongs of Women."[8] Lucretia Mott called on Mary Grew and informed her that an application had been made to the trustees of the Hovey Fund for financial assistance. Their reply was to the effect that an appropriation would be made for this purpose if certain Philadelphians decided that it was expedient. Mrs. Mott believed that Sarah Pugh and Mary Grew should be consulted, but she thought more highly of Miss Dickinson's speaking than they did and was not so much concerned about "her want of culture, & her extreme youth." Sarah Pugh and Mary Grew agreed in thinking her "an extraordinary girl, *earnest* & true, & promising much." Mary Grew thought that the fulfillment of Anna Dickinson's promise would depend very much on her education during the next few years. "If she could have the benefit of good school training, & wholesome criticism, for three or four years, she would probably, become a very valuable advocate of Reform." In conclusion, Mary Grew told Phillips that she would not object to his using his influence to get aid for Anna Dickinson from the Hovey Fund.[9]

In his most recent letter to Mary Grew, Phillips had added as a postscript the words "What glorious times!" She was glad to hear that, despite the hazard he had been subjected to by a Boston mob, he had "bated not one jot of heart or hope." The same day she had received a letter from Mrs. Garrison, exclaiming "What terrible times!" In Mary Grew's view, they were "not half so terrible as times of moral stagnation." It seemed to her that the antislavery cause was now proceeding "without any special help from anybody." President Lincoln had said he "would run the machine as he found it." Mary Grew guessed that he would find that "the machine will run him."[10]

In April Mary Grew wrote in a letter to Elizabeth Neall Gay that the married women's earnings bill had been reported from the Judiciary Committee to the state Senate and "after nearly a whole day's discussion, in which it was earnestly advocated by some of the members, it was rejected by a majority of only two votes." She thought it would pass at the next session.[11] Such a law was not actually passed until 1872.

On 12 April 1861 South Carolinians fired on Fort Sumter and the Civil War began. Meeting in Philadelphia five days later, the executive committee of the Pennsylvania Anti-Slavery Society earnestly discussed this turn of events. There was "but little doubt expressed by any, that the ultimate result would be the Abolition of Slavery," despite the ambiguous position of the federal government on this issue.[12] Mary Grew agreed with her colleagues on this point. In June she spoke at a meeting of the Philadelphia Female Anti-Slavery Society, reviewing the history of the antislavery movement in the Pennsylvania metropolis and emphasizing the importance of continuing to sustain the *National Anti-Slavery Standard* as a vehicle of abolitionist sentiment.[13]

Mary Grew's friendship with the Garrison family grew stronger during the Civil War. In 1858 Garrison had referred to "our dear and cherished friend Mary Grew, who belongs to the household of *our* saints."[14] On 12 April 1861 she sent the Garrisons a piece of cake from James and Lucretia Mott's golden wedding celebration.[15] In the summer of 1861 she again visited the Garrison family in Boston. Writing afterward to William Lloyd Garrison, Jr., she declared, "One of the joys of my life is that I am permitted to be 'at home' in your father's family; and my interest in his children increases, as, with increasing years, life widens and deepens around them."[16] In September she gave an account of her visit to Boston for her associates in the Philadelphia Female Anti-Slavery Society, reporting that most of the abolitionists to whom she had talked were "hopeful that the righteous retribution which has come upon the Nation for the Sin of Slavery will result in freedom to the Slave."[17] Garrison attended the annual meeting of the Pennsylvania Anti-Slavery Society at West Chester on 24–25 October 1861. Mary Grew was there, serving on the business committee, and a long letter from Henry Grew, who was too ill to attend, was read to the convention.[18] Mary Grew helped to entertain Garrison when he visited Philadelphia after the close of the West Chester meeting.[19]

On 5 October 1861 a notice appeared in the *National Anti-Slavery Standard* asking support for "The Twenty-Sixth Pennsylvania Anti-Slavery Fair and National Bazaar." While it was signed by two or three dozen women, it was probably written by Mary Grew. "Our thirty years' war for freedom," it declared, "seems about to culminate in victory." However, it went on to say, "many a battle has been lost by too much haste in accounting it won. Until its proclamation of liberty to the slaves proves that this nation has discovered, and is willing to acknowledge, the real cause and only true remedy for the Southern rebellion and consequent civil war, the American Abolitionists will continue to hold their solemn responsibility to the slave, and to the country."[20] There was some disagreement within the Philadelphia

Female Anti-Slavery Society over whether this fair should be held. The question was debated by the members on 14 November 1861, and the majority decided in favor of going ahead with it.[21]

The steering committee for the fair included Sarah Pugh, Mary Grew, Lucretia Mott, and Margaretta Forten. It was held in the Large Saloon of the Assembly Buildings on 17–20 December. After expenses, it yielded the sum of $1,188.01; gross receipts came to $1,350.[22] "If my influence can prevail to accomplish it," Mary Grew wrote Sydney Howard Gay, "*half the profits* will be given to the *Standard*."[23] Revenue from the fair exceeded the managers' expectations, since many women who had previously worked for this cause were now devoting their energies to relief for soldiers and freedmen. "The unusually fine weather, the absence of opposition in the public mind, the throng of sympathizing friends," the fair committee reported, "combined to make the time of the Fair a season of rare social enjoyment and gratification." Though the chains of the slave were not yet broken, the feeling that the time was not far distant when this goal would be achieved "gave gladness and hope, almost assurance, that our labors would ere long be crowned with success.[24] This was the last of Philadelphia's antislavery fairs. Before another one could be held, Lincoln had issued his preliminary Emancipation Proclamation.

Reviewing the momentous events of the year 1861, Mary Grew noted that at its beginning "the gaze of the civilized world" had suddenly fixed upon "a great nation dismembered by internal convulsions." European monarchs and the humblest Americans were asking alike, "What shall the end of these things be?"[25] Mary Grew was confident that the end was to be emancipation of the slaves. Already proposals for emancipation were being made and discussed on the floors of Congress. The South had announced that slavery was "the vital agent of the controversy." But the North lagged in taking up the gauntlet thus laid down. It had issued "equivocal proclamations" on the slavery issue. While the South was using its slaves in the war effort, the North was refusing the proffered aid of loyal black citizens. "The fact that slavery was the cause of this dismemberment of the nation" was "obvious to all excepting those who have shut their eyes to avoid seeing it."[26] Understanding the cause suggested the solution—emancipation.

Public opinion had altered: "After thirty years of persecution and calumny of themselves and their enterprise, abolitionists read with wonder, in prominent journals of this city, defences or apologies for both, and respectful tributes to men whose names had hitherto been used as a cry wherewith to rally a mob."[27] There was still danger, however, that the North might lose its new moral fervor and yield to "a compromise with wrong." It was "a dark sign of the times that the party in power" manifested "a higher devotion to the Union than to Liberty."[28] On the other hand, there were brighter signs. The soldiers of Potter County, Pennsylvania, had adopted a resolution declaring that "it was no part of the duty of the soldier to aid in returning fugitive slaves."[29] The first capital conviction in connection with the foreign slave trade had been obtained. The government had issued an order prohibiting the use of the jails of Washington as "slave pens." Facilities had been furnished to slaves escaping through the Northern states. The legislature of Pennsylvania had refused to repeal the laws that protected "the slave's right to freedom, when he is brought within her limits by his master." Whatever the shortcomings of the administration in Washington, it was still in advance of its predecessors on the matter of slavery.[30]

Mary Grew believed it was "folly" to trace the rebellion to any cause other than slavery and to think it could be suppressed by any means other than emancipation. She rejoined in "the vision of the slave's approaching deliverance." The aim of abolitionists during the past thirty years had been to effect this deliverance peacefully, "to redeem the nation from its sin, without this baptism of blood." This aim the nation had persistently and successfully opposed. Political parties had rivaled each other in their efforts to resist it, and the church had used "her wealth, her learning, her moral power, and the sanctity of her name, to thwart it."[31] For thirty years the abolitionists had striven to achieve "the redemption of the slave in time to save the land from civil war." The Philadelphia Female Anti-Slavery Society had contributed to these efforts through "the dissemination of truth by the press and the voice."[32] It was helping to finance the work of the Pennsylvania Anti-Slavery Society and the *National Anti-Slavery Standard*.

"A retrospective view of the anti-slavery enterprise from its initiation to the present hour," Mary Grew wrote in conclusion, "inspires us with gratitude, courage, and hope." While their hope of leading the slave peacefully out of bondage had been disappointed, the death blow of slavery had now been struck, and the providence of God was "leading the slave by another path to freedom." They commenced a new year "cheered by the bright vision of final victory looming up in the near future." The United States would stand "at last, glorious among the nations, a People exalted by Righteousness."[33]

Expecting the imminent end of slavery, members of the Philadelphia Female Anti-Slavery Society decided on 9 January 1862 that the cause would not require the aid of another fair. Sarah Pugh and Mary Grew were appointed to a committee to dispose of the property and goods remaining from the 1861 sale. At the same meeting four-hundred dollars was appropriated to the Pennsylvania Anti-Slavery Society and four-hundred dollars to the American Anti-Slavery Society, the latter to be used for support of the *National Anti-Slavery Standard*.[34] The twenty-eighth annual meeting of the Philadelphia Female Anti-Slavery Society was held 13 February 1862. Mary Grew read her annual report for 1861, which was adopted. She and Margaret Burleigh were appointed to arrange for the printing of 750 copies. At the same time an additional two-hundred dollars was divided equally for use by the Pennsylvania and American Anti-Slavery Societies.[35]

On January 1862 Mary Grew wrote Wendell Phillips at some length about the condition of Charles Greene, acknowledging the receipt of a check for fifty dollars for his benefit and commenting on his needs and his health. She said he needed some clothing and wished to buy a barrel of apples, at a cost of five dollars. She reported that Greene thought he was suffering from heart trouble and was taking digitalis, but she did not consider his condition very serious. She believed he should continue to run his little apothecary shop, since otherwise he would have nothing to do and "his life would be more wearisome than it now is." In the same letter she suggested the transfer of the funds that Phillips had sent her for her woman's rights project to Greene's account, "unless Mr. Irish, of our Senate, informs me that, in his opinion, something can be hopefully attempted, at the present session of our Legislature, to carry our bill for Women's Rights, which so nearly succeeded last winter." She expected to hear from Irish soon but had little hope "that any effort can be made in that direction in these times."[36]

On 13 March 1862 she introduced a resolution at the meeting of the Philadelphia Female Anti-Slavery Society pointing to the efforts being made in behalf of the slaves freed "by the advancing armies of the United States, and by the retreat of their rebel masters"; to the action of Congress and the executive in forbidding military and naval officers to return fugitive slaves and in abolishing "the slave pens" of the District of Columbia; and to the initiation of "various schemes of emancipation" as "the result of the anti-slavery labor of the last thirty years, and a most encouraigng token that the hour is at hand when the great cause which has so long been the peculiar care of abolitionists, will be adopted and cherished as the cause of the American Nation."[37] The resolution was adopted and sent to the *Standard* for publication.

On 8 May she presented a similar resolution hailing the abolition of slavery in the District of Columbia "as the first ripe sheaf of our harvest, joyfully and gratefully accepting it as ample recompense for our thirty years of anti-slavery labor" and declaring that "we wait with increased faith and confident hope, for the perfect consummation of the glorious enterprise to which the American abolitionists have devoted their lives."[38] This resolution was likewise passed and sent to the *Standard*. It was also sent to several Philadelphia papers, but these refused to publish it without pay.[39]

Mary Grew continued to be active in the Pennsylvania Anti-Slavery Society, serving on its executive committee. On 12 February 1862 this body directed her to draft a letter replying to Miller McKim's resignation as corresponding secretary of the society. He was leaving this position to go into freedmen's aid work. The following week Mary Grew presented a letter stating that McKim's resignation was received with "no ordinary feeling of regret." Years of working together with him in the antislavery cause had created "the strongest fraternal bonds." The work was not yet done; the cause still needed him and the society needed him. For twenty-two years he had been, in effect, executive secretary and business manager, one of the society's few paid employees. The society accepted his resignation "with most sincere reluctance." In her letter, Mary Grew paid tribute to "the fidelity, and zeal, and dilligence [sic]" with which he had served the cause "through all its vicissitudes." The society extended to him their best wishes for his "prosperity" and for "the abundant success" of all his "efforts to bless the human race."[40] The letter was approved and ordered sent to McKim with the signatures of the members of the executive committee.

McKim became general secretary of the Philadelphia Port Royal Relief Association. A large group of former slaves had gathered at Port Royal, South Carolina, behind Union lines, and needed assistance. On 5 March 1862 the executive committee of the Pennsylvania Anti-Slavery Society discussed the freedmen's aid movement, and Mary Grew was directed to prepare a resolution for the next meeting "embodying the feeling of the Committee respecting this movement."[41] On 12 March she presented the following resolution:

> Resolved—That this Committee hail with joy and gratitude, as a sign of the times indicating the approach of the Abolition of Slavery, the deep interest manifested by our citizens in the Slaves congregated at Port Royal and elsewhere, and that we heartily sympathise with the efforts in their behalf which have been inaugurated, by the Freedman's Relief Assocs. recently organised in this and other Cities."[42]

The resolution was adopted.

Early in the summer, Mary Grew wrote her friend Elizabeth Neall Gay that she would probably not be able to go to New York or New

England because of her father's "very feeble condition" and her sister Susan's sojourn with them in Philadelphia.[43] "You speak exultantly at the times," she continued. "They are glorious, & we should be jubilant. Not that every thing is going on as we wish; not that our politicians have suddenly turned saints, nor that Lincoln's cabinet is of the kingdom of heaven, such things are not expected by some reformers. It is enough to elicit our deep thanksgiving that, by events over which the govt. has or has not control; from motives pure, selfish, or commingled, the abolition of slavery is at hand. I cannot doubt this, so plain seem the indications."[44]

William Lloyd Garrison was in Philadelphia in June of 1862 and went to see "dear Mary Grew's father, who has been so very ill, hoping to see her also." He found "the venerable invalid" sitting up in his chair, poring over the Bible, and "looking very feeble indeed, though he is slowly recuperating as the warm weather advances." Garrison thought Henry Grew was glad to see him, and they spent half an hour together "in interesting conversation." Susan Grew was also present, and they were expecting Mary momentarily when Garrison had to leave.[45]

On Monday, 11 August 1862, the *Philadelphia Public Ledger* carried the following notice:

Died

In this city, on Friday, the 8th inst., *HENRY GREW,* aged 80 years.
His funeral will take place, from No. 116 North Eleventh street, on Tuesday, the 12th instant, at 9 o'clock A.M. His friends, and those of his family, are invited to attend.[46]

The *Ledger* carried no sketch of his life or obituary tributes. On 16 August the *National Anti-Slavery Standard* reported that his life had ended "gently and peacefully" and declared that "the anti-slavery cause never had a more unselfish and devoted friend than Father Grew." He had espoused that cause "in its very beginning" and had remained faithful to it "even unto death." In Henry Grew's character, said the *Standard,* "gentleness and childlike simplicity" were combined with "unbending firmness and integrity. . . . Faithful, under all circumstances, in testifying against wrong, his rebukes were always tempered with kindness to the wrong-doer." The *Standard* also paid tribute to his "patience under trials" and stated that "all who knew him instinctively said, 'Behold a Christian indeed, in whom is no guile.'"[47]

A correspondent for the *Standard* reported that Henry Grew's funeral was "an interesting and impressive occasion. . . . Addresses, from J. M. McKim, Mr. Green, Rev. Mr. Stewart, Dr. Child, Lucretia Mott, and Rev. Mr. Campbell, bore witness to his remarkable conscientiousness, his disinterestedness, his free and discriminating charity, his consistent advocacy of the brotherhood of man, his careful and conscientious rejection of the produce of the unpaid toil of the slave. . . ." "We feel that a good man has departed from among us—a good man and a minister of good," was that writer's conclusion.[48]

In the *Liberator* (15 August 1862) Garrison paid tribute to Henry Grew as "our revered friend" who for thirty years had been an uncompromising advocate of the cause of the slave and who "both with his voice and pen vindicated the safety and duty of immediate and unconditional emancipation." Garrison stated that Grew was "of a deeply religious nature, eminently conscientious and upright in all his ways, warm in his sympathies for suffering humanity in its various phases, generous in the distribution of his charities, and a truly good man, whose constant aim it was to glorify God and bless his fellowmen." In theological matters, according to the *Liberator,* Grew was "an independent thinker, true to his convictions, however unpopular they might be, anxious only to know and cherish the truth, and a preacher of practical righteousness." The *Liberator* concluded that he was "widely known, revered and beloved."[49]

Henry Grew's will, dated 19 January 1861, set up a ten thousand dollar trust fund for his fourth wife, Elizabeth Noble, who was to have the use only of the interest. At her death, the principal was to be distributed to benevolent societies. One thousand dollars each was to go to the American Baptist Free Mission Society, for publication of the Bible; the Children's Aid Society of New York City; the Five Points House of Industry in New York; the American Bible Union in New York, for publication of the Bible; and the American Female Guardians Society of New York, for its Home of the Friendless. Five hundred dollars each was to go to the following:

1. The Northern Soup Society in Philadelphia
2. Southwark Soup Society in Philadelphia
3. Moyamensing Soup Society in Philadelphia
4. Union Benevolent Association in Philadelphia
5. Northern Association of the City and County of Philadelphia for the Relief and Employment of Poor Women
6. Rosine Association of Philadelphia (see above, p. 43)
7. Home for Destitute Colored Children
8. Pennsylvania Anti-Slavery Society

9. Philadelphia Society for the Employment and Instruction of the Poor

10. The poor of Birmingham, England.

The rest of his estate was to be divided into four equal parts for the benefit of his daughters Susan and Mary and his grandchildren. The latter included Susan G. Bingham, daughter of his son Henry J. Grew, and Howard M. Jones and Eliza Richmond, children of his daughter Julia. On 26 July 1862, two weeks before his death, Henry Grew added a codicil to his will directing that, "in consequence of the change of times" (wartime inflation?), only five thousand dollars of his wife's trust fund was to be given to benevolent societies, the other five thousand dollars to be added to his residuary estate for his children and grandchildren.[50]

At its first meeting after a three-month summer recess, the members of the Philadelphia Female Anti-Slavery Society adopted a resolution declaring that "in the death of our venerable and venerated friend Henry Grew, this Society feels the loss of a most faithful and earnest coadjutor." He had embraced the antislavery cause "when it was first agitated in this country" and had continued to give it "his faithful, consistent support to the day of his death, never faltering for a moment even in its darkest hours." The women expressed their desire to "so cherish his memory, as to strengthen our faithfulness to the cause we love."[51]

Replying somewhat belatedly to Garrison's letter of sympathy on the death of her father, Mary Grew wrote on 2 October that while his letter had lain long unanswered, along with many others, she had read it often and "every time" had drawn "fresh comfort from it." She knew that she had reason for "great thankfulness" and she was grateful that she and her father had been "companions for so many years." "All the beauty of his life," she wrote, "shines on me now." She told Garrison that her father's last hours were "full of peace and faith" and that an "angelic expression" had come upon his face as he drew his last breath. Lucretia Mott had said, "He is not here; he is risen." Mary Grew felt that her life had been so intertwined with that of her father "that it is as strange as it is sad to live on without him." She hoped he could communicate with her "in spirit."[52]

In the same letter to Garrison, Mary Grew commented on the preliminary Emancipation Proclamation, which Lincoln had issued on 22 September. "We are giving thanks for the Proclamation of Emancipation," she wrote, "wrung from a reluctant govt. trembling beneath the retribution of justice. Was ever man so blinded, *or so fettered* (I don't know which) as Lincoln?" She would hesitate to predict what the next three months might bring, but she believed that out of all the turmoil of the times would come two things, "by God's decree"—the abolition of American slavery and "the punishment of the nation for its sin." In conclusion, she wrote, "In all times of our personal affliction, or national calamity, the rock of our strength is our faith that 'the Lord God omnipotent reigneth.'"[53]

On 9 October 1862 the Philadelphia Female Anti-Slavery Society discussed the Emancipation Proclamation at its meeting. Lucretia Mott spoke of it as "a measure fraught with great good—though not all we could have wished, still affording cause for gratitude and triumph on the part of Abolitionists—if properly carried out a bright prospect was opening before us."[54] On motion, a committee was appointed to prepare resolutions on this subject for transmission to the president and the newspapers. Mary Grew and Abby Kimber were appointed to this committee.[55] By the time the two women reported to the society (8 January 1863), Lincoln had issued his final Emancipation Proclamation (1 January 1863), and Mary Grew was taking a more sanguine view of it. She proposed a resolution, adopted "after a slight amendment," hailing "with unutterable joy and gratitude, the Day of Jubilee which has dawned on the American Nation, and the Emancipation of millions of the American slaves in whose behalf this Association has for thirty years, hopefully labored." As members of the society had "sympathetically entered into their sufferings and borne their burdens, we are now partakers of the joy with which, casting off their broken fetters, they are rising, new born and exultant, into a life of Freedom." Her resolution called the Emanciptation Proclamation a harbinger of "the speedy abolition of Slavery in the remaining portions of the Union." This would represent "the consummation of our work; the fruition of our hopes" and "glorious" recompense for all their toil and sacrifice in the cause.[56]

At the same meeting Mary Grew proposed another resolution expressing sympathy for fellow members of the society who had lost relatives and friends in the war and hope that the bereaved might find "some consolation in the fact that lives dear to them were sacrificed in the cause of the slave's deliverance."[57]

Reviewing the events of 1862 in the *Twenty-Ninth Annual Report of the Philadelphia Female Anti-Slavery Society,* published in the spring of 1863, Mary Grew exclaimed, "The day of America's jubilee has dawned at last; and we who have watched and striven through the dark night of her despotism, now hail that dawning with joy and gratitude unutterable; and in faith and hope wait for the ascending of its sun to the zenith."[58] It was "a pleasant task to trace the tokens of our nation's progress during the past year." In March 1862 Congress had passed a bill forbidding any person connected with the army or navy to aid in the return of fugitive slaves to their masters. In April the president signed a bill abolishing slavery in the District of Columbia. Mary Grew recalled that in the 1830s it had been "accounted a bold action to sign a petition" to Congress on behalf of this object, that persons circulating such petitions were subjected to insult, and that the right of such petitioning had been denied by the House of Representatives. She reminded her readers of John Quincy Adams's heroic struggle for the repeal of this "gag rule." Abolition in the District of Columbia was speedily followed by a Congressional enactment prohibiting slavery in federal territories in the West (June 1862). The president had suggested to Congress a plan for gradual and compensated emancipation in the border states. On 22 September he had issued his proclamation for abolition of slavery in the Confederacy. On 1 January 1863 this measure became final. Congress had passed a bill authorizing the president to receive into the armed forces of the United States volunteers of African descent. There was renewed opposition to the foreign slave trade; an individual had been sentenced to death for participating in it, and a new treaty had been made with the British for its suppression. Another sign of progress, Mary Grew noted, was the recent decision of the United States attorney general that "free men of color, born in the United States, are citizens of the United States." "Thus, during the eventful year, has the abolitionist, in grateful joy, garnered the first sheaves from his long and patient sowing, accounting each an earnest of the full in-gathering."[59]

Great as these victories were, Mary Grew realized, much remained to be done. Enforcement of the Emancipation Proclamation would depend on future successes of United States armies. Something would have to be done about slavery in the loyal states. Black people were still being denied equal rights; in Philadelphia itself they were not allowed seats in the streetcars. The president was talking of colonizing blacks "in distant countries." There were disloyal men in the North working for the Confederate cause. Abolitionists would have to remain at their posts until the freedmen were enfranchised. The Port Royal experiment, she thought, demonstrated that the freedmen were willing to work and able to take care of themselves. "To the work which remains for us to do," she concluded, "we joyfully address ourselves: devoutly thankful for all that has been attained, and strong in faith that the hour of final victory is at hand, when the abolitionist may put off his armor, and sing, 'Jehovah hath triumphed, His people are free.'"[60]

Mary Grew was ill again in the winter of 1862–63. "In consequence of the illness of the Cor. Sec.," the Philadelphia Female minutes for 12 February 1863 recorded, "the Annual Report was not presented."[61] It was not presented until 9 April 1863 and not printed until several weeks after that. This illness may have been related to the death of her father. She unburdened herself in a letter to Elizabeth Neall Gay dated 24 May 1863. Acknowledging the receipt of several letters from Mrs. Gay over a period of some months, she wrote that they would have been "answered long ago had I been able to find time and strength therefor. . . . Sorrow reveals our true friends to us, and my father's departure from me (I do not like to call it death, for, surely, he lives more intensely now) elicited from many dear friends letters of sympathy which were and are very precious to me." She had been able to reply to few of them, "for my time & thoughts have been very closely occupied since last August, with new cares & responsibilities, and with some which I once shared with my beloved father, and now bear alone, and, also, with sickness & death around me." She would not write Elizabeth a detailed account of "these things" but would talk to her about them when she saw her as she hoped to do in July, if not before. "Perhaps you heard of Margaret's illness in the Fall, (her first real illness), and of mine, afterwards; &, recently of poor Mrs. Grew's death. That was a release which she greatly desired."[62] She was deeply appreciative of the Gays' invitation to her to go and "find rest & healing with you & Sydney in your quiet home, & within the atmosphere of your sympathy, sympathy born of your own keen suffering." She would gladly have accepted it if she could have, "but it was impossible." She hoped that Sydney and Elizabeth could come to Philadelphia for their niece's wedding shortly, but in any case she would plan to see the Gays in their home on Staten Island "when I leave this hot city, for the summer. . . . I have a great deal to say to you both," she concluded, "but it must wait." She had "neither time nor strength" to attend the annual meeting of the American Anti-Slavery Society. She was sending with this letter the annual report of "the Old Female." The letter was signed "Yrs. lovingly, Mary Grew."[63]

In the summer of 1863 Mary Grew visited her sister Susan and various nephews, nieces, and cousins in New England and western New York. When she found the end of September approaching, she felt she should rush home by the shortest route and did not go to New York City to see the Gays. She came through Elmira and "over that road so magnificent in its scenery, the Catawissa."[64] She arrived home on 2 October, just too late for the wedding of the McKims' adopted daughter, Annie, and just in time to greet Margaret Burleigh on her return from the funeral of a beloved niece in Massachusetts.

In November 1863 Mary Grew was again complaining of illness. "An attack of blind headache & its debilitating effects" had prevented her from acknowledging sooner the receipt of a book from Wendell Phillips. In the same letter to Phillips she dealt with some problems concerning Charles Greene and with her impressions of Phillips Brooks, later to be famous as pastor of Boston's Trinity Church, who was then serving as a young Episcopal minister in Philadelphia. He was one of Wendell Phillips's cousins. "You would not be ashamed of him if his name was *Wendell* Phillips Brooks," Mary Grew wrote. "You know he has made a sensation here for some time past, as a *live* Episcopal minister; but he is doing more than that now." At a meeting in behalf of "the western contrabands, the other night," he had made "a firstrate speech, thoroughly anti-slavery, anti-prejudice against color, fervent & hearty as *you* cd. desire." She had been particularly impressed with two sentences from his address: "We hear a great deal about radicals & radicalism. In God's name, let us try to get back to the radicalism of our Master; a radicalism so deep that it cuts to the root of every sin." She had heard a sermon by him a few Sundays ago that made her suspect "he has tendencies to radicalism in some other directions than those of Moral Reform."[65]

The highlight of Mary Grew's life in 1863 was her participation in the Third Decade celebration of the founding of the American Anti-Slavery Society, held in Philadelphia on 3–4 December. She was one of the speakers, taking as her topic the history of female antislavery societies. Not everyone could be allowed to speak, Garrison told Miller McKim: "There are certain persons who must have precedence of others. For instance—Wendell Phillips, S. J. May, Lucretia Mott, Mary Grew, Robert Purvis, and Beriah Green." Green had presided over the founding of the American Anti-Slavery Society in 1833 but did not attend the thirtieth anniversary meeting. Garrison expressed the hope that "dear Lucretia Mott, Mary Grew, and Robert Purvis will not fail to speak,—ably representing, as they would, by their sex and complexion, those features of our struggle of which we have all been so jealous and so proud."[66]

Of the forty-five survivors among the founders of the American Anti-Slavery Society, eleven were present for this celebration. Garrison gave the opening address and introduced the reading of letters of regret from Arthur Tappan, John Greenleaf Whittier, Theodore and Angelina Grimké Weld, and others. The Reverend William H. Furness read the Declaration of Sentiments, which Garrison had written for the society in 1833. J. Miller McKim, the Reverend Samuel J. May, and Lucretia Mott gave reminiscences of the first convention. The role of women in that convention was pointed out. Mary Grew rose to inquire why the women's names had not been signed to the

Declaration of Sentiments. May replied, "Because we had no conception of the rights of women. Because it would then have been thought an impropriety; a thought at which we all laugh now."[67] Charles C. Burleigh spoke on what still needed to be done. Robert Purvis spoke on discrimination against free blacks. Frederick Douglas argued the need for Negro suffrage. Other speakers included the Reverend Henry Ward Beecher, Stephen S. and Abby Kelley Foster, Susan B. Anthony, Lucy Stone, Theodore Tilton, and Henry Wilson.

Mary Grew's address was reported in the proceedings under the title "Annals of Women's Anti-Slavery Societies." It was read to the convention on the afternoon of the first day. She pointed out that thirty years earlier a "trumpet-call" had summoned the American people to "moral warfare" against slavery. A "few earnest women" had responded and organized societies based on the principles that slavery was a great "national sin" and that "immediate emancipation" was a "right and duty." She thought the first of these organizations was founded in Reading, Massachusetts, in March 1833, followed by the Boston Society in October and the Philadelphia group in December, about the same time as one in Amesbury, Massachusetts. It was fortunate that they did not count the cost or the number of years this struggle would entail. Mary Grew emphasized the connection of the movement with civil liberties. She recalled the Boston mob that had driven the antislavery women out of their meeting room and threatened Garrison with lynching in October 1835. She discussed the three national conventions of antislavery women held in 1837, 1838, and 1839, the second of which had provoked the burning of Pennsylvania Hall in Philadelphia. The women had fought for freedom of speech and assembly and then for the freedom to work together with men in the antislavery cause, which was recognized by the American Anti-Slavery Society in 1840.[68]

She spoke of the annual fairs in Boston and Philadelphia, which had done so much to provide pecuniary and moral support for the antislavery organizations. She called them "Passover Festivals, whither 'our tribes went up' with gladness, and found refreshment and strength." She recalled the ejection of the Philadelphia fair of 1859 from its rented quarters and the successful defense of their right of assembly in 1860. In a ringing conclusion, she declared it was fitting that those who "side by side" had "toiled and fought for thirty years" should come together now to grasp each other's hands in fraternal congratulations and to express their thanks that "America's Day of Jubilee has dawned, and its sun is high in the heavens. . . . With its glory streaming down upon us, and the song of our ransomed brethren in our ears, we bow in adoration before the Power and

Wisdom and Love which is guiding this mighty revolution, and cry; 'Thy will be done on earth as it is done in heaven.'"[69]

In her annual report for 1863 Mary Grew stated that the year had been "bright with evidences of the Nation's progress towards a full apprehension of justice to the colored man." Especially notable was the fact that the federal government had authorized the formation of Negro regiments to fight in the war and had promised "the same protection of all its soldiers."[70] The military governor of Tennessee, Andrew Johnson, had issued an order that a fugitive slave could be returned to her master only if she were "*willing* to return." This represented quite a change from the days when abolitionists had been accustomed to "wait and watch, in agonizing suspense, through days and nights, for the decisions of United States Judges and Commissioners, upon fugitive slave cases in Northern cities; and to listen, in more agonizing certainty, to the doom which they pronounced."[71] Also remarkable was the fact that "our Government, while carrying on a great war, is able and willing to attend to the education of the slaves whom the war is emancipating." There were even efforts, as at Port Royal, to provide the freedmen with land.[72]

The president had made clear in his annual message on the State of the Union that pardon was to be offered only to those rebels who promised to honor the Emancipation Proclamation. Bills had been introduced in Congress to repeal the Fugitive Slave Acts of 1793 and 1850, to declare all slaves "free citizens," to prohibit the holding of persons in servitude except by contract, to guarantee equal payment of black and white soldiers, to establish a Bureau of Emancipation, and, "best of all," to amend the Constitution to prohibit slavery everywhere in the United States. Public opinion was now more favorably inclined toward blacks, especially toward their enlistment in the armed forces. There had been a "prompt and liberal response to the cry of the Freedmen for aid."[73] In Philadelphia alone nearly one hundred thousand dollars had been contributed for this purpose. The border states were preparing to abolish slavery. The church, which "by virtue of its high name and claims, should ever be the leader of moral reforms, but which in every age has been dragged forward," was taking a more favorable stand toward "the cause of Human Liberty and equal brotherhood."[74] The Pennsylvania convention of the Protestant Episcopal church had decided to give representation to Philadelphia's African Episcopal Church of Saint Thomas. Mary Grew singled out for special praise the work of "our townswoman, Anna E. Dickinson," in the antislavery cause.

She also declared that the year 1863 had demonstrated the capabilities of blacks as laborers and as soldiers:

Who asks now in doubt and derision, "Will the negro fight?" The answer is spoken from the cannon's mouth; it is written in the sunlight on flashing steel; it comes to us from Port Hudson's field of death, from Morris Island, and from those graves beneath Fort Wagner's walls, which the American people will surely never forget.[75]

She thought, "By the terrible discipline of civil war," God is educating this nation in a sense of justice, and in the knowledge of what constitutes its true safety."[76]

There was "a darker side of the year's history, from which we must not turn away." The nation's capital was "still disgraced by the capture and rendition of fugitive slaves." There was discrimination in pay, bounties, and pensions to black soldiers. Churches were not admitting black and white worshipers on equal terms. Blacks were denied admission to Philadelphia's street railway cars. Black men and women had to walk to neighboring Camp William Penn to visit sons, husbands, and brothers, to whom in many cases they were to "speak the words of a last farewell."[77] There was a danger that abolitionists would consider their work done. Slavery was not yet eliminated. A Constitutional amendment banning slavery everywhere in the nation was needed. The president was talking of compromise with the leaders of rebel states, suggesting that the interests of the freedmen might be turned over to Southern whites. There were traitors in the North. The legislature of Pennsylvania had considered a measure to prevent the migration of colored persons into the state. The Philadelphia Female Anti-Slavery Society had sent a remonstrance against it.[78]

However, as usual, Mary Grew ended her report on a hopeful note. The new year was "bright with promise." The path of "our just cause shines brighter and brighter as it approaches its perfect day. We confidently trust that this shall be the year of its complete triumph, and that a national decree of universal emancipation will consummate our labors."[79]

On New Year's Day 1864 Mary Grew introduced a resolution at a meeting of the executive committee of the Pennsylvania Anti-Slavery Society to the effect that the organization should continue with its policy of "moral warfare" against slavery but should also "watch with undiminished vigilance, and criticise with unswerving justice, every political party and leader and measure, in all their relations to the cause of the Slave's emancipation."[80] The resolution was adopted and ordered sent to the *Standard* for publication.

On 17 January 1864 Mary Grew addressed a long-postponed letter to Elizabeth Neall Gay, expressing her concern over the illness of the Gays' daughter Sarah, of which she had just learned. "For a long time," she wrote, "I have very much wanted to hear from you & to write to you; but the pressing demands of business of one sort & another, which will not, cannot be put aside, have prevented me from following my inclination in this and many other matters." With regard to Sarah's illness she remarked, "So fragile are the earthen vessels in which we hold our hearts' treasures, that the least touch of sickness, the least exposure to danger, makes our pulses throb with alarm; and our only strength is in our trust in Him who holds us & them in His fatherly embrace."[81]

In the same letter Mary Grew also commented on the state of the nation. "Your last letter to me speaks of the solemnity & the glory of the times," she noted. "How, even in the interval, have they become more glorious, more solemn" . . . What responsibility rests on the Nation now, (& because on the Nation, on all on us) as the time of adjustment, & reconstruction, & reconciliation seems to be approaching! And how earnestly do we all pray, God keep us from a false peace!"[82]

Writing to William Lloyd Garrison on 24 February 1864, she expressed her sympathy in connection with Helen Garrison's illness and again commented on national affairs; "For my own part, I am constantly inclined to sing anthems of thanksgiving; not that I think the work wholly done, and the time of our discharge arrived, but I am full of hope & faith that it is very nigh, even at the door." In this letter she again took note of the work of Phillips Brooks ("God bless him!"), who served two Philadelphia churches between 1859 and 1869 before becoming pastor of Boston's famous Trinity Episcopal Church. She regarded Brooks as "the most promising occupant of any Philadelphia pulpit." Speaking of abolitionists, he had asked her "why she didn't stay in the church? "Ah!" she wrote, "if we had;—where would now be the church or the State, or the slave, or such men as he?. . . . Our cause is gloriously justified, & the world is acknowledging that God has been its leader."[83]

A few days later she sent a letter to William Lloyd Garrison, Jr., the Garrisons' second oldest child, congratulating him on his engagement to Ellen Wright. In this letter she said, "I am not one of those persons who believe or fancy that marriage is, *per se,* happiness, but a true marriage is one source of the highest earthly happiness." As she was sure that young Garrison had "a high ideal of the relation" and could reasonably assume that he had chosen wisely and, from her knowledge of him, she was confident that he would be a good husband, therefore it was "quite right & proper" to congratulate him. When she said that he was well qualified to be a good husband, she thought she said "a great deal for that manner of man is rare. . . . Men, just, generous, good, in many other relations of society, often fail sadly in this relation; not, I think, by reason of unusual depravity, but in consequence of the low ideal of a wife's position, a husband's duties of the marriage relation, in which a false public sentiment has educated them." She thought that if, after the home training they had all experienced and "the beautiful illustration of marriage which you have seen all your lives, you should become other than good husbands, you would have no excuse for your delinquency." She knew Ellen Wright "a little" and considered her attractive, and from one who knew her well she had further confirmation that she was "what I should wish your wife to be." She was very hopeful "of & for you both. . . . Neither of you regard marriage as a pastime, or life as a long holiday; and so you may [be] trusted, doubtless, to work out, together, your own salvation." Young Garrison's prosperity and happiness would be "subjects of deep concern to me, for the tie which binds me to your father & mother & to their children, is stronger than that of consanguinity."[84]

Two months later she wrote William that she had seen "your Ellie" the previous Sunday and that she had "walked straight into my heart. . . To be sure, the door was wide open, but, then, it didn't certainly follow that she would enter in & take possession." She seemed different from what she had hitherto been, "one of many bright, interesting young women of my acquaintance." She was "now an object of my especial interest & love; & how my heart blessed you both."[85]

In March 1864 Mary Grew took note of how public opinion regarding Garrison and other abolitionists had changed. "It is vastly entertaining," she wrote, "to see how Forney's 'Press' . . . quotes from the Liberator, & extols Mr. Garrison as a man of the soundest judgment, . . . and repeats again & again, that he is in favor of Lincoln. Verily, the abolitionists have wakened up to find themselves famous."[86]

In April she wrote Wendell Phillips regarding the financial affairs of Charles Greene and his wife and commented incidentally on the state of the nation. "Things look rather dark, now, I think, at Washn., worse than they do in the field, even." She did not believe that God was going to allow "this Nation to succeed until it does justice to the black man. . . . I am glad that the Nation has, in you, a faithful censor, (so greatly needed in this crisis of its fate), but I cannot go *as far* as you do in your censure of Lincoln."[87]

In May she attended the annual meeting of the American Anti-Slavery Society in New York City. She spent a morning discussing public affairs with Garrison, George Thompson, Theodore Tilton, and Oliver Johnson.[88]

On 1 June 1864 she offered two resolutions at a meeting of the executive committee of the Pennsylvania Anti-Slavery Society, which were approved and ordered to be sent to the *Standard* for publication. The first one expressed confidence in "the peculiar adaptation of spiritual weapons to the destruction of moral evil. . . . It is of the utmost importance to the cause which we have espoused, that we continue to wield them faithfully, and to rely upon them, until that cause shall be completely triumphant." The other declared that while differences of opinion on current political questions were "natural and inevitable," they did not touch "the essential principles of our enterprise," and could not "divide its true friends." While they adopted no political platform, they considered it the duty of antislavery societies "to watch with undiminished vigilance, and criticise with unswerving justice, every political party and leader and measure, in all their relations to the cause of the Slave's emancipation."[89]

As was her custom in later years, Mary Grew left the heat of Philadelphia in the summer of 1864, visiting friends and relatives in New England and spending some time at "New Russia" in the Adirondacks. "We are pleasantly & comfortably established here, in a large farm house." Margaret Burleigh and her sister Susan were with her. "The situation is high; how high I have not been able to ascertain; yet we are in a valley, with mountain peaks all around us." Even there the weather was hot, and she had sprained her foot. She spoke of "the diminution of my strength, by loss of my accustomed exercise."[90]

"How sad is the aspect of the war, just now!" she exclaimed. "And not less sad the prospect in our political horizon, I think. Will not these disasters to our armies strengthen the Democrats in the approaching election?" This was in a letter to Elizabeth Neall Gay, 9 August 1864. "I hear that Lincoln grows less popular, daily, in Phila. If this be true, it is to be regretted, I think; for however far from our ideal he may be, what better man is likely to succeed him?" Her hope and trust for the country was that God was "saving it through discipline, and that he is ordering all events to that end."[91]

While Mary Grew was on vacation, word arrived that the Garrisons' third son, Wendell Phillips Garrison, had become engaged to Lucy McKim, daughter of J. Miller McKim and his wife, Sarah, who were among Mary Grew's closest friends and associates. "'Pleased'!" she wrote to the young man, "I am more than pleased, my dear Wendell. I am joyful and thankful in the thought of your happiness. And I do think you are richly blessed in the love of such a woman as Lucy McKim. She is very dear to me." But then, her mother and father had been her dear friends during all of Lucy's life, "and you know something of the strength of the bond which unites me to your father &

mother." It was "natural" and "inevitable" that this impending marriage should "deeply stir my soul with feelings akin to maternal love &
pride & joy!"[92]

Pennsylvania held state and local elections on 11 October 1864.
"The city, of course, goes for the Republican party," she wrote Wendell Phillips the next day, "but only (as I hear) by the usual majority. I
expected a greater majority." It was reported early that morning, on
the street, that the state had gone Democratic, but she did not believe
this. "Indeed, it cannot yet be known. The returns, last night, came in
more slowly than usual." The Union party expected a heavier vote in
November than in this election, she reported. "We shall see." She
could not believe that the North would give up control of the government to the Copperheads. She did not regard the issue as between
Lincoln and McClellan but "between two great parties, one of whom
represents the slave power; and the other, though far enough from
being true to liberty, is pledged to a certain degree of opposition to
slavery." She trusted the antislavery leaders in the Republican party far
more than she did Lincoln, and she hoped much from what he would
be *"compelled"* to do. She was glad that Frémont had withdrawn his
name, because his election was impossible and a third ticket would
weaken the Republican and strengthen the Democratic party. She
agreed with Phillips that moral and not political warfare was the
special mission of abolitionists and that their duty was to watch and
criticize all parties, but she thought they must wish success to the
party "most friendly to the cause of human freedom." Some of her
associates mourned over "the indiscriminate eulogy of Lincoln," but
the fact was that the "quadrennial fever wh. visits the nation" had
touched even abolitionists pretty deeply this time. She would be
thankful when the November election was over. "Until then, may God
help us, amidst our different opinions, to 'keep the unity of the spirit
in the bond of peace'! . . . Our work is not yet done."[93]

On 11 November 1864 Mary Grew attended the annual meeting of
the Pennsylvania Anti-Slavery Society in Horticultural Hall, West
Chester. There were morning, afternoon, and evening sessions. James
Mott presided. Mary Grew presented a series of nine resolutions "for
consideration and discussion." The first one expressed satisfaction
over the antislavery gains of the past year: repeal of fugitive slave laws,
prohibition of the coastwise slave trade, admission of blacks as witnesses in federal courts, treatment of blacks like white prisoners of war
by the Confederacy, abolition of slavery in Louisiana, and admission
of Nevada as a free state. The second one rejoiced in the result of the
recent presidential election. The third praised the progress of the
freedmen in South Carolina. The fourth deplored the exclusion of free

blacks from railroads and other places of public accommodation. The fifth demanded "absolute justice" for the freedmen. The sixth declared the abolitionists' intention to address themselves "at once" to the work of persuading Congress to pass an amendment to the Constitution abolishing slavery throughout the United States. The seventh contained a promise by the reformers to "remain at our posts" until "the interests of the slave" could be adequately protected. The eighth mourned the deaths of antislavery Congressmen Joshua R. Giddings and Owen Lovejoy. The ninth, and last, expressed gratitude to God for the success of the antislavery movement. The report of the meeting in the *National Anti-Slavery Standard* does not indicate the disposition of these resolutions. At the afternoon session Reuben Tomlinson spoke on his work with the freedmen of South Carolina. At the evening session Mary Grew was one of seven speakers; the others were James Mott, Lucretia Mott, Edward M. Davis, Robert Purvis, Dr. F. Taylor, and Oliver Johnson. She was again chosen as a member of the executive committee of the state society.[94] Of this convention Lucretia Mott wrote, "Our West Chester meeting was well attended, and more interesting than we had feared it would be. Reuben Tomlinson was very good with his Port Royal experience; Mary Grew, excellent, as usual."[95]

On 8 December 1864 the Philadelphia Female Anti-Slavery Society, with Sarah Pugh as president, resolved to send a memorial to Congress asking that the United States Constitution be amended to abolish slavery throughout all the states and territories. Mary Grew and Sarah Pugh were appointed as a committee to prepare it. At the 9 February meeting, Mary Grew reported that this petition had been sent.[96] By that time, Congress had acted. On 31 January the Thirteenth Amendment cleared both houses of Congress and was sent to the states for ratification.

"Glory! Hallelujah!" Mary Grew wrote her sister Susan on 1 February 1865. "That we should have lived to see the day! . . . With palpitating hearts we rushed for this morning's newspaper; and the fulfillment of all our hopes, the dissipation of all our fears, is almost overwhelming. Almost! It is quite." She could scarcely think, speak, write, or *do* anything; she could only feel. She found it hard to grasp the full meaning of the statement: "The Congress of the United States has abolished American Slavery." Her annual report was about half written, and she felt like putting it into the fire and writing instead thereof, "Lord, let now thy servants, the abolitionists, depart in peace, for our eyes have seen, our ears have heard, our souls have felt, thy salvation!" "With choking voices" the members of her household had read "the glad tidings" to one another. "What ample recompense for all the toil of the past thirty years, is this consummation!" But what was the use of writing more than a word of greeting and congratulations "when one has no language which will hold the heart's rushing tide of joy!" She could not answer Susan's letters that day. "Nothing seems of any consequence today, but the glorious fact that the slaves are FREE."[97]

The same day she took time to write a congratulatory note to William Lloyd Garrison, who had inaugurated the radical abolitionist movement with the issuance of the first number of the *Liberator* on 1 January 1831. She was "glad and thankful" that he had lived to see "the glorious triumph of yesterday." There was not much to be said about such a triumph for the antislavery cause; "it moves our souls too deeply." For all his toil, struggle, and sacrifice, "how richly are you rewarded!" She wished that she could be in the Garrison family circle that day, to look into their faces and grasp their hands. Though abolitionists scattered throughout the land were sitting apart, "one tide of joy and gratitude is rushing through their hearts, and they are in blessed communion. . . . Verily, 'the Lord hath done great things for us, whereof we are glad.' "[98]

Mary Grew rewrote her annual report for 1864 to include passage of the Thirteenth Amendment. She reviewed the antislavery gains made during the year. Congress had repealed the Fugitive Slave Act of 1850. In March 1864 Arkansas had adopted a constitution prohibiting slavery. West Virginia had done the same. Louisiana acted on 5 September, Maryland on 1 November. Missouri had abolished slavery on 11 January 1865, and Tennessee was to take action on 22 February. The United States Senate had passed the Thirteenth Amendment on 8 April 1864, by a vote of 38–6, and the House had finally concurred on 31 January 1865, by a vote of 119–56. In the closing days of the session, Congress had prohibited the domestic slave trade and decreed that no witnesses were to be excluded from federal courts on grounds of color. A black man had been accepted as an accredited lawyer in the Supreme Court of the United States. The proposal in the Pennsylvania legislature to forbid the immigration of colored persons into the state had been defeated. The national government had ceased to aid schemes for black colonization. In summary, Mary Grew said, "The events which have startled and gladdened our souls during the past year, when contrasted with the condition of this nation four years ago, exceed the enthusiast's wildest dream of progress."[99]

There had been moral as well as legal progress. Large sums of money had been raised for freedmen's aid, and Northern teachers were thronging into the South to educate the former slaves. Churches had opened their doors to blacks, and ecclesiastical bodies such as the

General Conference of the (Northern) Methodist Church had adopted antislavery measures. Regiments of black troops marched through city streets, greeted by admiring crowds. Frederick Douglass has given a public lecture in the city of Baltimore, where he had been held as a slave. George Thompson, the fiery English abolitionist, who had been driven out of the United States in 1835, had made a triumphant tour of the country in 1864.[100]

There were still things the nation should be ashamed of. Mary Grew thought it was a disgrace that black soldiers were being paid less than white. She thought the exclusion of blacks from Philadelphia street railway cars was outrageous. The Female Anti-Slavery Society had petitioned the railway presidents to do away with this discrmination, and one or two of the companies had admitted blacks to some of their cars. Blacks were seated separately in churches. Blacks had not been given the privileges of citizenship. The Female Anti-Slavery Society had petitioned Congress to require as a condition for the readmission of the seceded states the establishment of a republican form of government in those states, with no distinction in the rights of citizenship based on African descent. "It is the old battle between Democracy and Aristocracy," Mary Grew wrote.[101] She noted that Congressman William D. Kelley of Philadelphia had been "ably and eloquently" defending "the necessity of protecting the enfranchised slave with the suffrage."[102]

Mary Grew thought that abolitionists should "stand at their posts a little longer," at least until the Thirteenth Amendment had been ratified. Finally, she took note of the deaths of several abolitionists during the preceding year. "These, our fellow-laborers, who have received their discharge before us, wait in heaven as we on earth, with ear attent, to catch the first tones of our new, unflawed Liberty Bell, (sweetest music that ever went up to God from America), which shall" she wrote,

> Ring out the darkness of the Land:
> Ring in the Christ that is to be.[103]

5
Battling for Negro Suffrage (1865–1867)

WITH Congressional passage of the Thirteenth Amendment, many abolitionists, including William Lloyd Garrison, felt that the time had come to dissolve the antislavery societies. Others, led by Wendell Phillips, believed that this should not be done until the freedmen obtained the right to vote. The executive committee of the Pennsylvania Anti-Slavery Society took up this matter on 1 March 1865. Mary Grew read a letter from Samuel May, Jr., on behalf of the American Anti-Slavery Society, "containing several queries as to the proper time for dissolving that Society and discontinuing the publication of the Anti-Slavery Standard." The opinion of the Pennsylvania committee was solicited, but it did not take action on the matter at that meeting.[1] On 26 April 1865, on motion of Mary Grew, the committee passed a resolution declaring that it was "inexpedient and unwise" to dissolve the American Anti-Slavery Society at that time.[2]

The Philadelphia Female Anti-Slavery Society also took up this issue. It was discussed at their meeting on 13 April 1865, but no direct action was taken. Instead, this group unanimously adopted two resolutions proposed by Mary Grew that dealt tangentially with the question. The first of these declared that "in the grand and marvellous events which are thrilling the hearts of this Nation we see the hand of God leading the American Slaves, step by step, from their long and cruel bondage up to Freedom and victory over the oppressor." Furthermore, they saw "the beginning of a new and glorious era, in which the principles of Liberty, Justice, and Democracy, so long and loudly professed, shall be nobly illustrated on our National life." They devoutly thanked "Him in whose name and whose strength we have labored, that the Anti-Slavery Enterprise has culminated in glorious success; and that the hour when we may, in triumphant joy and profound gratitude, disband this Association is, evidently, very near at hand." The second resolution declared that "while we await only the announcement that American slavery is abolished by the Constitutional law of the land; we re-assert our conviction that justice to the emancipated Slave, and the safety of the Nation, require that the

States which have rebelled against the Government, in the interests of Slavery, shall be permitted to return only upon the condition that under their State Constitutions citizenship shall be conferred on black and white men equally."[3] On motion of Lucretia Mott, it was directed that these resolutions should be presented to the American Anti-Slavery Society at its next annual meeting. Sarah Pugh and Mary Grew were appointed to present them.[4]

Writing to Samuel May, Jr., on 29 April 1865, Mary Grew explained the action of the executive committee of the Pennsylvania Society. "The sentiment decidedly expressed in our meeting," she reported, "was what I wrote to you before; that the Am. Socy. should not be dissolved until the [Thirteenth] Amendment is ratified." However, she had used the words "at present" in her motion because "in these revolutionary times, one can foresee nothing; & it is enough to speak confidently of the present hour."[5] She hoped to see May shortly at the annual meeting of the American Society in New York. At that meeting Garrison introduced a resolution for dissolution of the society. Phillips introduced a counterresolution calling for its continuance. Garrison's resolution was rejected by a vote of 118–48, Phillips was elected president, and the society continued until 1870.[6]

In the summer of 1865 Mary Grew and her friend Margaret Burleigh spent several weeks in Massachusetts. Passing through New York City on the way, Mary Grew visited Parker Pillsbury and told him "how much we in Phila. like his management of the Standard."[7] The two women decided to vacation on Clark's Island, off Plymouth. While there Mary Grew wrote a letter describing her experience. The days had passed rapidly, she reported, and she had accomplished very little. "Every thing seems to depend on the tide, and to be governed by it. So, if the tide suits, off we go in the morning early, across the bay, in some direction, come back to dinner, & tired enough to need the afternoon for rest. As for evenings, there never seem to be any, at such places. I always go to bed as early as possible. When we don't go out sailing in the mornings, we sometimes stroll around the Island, & sit out of doors & try to read or write; come in to an early dinner, & avail ourselves of the afternoon tide, for a sail."[8] The vacationers had visited Standish's Hill, had stood on the foundation stones of Miles Standish's house, and had seen some of the relics of his time. They had visited Plymouth Rock and Pilgrim Hall on the day of their arrival. "With our continual goings out & comings in," Mary Grew wrote, "I became rather exhausted, and found little time or strength for writing letters. Two or three days I was compelled to devote to rest."[9]

"We like this place," she reported, "and our host, & the visitors very much." Their host, Edward Watson, was "a rare character; a man well worth knowing, who welcomes and appreciates true reformers, and persons who do their own thinking; 'the advanced guard,' as he calls them." The boarders whom they had met there were "generally, persons of culture and free thought, whom it does one good to see."[10] Among these were "Mr. & Mrs. Goodwin of Cambridge. . . . Mr. G. is the Greek Professor at Harvard; Mrs. G. was Miss Jenks of Phila,; she is a cousin of Mrs. Furness. They are charming persons; & have a lovely baby. . . . Almost every body here claims descent from some Pilgrim Father or Mother; & there are so many Pilgrim relics and traditions around us that we almost fancy we are living in the old Pilgrim days, & would not be much surprised to see Miles Standish, Gov. Bradford, or Elder Brewster, suddenly appear." This was the island upon which the Pilgrims had first landed and spent their first Sunday after their arrival in North America, before they landed at Plymouth. There was a large rock on the island that the residents associated with the Pilgrims, "naturally supposing that they climbed it, or possibly, used it as a pulpit for their long Sabbath services. . . . Professor Stevens, from Philadelphia, carried off a large piece of it, the other day, as the next best thing to a bit of the Plymouth Rock, which latter cannot now be had for love or money."[11]

Leaving Clark's Island, Mary Grew and Margaret Burleigh went to Nantucket for a week or two, then toured the Cape and took a steamboat from Provincetown to Boston. Mary had written Wendell Phillips for letters of introduction to people on the Cape. "Some good anti-slavery friends" on Clark's Island had told her enough about the people of the Cape, "especially the Comeouters there, to interest us in them."[12] In Boston it appears that the two women visited William Lloyd Garrison; their disagreement over dissolution of the antislavery societies did not seem to have destroyed their friendship.

Attending the first meeting of the Philadelphia Female Anti-Slavery Society after the summer vacation, on 14 September 1865, Mary Grew spoke on the necessity of granting black men the right to vote. She read a letter which had been written to the *Philadelphia Press* indicating that there was a common purpose "to guard the newly-acquired liberties of the freedmen by other securities, while *withholding* that chief security of a freeman's rights, the suffrage." She regarded this as "a dark sign of the times." Abolitionists had a duty to demand suffrage for the freedman as "the *only* security of any real liberty for him." She was instructed to write a letter to the city newspapers expressing these sentiments.[13]

On 27 October 1865 Mary Grew attended the twenty-ninth annual meeting of the Pennsylvania Anti-Slavery Society in Horticultural Hall, West Chester, and took a prominent part in the proceedings.

James and Lucretia Mott, Thomas Garrett, Robert Purvis, Sarah Pugh, Edward M. Davis, and others "well approved for long years of faithful service, were there, vigorous, courageous as ever, and determined to see complete victory crown their warfare unless released from it by death."[14] The *National Anti-Slavery Standard* reported that Wendell Phillips was "the great attraction" at the convention. "Miss Anthony of Rochester and Miss Grew made brief but most forcible speeches; and the occasion, on the whole, was not soon to be forgotten."[15]

Following in Garrison's footsteps, Sarah Pugh introduced a resolution to "close the operations and existence of this Society with the present annual meeting," but it was defeated. Arguing against this proposal, Mary Grew pointed out that friends of the cause in Congress were saying, "help us, back us; we need the agitation which you are keeping up . . . do not dissolve your societies."[16] Liberty was not secure in the South, she said; "everything depends on how the Government shall be reconstructed and upon what conditions the revolted States shall be allowed to return. . . . Now, my friends, what ought we to do? We should endeavor to urge the conscience of the nation up to the very highest standard of the Right and Justice; we should demand for the slave yet in chains and for the freedman the protection of the suffrage."[17] Another resolution, proposed by Alfred H. Love, would have changed the name of the organization to "The Pennsylvania Equal Rights Society," but it, too, was defeated.[18] While Mary Grew disagreed with Garrison on the matter of dissolving the antislavery societies, she introduced a resolution, adopted unanimously, that praised his devoted commitment to the cause of abolition.[19]

On 7 November 1865 Mary Grew addressed a note to Ann Greene Phillips, presenting an anecdote regarding social reform. "I must tell you of the remarkable influence upon the formation of character exerted by that poem of our venerable collateral ancestor . . . which we were refreshing ourselves with when I saw you last summer." Afterwards in Buffalo, Ann Gardner had told her that she had been familiar from childhood with the poem "Should I Kill Thee, Crawling Spider?" From early years to this day, Gardner never was about to crush one of "those helpless creatures," but that expostulation came forcibly into her mind. "But," she added, *"I always killed the spiders."* Mary Grew thought that this little illustration of "how our good words as well as deeds 'live after us' and 'bear fruit' might be interesting and encouraging to Ann and Wendell in their philanthropic efforts."[20]

The executive committee of the Pennsylvania Anti-Slavery Society met on 30 November 1865. The list of officers for the ensuing year, which had been chosen at the West Chester convention, was announced. Mary Grew was included as a member of the executive committee. At the November meeting the subject of printing petitions to Congress, praying that body "to employ suitable means to secure such an amendment of the United States Constitution as will effectually prevent every State from making any distinction in the civil rights of its naturalized and native born citizens on account of race, color, or descent." After "due consideration as to its importance, as well as to the number of copies which should be put into circulation, and the probable expense," the matter was referred to Benjamin C. Bacon and Mary Grew, giving them power to act.[21] They were to have petitions printed and to arrange for their circulation.

On 18 December 1865 the Thirteenth Amendment, abolishing slavery everywhere in the United States, having been ratified by twenty-seven states, was formally proclaimed in effect. "The People have said Amen! and the great deed is done," Mary Grew wrote her sister Susan on the nineteenth.

> American Slavery is abolished BY LAW. . . . Having read the official announcement in this morning's paper, nothing else seemed worth reading; and I am still in a happy state of ignorance of all else which the paper may contain. . . . Our hearts are too full for much utterance, and I came upstairs to sit in my room in silent thankfulness. The news came just in time for Margaret to carry it in her heart as she went to town. As I opened my Testament to read a while, the first words which caught my eye were: "Who hath delivered us from so great a death." I read no more, but shut the book, and gave myself up to quiet meditation on the greatness of the deliverance.[22]

It was true, she went on, that they had been, for months, watching and counting the steps which led to this end. They knew that it was at hand, "yet not the less for that, did the sudden thrill of joy run through our nerves and kindle our souls, when the official words were said; even as at the altar a thrill of intenser joy, and deeper solemnity fills two young hearts, when the vow, long before made, is irrevocably spoken. O blessed marriage of America and Liberty!"[23]

It was also true that the transition state of the emancipated slaves would be "full of pain and peril . . . that our utmost vigilance will be needed to protect them against the baffled rage of their former masters, who would gladly give them *only the name* of freedom; for all the people have not said Amen. But having gained so much, shall we doubt that our victory will be complete if we are faithful?" That morning she felt sure that all they asked would come—"full protection of 'equality before the law,' for white and black men, the only protection now sufficient for the freed slave." It might not come at once; it would not come without "earnest conflict . . . but on this joyous day, we may say with all our hearts, 'We trust the future, having known the past.' "[24]

Mary Grew did not pretend that she realized fully "the greatness of the fact which has transpired," but it pervaded her soul sufficiently "to make Heaven seem nearer and life nobler; and to awaken profound gratitude that one great task to which I set myself in youth, is accomplished." At first she had expected to live to see its accomplishment, but she had relinquished that hope "many years ago," and it had revived only at the commencement of the war.[25]

"Are you not glad," Mary Grew wrote Susan, "that the official notice of the Ratification, is announced before *The Liberator* is given up?" It seemed to her fitting that "Mr. Garrison should hang out that flag" at least until slavery was abolished by law. She was glad that the deed was done just in time for him to announce it.[26] The final issue of the *Liberator* appeared 29 December 1865.

"Of course, you are watching Congress," she concluded, "and rejoicing, as we are, in the moral strength which they have, thus far, manifested. They *do* seem likely to redeem those Halls from the infamy of past years of legislation. Did you see the telegram of the Governor of Oregon to the Sec. of State? It announced the ratification of the Amendment, by Oregon, & ended with, 'Glory to God!' "[27]

On 27 December 1865 the committee "on the Suffrage petition"— Benjamin C. Bacon and Mary Grew—reported to the executive committee of the Pennsylvania Anti-Slavery Society that three thousand copies had been printed and were being circulated for signatures. Letters were read from Susan B. Anthony and Parker Pillsbury, respecting the calling of a special meeting of the American Anti-Slavery Society to consider the expediency of so altering the name of the society as to be "more in accordance with the changed character of slavery and to add suffrage for women as one of its objects. . . . After an animated discussion upon these topics," the matter was referred to a committee consisting of Sarah Pugh, Margaret J. Burleigh, and Mary Grew to report a resolution to the next meeting for further consideration and final action.[28]

This committee reported on 3 January 1866. It hailed the ratification of the Thirteenth Amendment, "this grand triumph of our cause," with "profound joy and gratitude to God who has wrought out so great a deliverance for the millions of slaves in our land." However, the report said, "the spirit of slavery" still existed and was manifested in legislative action and the press of the South as well as in "the personal cruelty practised by the recent slave masters upon their victims." The only way to protect "the personal liberty of the black man in the South" was to put the ballot in his hands. On recommendation of the committee, the society's executive board resolved "that we will now address ourselves to the completion of our work, by advocating and demanding in the name of justice and humanity, that in the reconstruction of Southern State Governments, suffrage shall be bestowed without distinction of color; that the enfranchised slave may thus be invested with sufficient political freedom to protect his personal freedom."[29] No action was taken on the proposals to change the name of the American Anti-Slavery Society and to support suffrage for women.

In January 1866 Mary Grew wrote the report of the Philadelphia Female Anti-Slavery Society for 1865. In this document she pointed to the antislavery gains of the year, most notably, of course, the ratification of the Thirteenth Amendment. Language failed to portray "the magnitude of the triumph," she wrote, "or to reach the heights and depths of our glad thanksgiving."[30] She also noted that several Southern states had abolished slavery of their own volition. Progress was being made in educating the blacks; in Charleston the public schools had been opened to white and colored children "on equal terms." Congress was about to give the franchise to blacks in the District of Columbia. Illinois had expunged its "infamous black laws" from the statute books. Colored men were being appointed to public office. The House of Representatives had refused admission to delegates from the rebel states, and bills had been introduced to provide equal protection for blacks. There was a movement to give them the right to vote. Congress had given the Freedmen's Bureau a new lease on life.[31]

"Is the triumph of our cause complete?" she asked.[32] No, the spirit of slavery was still evident, not only in the South but in the North. The southern states had passed severe "Black codes," limiting the rights and privileges of the freedmen. Former slaveholders were determined to establish a system of peonage in the place of slavery. The Southern press was filled with racial hatred. Andrew Johnson's plan for Reconstruction did not provide for Negro suffrage. Even in the North many states, Pennsylvania among them, denied black men to the right to vote. Rhode Island had banished black children from her public schools.[33] Philadelphia had closed the doors of her city railroad cars "and the pews of her churches" to black people. What was needed was to bestow upon the black man "sufficient political liberty for the protection of his personal liberty."[34] This could not be accomplished without giving him the ballot.

Mary Grew was convinced that the government could not be

trusted to complete the work of emancipation. Nor could the army. Certainly not President Andrew Johnson. Not even the Republican party. Nor the Church. Only the abolitionists could be trusted with this task. Some said they should turn over their work to the freedmen's aid socieies. "Vast and important as this work is," Mary Grew declared, "it is not the work to which, *as abolitionists,* we are pledged, viz.: *the completion and security of the slave's freedom.*"[35] They would work to transform public sentiment through circulation of the *Standard* (the last surviving antislavery newspaper), through communictaions to the secular press, through petitions to Congress, through "words of remonstrance, warning, approval or censure," with a view to "converting the Northern heart to a sense of its obligations to those whom it has so long oppressed; and to a steadfast purpose to fulfil those obligations."[36]

"Abraham Lincoln fell by the assassin hand of slavery," Mary Grew noted in her conclusion. "Then men knew that American slavery was not dead."[37] While the people buried their martyred president "with the highest funeral honors which a people can bestow, the tears of affection, his successor vowed to carry on the work which he had begun." The hopes Andrew Johnson had first aroused had been followed by anxiety as "the friends of freedom" watched his course. Those hopes faded, the passing months were marked by "downward progress," and the new president had betrayed the Negro. "Doubtless we took counsel of our fervent wishes rather than of our cooler reason, when we expected that the national decree declaring slavery abolished would at once annihilate the system so inwrought with the nation's heart and life, and that the transition from slavery to actual freedom would be rapid and brief." However, the abolitionists would not pause to portray their disappointment in "impotent words of regret"; they would "meet the demands of the present hour with the strength and courage which has borne us through the past; looking hopefully to the future with unshaken faith that He, who with a mighty hand and outstretched arm hath brought the American slaves out of the Egypt of their bondage, will turn back their pursuers, and guide them safely through their perilous passage to perfect freedom."[38]

On 4 January 1866 Mary Grew addressed a letter to Wendell and Ann Phillips. She enclosed a letter she had found among her father's papers that she thought might be of interest to them, but did not comment on its contents. She reported that she had recently visited Charles Greene and found him "not so well as usual, apparently suffering rather more from the disturbed action of his heart; yet not sick, or unable to go out as usual."[39] Most of her letter concerned the affairs of the American Anti-Slavery Society and its organ, the *National Anti-Slavery Standard*. The executive committee of the Pennsylvania Anti-Slavery Society was solicitous to know who was going to succeed Parker Pillsbury as editor of the *Standard*. They regretted his withdrawal from the paper and "likewise, his failing health." He had done good service in the editorial chair. James and Lucretia Mott, she said, were desirous that Charles K. Whipple should be Pillsbury's successor. "Do you favor the suggestion," she asked the Phillipses; "and would he accept the office? . . . He has been in our cause so long, & knows it so well, and has so thoroughly proved his fidelity and ability, that we could certainly trust this most important responsibility in his hands."[40]

Congressman William D. Kelley of Philadelphia had asked her if the *Standard* would be sent to members of Congress this winter, as it had been the previous winter, adding that it was *"highly important"* that they should have it." She had written to Pillsbury about the matter; he had replied that he did send some copies to congressmen and would have sent more had he remained in New York. "It is certainly very important that all the members who will read it, shall be supplied with it." She asked Phillips to let her know if the executive committee of the American Anti-Slavery Society would order that this should be done and what number they would send.[41]

The day before Mary Grew wrote, Pennsylvania's executive committee had appointed Edward M. Davis to write to members of the national executive committee regarding the proposal to move meetings of the American Anti-Slavery Society from New York to Boston. "I presume he will write to you. So we need say no more than this," she wrote; "that we don't like the idea of the Meetings of that Soc'ty being removed from N.Y. to Boston; & thus, at this season of the year, being put out of reach of Pennsylvanians." There were "very important topics demanding consideration & action on the part of abolitionists now; & a Meeting of the Am. Soc'y seems very desirable; but if it is to be anything more than a meeting of New England abolitionists, it should, surely not be held in Boston." Mrs. Mott had suggested that the meeting of the Massachusetts society should be held first, to be followed by a meeting of the American Society in New York, at which they might have the benefit of the sentiments and proposed plans of action elicited at the former. "There is an immense work to be done by us yet," Mary Grew wrote, "and there is no time to be lost." Congressman Kelley had said to her the other day, "Every word of compromise spoken in the North weakens us in Congress." She had not intended to write such a long letter, and she wished she could talk of these matters with Wendell and Ann in person, instead of writing. She trusted that whatever was done would be "for the best."[42]

On 11 January 1866, at a meeting of the Philadelphia Female Anti-Slavery Society, Mary Grew reported that in pursuance of the directions of the society, she had applied to the editor of the *Public Ledger* for the gratuitous publication in his paper of an article advocating Negro suffrage. The application being refused, she had purchased the insertion of a short article on this subject. At this meeting the society decided to petition Congress for an amendment to the United States Constitution that would prohibit the states from "making any distinction in civil rights and privileges among naturalized citizens or persons born on its soil on account of race, color or descent." Mary Grew was appointed to prepare such a petition for signatures and to forward it to Congress.[43]

On 17 January 1866 Mary Grew wrote to Elizabeth Neall Gay regarding the matters of dissolving antislavery societies and of Negro suffrage. "'The Old Female' proposes, as you will see by the Standard, to discuss on the 25th inst. the very serious question of the propriety of giving up the ghost. Whether or not the time has come for this, will be, I suppose, decided, by her own wisdom, or foolishness, on that day." Mary Grew urged Elizabeth Neall Gay to come to Philadelphia for this meeting and "assist in keeping the breath of life in her, or help her to sing her 'Nunc dimittis.'" If she could not come, would she send a letter embodying her opinions and sentiments on the matter of further need for the society "in this mundane sphere"? Sarah Pugh had told Mary Grew that Elizabeth Gay had once expressed an intention of coming to Philadelphia should such a crisis arise, "and we all think it would be an excellent arrangement for you and the children to make a visit to your numerous friends, at this time, & remain until our next, & perhaps our last, Annual Meeting. . . . The Old Female assures me that she will not draw her last breath (in case she concludes to expire) before that Meeting is held; which will be on the second Thursday of February." Regardless of the uncertain future of the society, Mary Grew was writing its annual report as usual. "On one point, I am clear," she told Mrs. Gay, "i.e., that our work is not done; that freedom is not *secured* to the black man; & will not be so, without the suffrage; and that *we,* the old abolitionists, under some name or other, & in some organization, have got to fight out this battle for him."[44]

On 25 January "The Old Female" decided against dissolution and against changing its name. It was to continue until the Fifteenth Amendment was added to the Constitution. On 1 February Mary

Grew reported that the society's petition to Congress regarding civil rights for blacks had been presented to Congress by Senator Charles Sumner. Sarah Pugh declined reelection as president of the society, and Lucretia Mott was chosen in her place. On 8 March Mary Grew presented a resolution of regret at Sarah Pugh's decision and expressed appreciation for her many years of faithful service as president. On 12 April she introduced a resolution hailing the passage of the Civil Rights Bill over Andrew Johnson's veto, which was adopted and ordered sent to the *Standard*. The resolution expressed her view that the two-thirds vote of Congress in behalf of this measure was "an indication of the purpose of that body to resist successfully the assaults upon Justice and Human Liberty, made by Andrew Johnson." It also entreated those members of the House and Senate "whose zeal and persistent labor accomplished the passage of this Bill, that they will to the utmost extent of their power, secure its practical enforcement in every part of this country." A second resolution declared that the thanks of the nation were due to "those Senators and Representatives of the Thirty-Ninth Congress who are so bravely battling for Liberty and Human Rights against the President of the United States who has betrayed the Party who elected him, a People who trusted him in the hour of their bereavement and peril, who has broken his solemn promises of protection to the oppressed millions of our land, and joined himself to their oppressors."[45]

On 4 May 1866 Mary Grew wrote to Ann Phillips regarding family papers and the upcoming annual meeting of the American Anti-Slavery Society in New York City.

> I was very glad to learn from Wendell's letter that the old letter, written by our uncle Charles, gave you all so much pleasure. I *have* looked in all the repositories of my father's papers, I believe, for something more of similar interest, but in vain. The only hope that I have left, of finding anything of the sort, is from a package of very old papers, which were left, many years ago, in Hartford. Probably, they are destroyed or lost, before this time, but the recollection of their existence, & the *possibility* of some relic of your mother being among them, induces me to make inquiry concerning them.

She went on to tell Ann that she had "a relic of your early days," which she would give to Wendell the following week, when they met in New York. "*He* will value it, & it may interest you to see it."[46]

In the same letter Mary Grew inquired whether it had occurred to Wendell Phillips to invite General Rufus Saxton to the anniversary meeting. "He is staying, just now, at the water cure in Northampton." Saxton had been military governor of the South Carolina and Georgia

offshore islands and assistant commissioner for the Freedmen's Bureau in South Carolina; he was a native of Massachusetts and "an
abolitionist sympathizer."[47] "He is in hearty sympathy with our cause,"
Mary Grew declared, "& he or his wife said to me that they might
possibly attend the Meeting. His presence there would help." Someone had told General Saxton "a while ago" that Wendell Phillips's
eulogies of him had probably hindered his promotion. Saxton had
replied, "I would rather have Wendell Phillips' approval than a Major
Generalship." Saxton told Mary Grew a few weeks earlier that he had
recently received a letter from his father, who wrote to him, "I would
rather have Wendell Phillips speak well of you, than see a thousand
stars on your shoulder." "Sensible old gentleman, isn't he?" Mary
Grew concluded.[48]

Mary Grew attended the annual meeting of the American Anti-
Slavery Society, which convened in New York City on 8 May 1866,
served on the nominating committee, participated in the discussions,
and gave a speech. She was chosen one of the vice presidents for the
ensuing year. In her address she made an appeal for funds to support
the work of the society and for Negro suffrage. She brought a message
from Lucretia Mott, who had lost her voice due to a cold, commenting on the huge contributions being made to freedmen's aid societies.
"She asks you to remember that the treasury of this Society has not a
tenth part as many contributors, and that it needs, at this moment,
help far more than any other association which has pressed its demands upon you. She would have you imitate the munificence which
has filled those coffers." Mary Grew herself had heard it said not long
before in Philadelphia, "and I dare say you hear it said every day," that
if the abolitionists could go before the public and request support for
"this or that specific work to do, we could raise money enough; but
that in fact we have nothing to do; that our work is done, and we do
not know it; that the Temple of Liberty is built, and we do not see it."
The abolitionists were well aware of the great victory that had been
won, but it was not enough. The Temple of Liberty was still "un-
roofed," and "millions of emancipated ones are crowding into it for
shelter. . . . We want to roof it. Will you *give us the money?*" This
question brought applause from the audience. The work of an abolitionist was "like the building of a bridge. . . . It is finished, all but one
span. One arch only is wanting. But while that arch is wanting, of
what avail is the bridge?"[49]

She went on:

> Now what is the remaining work which we ask you to help us do? It is
> to secure the personal freedom of the emancipated millions by giving them

the suffrage, by making them American citizens indeed and in truth. We appeal to every man who glories in his citizenship, and who feels a pride and joy as he holds the ballot in his hand as a symbol of that citizenship, to give, by every means in his power, that right to his colored brother which he values for himself. . . . We appeal to every woman too who knows its value by the injustice which denies it to her, to work diligently and faithfully to give it to every black man in the land.

Until this work was done, until absolute security was obtained "for the personal liberty of the colored race in this country," the work of the American Anti-Slavery Society was not completed.[50] Mary Grew implored members and friends of the society to "Give generously, sparing what you can from your luxury, from your convenience, from your comfort even, for your brother's necessity, for your nation's need; and God shall return to you good measure, pressed down and running over."[51] There was applause as she finished.

On 26 May 1866 the *National Anti-Slavery Standard* carried an editorial by Mary Grew entitled "The Situation," in which she developed further the need for the American Anti-Slavery Society to continue its work. "It is not the Abolitionist alone," she wrote, "who says that this is an hour of peril, a crisis in the nation's life." From their places in the Senate and the House, the nation's legislators were "sounding their notes of warning, and bidding the people beware lest their victory in the strife of arms be succeeded by defeat in a contest of diplomacy." In the presidential chair sat a man "whose heart is in sympathy with the rebels whom he is sworn to resist; and who is using his immense power to bring into Congress representation of eleven States, as disloyal in heart to the United States government to-day, as they were when they fought Grant and Sherman on the battlefield." The Southern states were "as loyal to slavery to-day as they were when they seceded from the American Union in order to found a Confederacy of which slavery should be the corner-stone." The present incumbent of the presidency designated the opposition of Congress to his measures "as opposition to *the government*." He was betraying the party who had elected him to power and was continually violating "his solemn pledges of protection to the persecuted colored population of the South."[52]

Noting that there were three factions in Congress—Democrats, regular Republicans, and Radical Republicans, Mary Grew said the question before the nation was whether Andrew Johnson would be able to garner sufficient support to execute his policy. Would he succeed "by the immense power of his official patronage (power which ought not to be placed in the hands of one man) in buying a sufficient number of invertebrate Congressmen to fatally weaken the hands of the stronger and better portion of the Republicans? . . . And will the radical members of Congress . . . be true to their solemn trusts and loyal to absolute justice, which is the highest law?" On the answer to these questions hung "the nation's destiny." It was the duty of abolitionists, she reiterated, to continue their work until they had achieved whatever was necessary to complete and secure the slave's freedom. "Our task is still, as it has ever been, to inspire the nation with a sense of justice towards the black man, which should work out for him his complete freedom." They had a duty to guard the rights of blacks "with vigilant fidelity." The black man must be clothed with "a citizen's power to protect his freedom." The Civil Rights Act was not enough. The freedman must have "the suffrage of a freeman." Not until his personal liberty was "hedged about with all the defenses necessary to its secure possession is he *really free*, and not till then, is work of the American Anti-Slavery Society done."[53]

In June 1866 the Philadelphia Female Anti-Slavery Society appointed Mary Grew and Lucretia Mott as a committee to arrange a course of lectures for the following year to raise money for the cause. They decided to invite General Benjamin F. Butler, General John Charles Frémont, Senator Charles Sumner, and Wendell Phillips to come to Philadelphia for this purpose. On 7 June Mary Grew addressed a letter to Phillips, requesting that he write to Butler and Sumner asking them to grant the women's request. "You can say some things in a private letter," she wrote, "about our need of money to sustain the Standard, which could not well be said in our more formal letter of invitation. As they are your personal friends, we rely greatly on your influence with them."[54] They had asked Edward M. Davis to use his influence with General Frémont. "We want to raise $1500. if possible. We certainly ought to raise $1000. with four such lecturers. Of course, the profits, whatever they may be, will go mainly to the Standard. In fact, the whole of the sum will; for whatever small portion *may* be needed towards sustaining our office agent, etc. will be devoted to the same end, as these are kept in operation for the sake of sustaining that A.S. Soc'y."[55] Mary Grew noted that the day for antislavery fairs "has gone by with us here" and that "a course of lectures seems to be our only resource now, for increasing our funds. . . . Of course, we rely on you for the best lecture of the course, but this we shall not mention to the other three gentlemen. Please let us know what time will suit you. I suppose we must take Mr. Sumner on his way to Washington," she said, "if we are fortunate enough to get him at all. . . . Mr. Davis thinks that it would be well to have all the lectures between the middle of Nov. & the middle of Dec. but we may not be able to get all our lecturers in those weeks."[56]

In the same letter Mary Grew noted that Aaron M. Powell, new editor of the *Standard,* was to be in Philadelphia that day and she was going to see him "and talk about the Standard, etc. . . . We all like the changes in the appearance of the paper very much," she continued. "Thus far, certainly, Mr. Powell has managed it well."[57] She informed Phillips that her post office address during the summer would be "Care of Mr. Edward T. Steel, No. 4 North 2nd St. Phila. . . . Wherever I may wander, letters directed in that way will be forwarded to me."[58]

On the same day she wrote Phillips, Mary Grew addressed a letter to Edward M. Davis, notifying him that she had prepared the letters of invitation that morning. "I supposed that the sooner our letters were sent, the better." She asked Davis to make sure that his copyist filled correctly, in each letter, the blanks she had left for the "three other" lecturers. She also asked Davis to read her letter to Wendell Phillips; "and if you have anything further to say to him, you can add it."[59]

Writing to "Dear Friend" (Mrs. Aaron M. Powell) from Brattleboro, Vermont, on 6 August 1866, she expressed her concern over the news of Mr. Powell's "prostration and illness." She said she was "more sorry than surprised." She had been "extremely anxious about his health ever since he assumed the care of the paper." She trusted that "we have not seriously injured him by putting such a burden upon him. . . . The almost unprecedented heat of July was enough to prostrate any one in the atmosphere of a large city." She hoped Powell was recovering "in the better air of Ghent, and able to enjoy something of the rest & quiet which his absence from New York will give him." She hoped he would not attempt to return until he was "quite restored, & fully equal to the effort to resume his labors. . . . For *our* sake, as truly for his own, this is desirable. His life and health are too valuable to the cause of Freedom, to be trifled with by attempts at overworking himself." It was her intention to send something to the *Standard* every week while he was absent from his post. Just yesterday she had mailed such an article to New York. She noted that Wendell Phillips was doing "an unusual amount of work for the paper. . . . How really *grand* is his *Appeal to Am. Clergymen!* . . . The paper *grows* in excellence, and its publication seems to me, now, so important to the moral health of the nation that I tremble lest some untoward event should befall it." She hoped Mrs. Powell would keep her informed of her husband's condition.[60]

On 18 August 1866 the *Standard* carried an article by Mary Grew commenting on a statement Secretary of State William H. Seward had made to the effect that the Union would be restored only when "loyal men are admitted as representatives of the loyal people of the eleven States so long unrepresented in Congress." She wondered whether he included the freedmen among these "loyal people."[61] On 25 August 1866 the paper carried her article on "Governmental Powers," in which she took as her theme the famous quotation from the Declaration of Independence regarding governments deriving their just powers from the consent of the governed. She thought that either the nation did not believe this or that it did believe its government was "a very unjust one." Half the white population (women) and almost all the blacks were being governed without any means of expressing their consent. "Woe unto you, hypocrites!" she exclaimed. She thought the question of the day was whether the United States was to rise to "true national greatness and real prosperity" or perish "with a lie in its right hand."[62] By 15 September Aaron Powell was at his post again.

On 13 September, 11 October, and 8 November 1866 Mary Grew and other members of the Philadelphia Female Anti-Slavery Society again expressed their concern over the exclusion of colored people from the city streetcars. On 12 December she was directed to prepare a petition to Congress for "Universal Suffrage," which was adopted on 14 February 1867, signed by the society's officers, and ordered to be forwarded to Washington.[63] On 11 October 1866 Sarah Pugh resigned as treasurer of the Pennsylvania Anti-Slavery Society. She did not agree with the majority of its executive committee regarding the need for continuing the antislavery societies. Her resignation after twenty-three years of service was reluctantly accepted. Mary Grew prepared a resolution, which the committee passed, to express their "high appreciation of her services, and of her sympathy and co-operation with us during many years of our Anti-Slavery struggle; and our deep regret that we must be deprived of such co-operation."[64] Mary Grew was chosen to the treasurer's position at the annual meeting of the society in November.[65]

Robert Purvis, Edward M. Davis, and Mary Grew served on the committee to arrange this meeting. They were able to engage the hall of Franklin Institute in Philadelphia for this purpose. The meeting was held on 22 and 23 November. Mary Grew served on the business committee. The society called for the impeachment of Andrew Johnson, "one who has betrayed alike the colored and the loyal white men and women of the nation." A thorough reconstruction was demanded of Congress, the members declared, "one which shall guarantee both education and the ballot to the freedmen" and insure for the Southern states a truly republican form of government. Susan B.

Anthony spoke on behalf of woman suffrage at this meeting.[66] On 5 December 1866 the executive committee of the Pennsylvania Anti-Slavery Society adopted petitions for "impartial suffrage" and for the impeachment of Johnson, to be circulated for signing.

On 13 December 1866 the Philadelphia Female Anti-Slavery Society decided, as another means of raising funds for the cause, "to hold a Festival, which shall be another re-union of the Abolitionists and friends of Freedom such as we used to have in the time of our Anti-Slavery Fairs, bringing city and country friends to-gether without the labor of a Fair."[67] This festival was held on 17 January 1867 in National Hall. Mary Grew served as chairman of the committee that arranged it. Also on 13 December the female society adopted a resolution proposed by Mary Grew to send a petition to Congress asking for universal suffrage. Mary Grew prepared this petition, which was approved by the society on 14 February 1867, ordered signed by the officers, and forwarded to the nation's capital.[68]

In her annual report for 1866 Mary Grew reviewed the record of the Thirty-ninth Congress and found it wanting. "The weakness of Congress and the treason of the acting President" had "revivified the spirit of the rebels," and a new campaign had been organized under the leadership of Southerners and Andrew Johnson "for the purpose of winning back all that the slave-power had lost upon the battle-field."[69] It was true that Congress had passed the Civil Rights Bill and the Freedmen's Bureau Bill over the president's veto. These measures she approved. However, it had permitted Andrew Johnson to "restore Tennessee to her forfeited rights as a sovereign State in the Union" and to "exclude from the rights of citizenship a class of men who had been true to the Union when she had been false to it." She thought the suffrage provision of the Fourteenth Amendment, providing for reducing representation in Congress for any state denying the right to vote to any male inhabitants over the age of twenty-one, was completely inadequate and constituted a "breach of faith with a class of men who battled bravely under the United States flag in the hour of the Nation's extreme peril."[70]

She thought Andrew Johnson should be impeached and removed from office. He had responded to Congressional measures designed to protect blacks by vetoing them; he had declared their sponsors to be "traitors and assassins." He had given "aid and comfort to the murderers in the New Orleans massacre." He had revoked a military order that "forbade the public whipping of colored men and women in North Carolina." He had proclaimed peace "when there was no peace." His purpose was to restore to state sovereignty and congressional representation "rebels fresh from the battle-field, so unrepentant of their treason that they still make it unsafe for loyal white men to dwell on their soil, and still treat the negro with insult and cruelty." Was the Negro's freedom safe under the protection of such an executive officer? "Of Andrew Johnson it may be said that his treachery to his party, his disloyalty to his country, his treason to Humanity have risen to such colossal magnitude that the name of Jefferson Davis dies out of men's thought."[71]

She thought the record of the Johnsonian governments in the South demonstrated the necessity of unequivocally granting the suffrage to blacks. An indication of what could be expected of Southern white governments she found in North Carolina, "where negro men and women are publicly whipped in the most cruel manner, for slight offences, in order to disqualify them for voting at some future day; there being a law of that State which deprives a person, who has been publicly whipped, of the right to vote."[72] A black man had been shot and killed in Lexington, Virginia, by one of General Robert E. Lee's pupils at Washington College; he was acquitted on grounds that the Negro had "insulted" him.[73] The Southern states had enacted Black Codes, which "differed very little from the old slave laws." In Louisiana, for example, freedmen who were employed on a plantation were forbidden to leave it for the purpose of visiting their friends, and friends were forbidden to visit them. Unemployed freedmen who had not made contracts during the first ten days of January were declared "vagrants" and could be sold to planters for one year or compelled to work upon the public roads or levees "without contract or fair wages." Persons could be published for "tampering with, enticing away, harboring, or feeding, or secreting laborers, servants, or apprentices."[74] The freedmen were required to carry passes. Florida had provided for arming whites and disarming blacks. It prescribed the lash as a penalty for "trifling offences." Failure to perform assigned work, violation of contract, and "disrespect to the employer or his agent" were made crimes for which freedmen could be sold into servitude for one year.[75]

Mary Grew was convinced that the federal judiciary could not be relied on "in this great conflict between the spirit of slavery and the spirit of Liberty." Recent decisions of the Supreme Court had "startled the Nation, awakening alarm among the friends of freedom, and inspiring with joy the rebels and their Northern allies."[76]

Mary Grew believed that the ballot could be secured to the freedmen only by the federal Constitution and "an Executive Officer loyal to that Constitution. . . . To obtain such amendment of the Constitution as will secure it is the work of the present hour."[77] She hoped that the Fortieth Congress would present to the American people for ratification such an amendment to the Constitution as would give the ballot to the Negro "and enable the Federal Executive power to defend him in the exercise of it." She also hoped it would remove from the presidential office "the man who has defied its laws and betrayed the Nation."[78]

Mary Grew was also concerned about equal rights for Negroes in the North. She devoted several pages of her annual report for 1866 to the problem of Philadelphia Negroes being excluded from the city streetcars. "On this subject," she noted, "the churches and clergy of this city have signally failed in their duty. Eager, zealous, prompt to do battle against the running of our city cars on Sunday, they have scarcely been disturbed by this wicked and cruel practice of excluding their fellow-citizens and fellow-christians from those cars on account of their complexion." She found three exceptions among the city's clergymen: "The persecuted colored man of this country has reason to remember and to bless the names of Rev. William H. Furness, Rev. B. F. Barrett, and Rev. Phillips Brooks."[79] Early in 1867 the state legisalture passed a law forbidding this type of discrimination.

Concluding her report, as usual, on a hopeful note, Mary Grew declared:

> The complete and final victory of our cause is certain. We believed this in its darkest days; we are not less assured of it, now, when faith is changing to sight. The light which, from around and above us, is poured upon our path, throws its beams far into the future, and in that light we see our beloved country purged from all stains of oppression, emancipated from all bonds of caste, regenerated by supreme love of justice, ruling itself in righteousness, and sending up to heaven, from every hill and valley across the broad continent, the acceptable worship of a "People whose God is the Lord."[80]

6

Dissolving the Antislavery Societies (1867–1870)

MARY Grew's annual report for 1866, published in February 1867, included an account of the "Festival of the Friends of Freedom" held under the auspices of the Philadelphia Female Anti-Slavery Society in National Hall, Market Street, on 17 January 1867. Two hundred fifty circulars had been distributed in the city and county, requesting contributions of money and supplies. Two thousand circulars of invitation had been printed for distribution. The admission charge was fifty cents. Application had been personally made to several caterers for provisions, and they had responded generously. The festival was held in the evening, and despite a snowstorm, so many people attended that, "but for the great size of the hall, the guests would have been uncomfortably crowded. . . . The managers were gratified with the result of their efforts." Mary Grew was chairman of the committee on arrangements. The hall had a pictured ceiling and was brilliantly lighted. The walls were hung with "the well known banners which have adorned so many of our Anti-Slavery Fairs." The refreshment table had as its centerpiece a pyramid of flowers donated by Abraham L. Pennock, Jr., which produced "a fine spectacular effect." Instrumental music was supplied by the Delmonico Cornet Band, songs were presented by Miss Elizabeth Greenfield and her pupils, and a "Stereorama" was exhibited in an anteroom.[1]

Among the objects of special interest at the festival was the table on which founding members of the American Anti-Slavery Society had signed its Declaration of Sentiments in Philadelphia's Adelphi Building in December 1833. In an interval between conversation and music the festival goers were addressed by Elizabeth Cady Stanton, Susan B. Anthony, J. Miller McKim, and Lucy Stone. Letters of regret were read from the Honorable Schuyler Colfax and the Honorable John W. Forney. "The abolitionists, young and old," Mary Grew reported, "seemed to enjoy heartily this rare opportunity of general social intercourse with so many fellow laborers."[2] After expenses, the festival yielded a net profit for the society of $403.62. "The experience of your Committee in the management of this Festival," Mary Grew noted in conclusion of her report as chairman, "has taught them how the expenses might be greatly reduced if a similar occasion should occur in the future."[3]

On 22 January 1867 Mary Grew wrote to Wendell Phillips concerning the affairs of Charles Greene, who had recently given up his apothecary shop, and she enclosed a contribution of $305 to the work of the American Anti-Slavery Society. "Three hundred dollars is the contribution of the Pennsylvania Anti-Slavery Society [Mary Grew was now treasurer], to the National A-S. Festival; and the remaining five dollars is my own contribution." She said she would gladly send more if she felt sure she could afford it, but her "larger contributions to the cause must be made through the Penna. & Phila. Female Societies; & also directly to the Am. Soc'y in May." Margaret Burleigh was unable to contribute anything to the national festival because her funds were too low. "Loss of health has compelled her to suspend her labors of school teaching." Mary Grew also reported to Phillips on the Philadelphia festival: "We had a good time at our Festival. I wish you could have been with us." She noted that Congressman George W. Julian did not come, "not being well," and that Congressman Schuyler Colfax had sent a letter of regret. "From Gen. & Mrs. Frémont, who were formally & earnestly invited, no word of response has been rec'd; wh. E. M. Davis thinks is unaccountable." Davis also thought that a check "will not serve you as well as a draft on Boston. . . . I can't conveniently get a draft today, and I have sent so many cheques to Boston & Providence, & always understood that there was no discount made on them, that I shall send this. If a draft is preferable, please return the cheque and I will get you a draft. I shall be glad if you will send me a line saying that it has come to hand."[4]

On 14 February 1867 Mary Grew presented a petition at the meeting of the Philadelphia Female Anti-Slavery Society asking of Congress "such an amendment to the Constitution as should establish Universal Suffrage."[5] The society adopted it and ordered it signed by Lucretia Mott as president and the other officers and forwarded to Washington. On 22 February the executive committee of the Pennsylvania Anti-Slavery Society adopted a petition on behalf of a measure to prohibit importation into the United States of sugar and other commodities produced by slave labor. Mary Grew and Benjamin C. Bacon were to prepare it for signature by the officers.[6]

On 14 March 1867 the Philadelphia Female Anti-Slavery Society appointed Mary Grew as a delegate to the international antislavery conference to be held in Paris in June. The conference was actually held in August, and Mary Grew did not attend. The executive committee of the Pennsylvania Anti-Slavery Society took up the matter on 26 June and appointed her to correspond with officers of the American Anti-Slavery Society with a view to preparing "a suitable address" to the international conference. The committee thought a written message to the gathering would be better than sending delegates. Wendell Phillips thought that the American Society should not support a conference from which women delegates were to be excluded.[7]

In the summer of 1867 Mary Grew vacationed in western New York State. Writing to Wendell Phillips from Buffalo on 23 July 1867, she answered his query as to why she had not been writing for the *Standard.* "Because I have collapsed," she wrote, "sunk into that miserable, good-for-nothing state, in which I am not fit for writing a letter to you." She *wanted* to write for "that most valuable & influential paper," and she had begun an article just before she left home that she had not been able to finish. "Perhaps one reason that I'm in so low a condition," she reflected, "is that I have not seen the Standard since I came out here. . . . I expect it daily, however. Then your editorials may revive me to that degree that I shall be inspired to write."[8]

Mary Grew had been instructed by the executive committee of the Pennsylvania Anti-Slavery Society to write to Phillips, in their behalf, urging him, "by all that is dear to our cause," to prepare an address to the Paris conference setting forth "the true position of the Am. Soc'y. & its auxiliaries; and the Nation's continued need thereof." Before Mary Grew had gathered energy enough to fulfill this commission, a letter had arrived from Phillips gravely proposing that *she* should do it. "Just as though *anybody* in the country knew what ought to be said, *exactly,* as you know it, or could say it as you can." The Pennsylvania committee thought that the position of the American Society would be misrepresented in England and France and that some statement from the Americans was called for. "They, also, wished me to say to you that in such statement they wd. like to have the comparative importance of our work & that of the Freedmen's Association clearly set forth; without, of course, detracting from the merits of the former. I state this because I was directed to do so; not because you need any suggestions on the subject."[9]

She hoped that Phillips would write such an address, "for it may enlighten some of those English & French people, who are either stupid or misled. As to our own folks at home, if the present condition of the nation, the testimony of Radical Congressmen, & of our daily papers; added to the arguments of Abolitionists, doesn't convince them of the need of our Society's existence, neither wd. they be persuaded if one shd. rise from the dead."[10]

Mary Grew had just come from Fredonia, where she was visiting her nephew, Howard Jones. "The people of that place," she observed, "are very anxious that you shd. bless them with your presence." In Buffalo she was visiting her niece, Mrs. J. F. Bingham, who was married to a minister. "Mrs. Bingham wanted yr. autograph, so I had to spare the signature from yr. letter. . . . I ought to supply myself with yr. autographs, when I travel. I might make something for 'The Cause.'" In this letter she also commented on the loss of Francis Jackson's bequest, which went to the freedmen's aid organizations instead of to the antislavery societies. "But abolitionists are accustomed to being ill-treated," she remarked philosophically, "& I for one, glory & rejoice daily; that the wrong-suffering rather than the wrong-doing is on our side."[11]

When Mary Grew returned to Philadelphia in September she plunged into preparations for another Festival of the Friends of Freedom. It was held on 8 November 1867, the evening of the same day on which the Pennsylvania Anti-Slavery Society held its thirty-first annual meeting in the hall of the Franklin Institute. The annual meeting was held in the morning. Mary Grew was appointed to the committee on finance. She also "spoke briefly on individual responsibility to the cause of freedom, and the duty of every member of the Society to work faithfully according to his ability, whether one, five or ten talents have been committed to him." In addition, she presented resolutions stating that events in the South made it clear that the work of the American abolitionists was not completed, that the work could not be left to the Republican party, which was following "a timid and faltering course," and that Andrew Johnson should be impeached and removed from office. She gave the treasurer's report but was not reelected to that office; she was succeeded by John K. Wildman. Finally, she read several letters to the convention from absentees.[12]

The evening festival was held in Horticultural Hall. The doors opened at five o'clock, and Wendell Phillips lectured in the upper hall at eight o'clock on "the present condition and needs of the country." The festival, including Phillips's lecture, yielded a net profit of $943 for the female abolitionists. Phillips also lectured in Kennett Square and in West Chester before he came to Philadelphia. Mary Grew wrote a report on the festival for the *Standard*.[13] While Phillips was in Philadelphia, she managed to persuade him to have his picture taken. Sending a copy to Ann Phillips, she remarked that Phillips had been called "the Chevalier de Bayard of American politics." She hoped that the picture would not get "smashed & bent in Uncle Sam's mail bags." The photographer had assured her that he sent pictures all over the country in this way. "Maybe you'll think it a good likeness, & maybe you won't. There's no knowing. I like it, & rejoice in the possession of one."[14] Margaret Burleigh added a postscript paying tribute to Phillips: "Never did I more rejoice in the clearness of his teaching and the beauty of his life, both public and private. A demonstration of the possibility and the loveliness of human virtue is worth more than untold stores of argument upon it."[15]

In her *Thirty-Fourth Annual Report of the Philadelphia Female Anti-Slavery Society,* published in February 1868, Mary Grew took pains to justify the value of such stocktaking. "An important element of success in any conflict is a correct estimate of the forces to be opposed." A careful survey of the situation was a profitable study at the close of one year of labor and the commencement of another. It was wise to look all their difficulties and dangers in the face and to recount all their victories, "neither exaggerating or under-estimating one or the other." Thus they would be able to "enter intelligently, hopefully and valiantly on the work before us. . . . Our ardent hope outran our judgment when we fancied that the close of four years of war would consummate our work and the glorious triumph of human freedom in our land."[16]

The question of the hour, she thought, was "simply this: Shall the colored man possess and enjoy his freedom, and his rights as a man; or shall he be deprived of a portion of such freedom and rights, on account of his color?"[17] There had been some signs of progress in the cause of freedom during the preceding year. Public meetings of colored and white men had been held in Savannah, in Charleston, and in Columbia, South Carolina, to discuss questions of state and national policy. Testimony of Negroes in a suit where both parties were white had been admitted in a court in Virginia for the first time. Chief Justice Chase had "set free from a new form of slavery, called apprenticeship, a certain child in Maryland." In Charleston the right of colored persons to use the streetcars had been established. In New Orleans black men sat on a grand jury. Above all, black men had participated in the state constitutional conventions called under the Military Reconstruction Acts of 1867. The *National Anti-Slavery Standard* was offered for sale in Southern cities. In Pennsylvania a state law had ended the exclusion of colored persons from railway cars.[18]

On the other side of the ledger, however, there were at least as many signs that the spirit of slavery and caste was very much alive. Southern states were contesting congressional Reconstruction legislation in the courts. They were denying the black man the ballot. Southern newspapers were filled with racist appeals. Over eight thousand "loyal white and black men" had been "wantonly murdered" in the South since 1865, and no efforts had been made to arrest and punish the murderers. A mob had assaulted and attempted to kill Philadelphia's Congressman William D. Kelley while he was addressing a meeting of citizens in Mobile, Alabama.[19] Large numbers of black children were held in virtual slavery through the system of apprenticeship. The city of Baton Rouge had opened its public schools to whites only. Coolie laborers were being brought from Cuba to labor on the plantations of Louisiana. Northern states were rejecting measures for Negro suffrage. In Pennsylvania there was a movement to repeal the law that had opened the cars to blacks. Pennsylvania had segregated public schools. There was danger that the Supreme Court would declare the Reconstruction legislation unconstitutional. Andrew Johnson was subverting this legislation. Mary Grew thought he should be impeached and deposed.[20] Shortly after this report was written, the president was indeed impeached by the House of Representatives for "high crimes and misdemeanors," the charges relating mainly to his alleged violation of the Tenure-of-Office Act.

Coming to the question of Negro suffrage, Mary Grew noted that the Fourteenth Amendment had been ratified by twenty-one states and declared in effect on 11 January 1868. It provided for the reduction of a state's representation in Congress to the extent that it denied the right to vote to male citizens over the age of twenty-one. She thought that the colored people of the South had conducted themselves with "wisdom and patience" while waiting for their rights. She believed that they had "fully disproved the charge that they had not sufficient intelligence to discern between the claims of opposing candidates." The Fourteenth Amendment was not enough. "The true Christian, the true patriot, must demand without ceasing that the black man's right to defend his freedom by the ballot shall be secured to him by the Federal Constitution, and not left to the poor protection of the laws or Constitutions of restored rebel States."[21]

The antislavery work must go on through its tried and true instrumentalities. The abolitionists would seek to promote "a correct public sentiment, and inspire zeal for righteousness in the hearts of the people, by publishing and proclaiming the truth, and the just demands of the colored man."[22] Their chief agency in this work was the *National Anti-Slavery Standard,* to whose sustenance their labors were principally devoted. Noting that James Mott had recently died, Mary Grew closed her report with a tribute to him and a forecast of complete success for the cause:

Walking in his steps, it is ours to finish the work which he began and faithfully continued. Then shall mingle with the last notes of our jubilee song, fervent thanksgivings that upon us was bestowed the high privilege of being workers in the grandest moral reform of the nineteenth century.[23]

Some time after her father's death, Mary Grew became a Unitarian. By 1868 she was preaching in Unitarian pulpits. "The world moves onward and upward," Sarah Pugh wrote in her diary on 5 January 1868, "or this year of grace would not have witnessed Mary Grew preaching to a Unitarian congregation in this conservative place [Germantown], and with great acceptance, spite of fears of friends and the forebodings of those who thought her wandering from her sphere. . . . I had not before heard her from the pulpit, from which she spoke with an unction and power that silenced caviling. The expressions of satisfaction and admiration were gratifying to hear."[24]

James Mott, who had been president of the Pennsylvania Anti-Slavery Society during most of its thirty-year history, died on 26 January 1868. Speaking at his funeral, Mary Grew paid tribute to the "incalculable value of the influence of such a life, extending from generation to generation." She also wrote a letter of sympathy to Mrs. Mott:

> Let it comfort you, dear friend, that this world of ours is, to-day, better for your life in it; better, because you two have lived together in it. Very rarely is the world blessed with such a light as shone—and shone so—from that wedded life. That light has not gone out. It will never go out. And every year that you will stay with us will help to keep it bright. If I were to try, I could never tell you, dear friend and teacher, how much you have done for me. The breaking of some spiritual fetters, the parting of some clouds which opened deeper vistas into heaven, I owe to you.
>
> Some day, perhaps, in this world or another, sitting at your feet, I can tell you more of this. Now, sorrowing in your sorrow, I can do little more than pray that you may be blessed and comforted, even as you have blessed and comforted others.[25]

On 3 February Mary Grew read a tribute from the Pennsylvania Anti-Slavery Society to the memory of James Mott, which was adopted by the executive committee and published without charge in four of Philadelphia's daily newspapers.[26] On 12 March the Philadelphia Female Anti-Slavery Society took note of his death. "A feeling of quiet sadness seeming to pervade the meeting," the secretary reported. "Mary Grew represented the importance of patient acquiescence in the changes which Time brings to us."[27]

Early in 1868 the women's society decided to send another petition to Congress asking that body to "take measures for securing a Republican form of government in the several States." Mary Grew was asked to prepare it. She reported on 13 February, and her petition was read, adopted, ordered signed by the officers, and forwarded to Washington. It begged Congress to "protect the rights of the colored people of the Country, by taking measures to secure to every State in the Union a Republican form of government."[28] On 12 March she reported that it had been forwarded to Congress.

On 21 January 1868 Mary Grew wrote Wendell Phillips of her concern about the *Standard,* which was, as usual, experiencing financial difficulty. She thought its problems would be discussed at the anniversary meeting of the American Anti-Slavery Society in May. The financial problems were made more serious by the loss of Francis Jackson's abolition bequest, which had gone to freedmen's aid rather than the *Standard.* Mary Grew thought it would be worth considering whether the paper could be published at considerably less cost in Philadelphia than in New York, and if it could, whether it would lose any prestige in being removed to this "'provincial town,' as those conceited New Yorkers call the city of Brotherly Love." She felt qualified only to make this suggestion, not at all to give an opinion upon it, since she did not know what the comparative cost of publishing in the two cities might be or whether Aaron M. Powell (the editor) would be willing to come to Philadelphia, or what weight other considerations might have. "In the present state of the country," she thought, "we can't afford to let the Standard go down, even if we should be obliged to issue it only once a month or twice a month."[29]

Garrison and Phillips had quarreled over the matter of dissolving the antislavery societies and over the disposition of the Jackson bequest, among other matters. Mary Grew expressed her sympathy to Ann Phillips on 3 May 1868 over a particularly bitter attack Garrison had made on Phillips in the *Standard:* "With what sadness & pain I read it and thought upon it, I cannot tell you. Wendell was then in the West, & I thought of you, at home, alone, reading these words of unkindness, of fierce invective from our dear old friend of former years. It is for Mr. Garrison that we are sad & sorrowful; how sad & sorrowful, I cannot tell you. But you do not need to be told."[30] Mary hoped to see Wendell at the meeting of the American Anti-Slavery Society in New York the following week. "And before that time, I trust, you & we will be rejoicing together over Andrew Johnson's conviction. Won't it be refreshing to see old Ben Wade, President?"[31] Johnson escaped conviction and removal by one vote.

Most of the Philadelphia abolitionists' attention in 1868 revolved about preparations for the annual meeting of the Pennsylvania Anti-Slavery Society and the annual festival of the Philadelphia Female Anti-Slavery Society. On 9 April Mary Grew suggested to the women's group the importance of making early arrangements for the festival. On 11 June she was appointed to head a committee to make these arrangements. On 17 June it was announced in the executive committee meeting of the Pennsylvania Anti-Slavery Society that Wendell Phillips had agreed to spend a week in Pennsylvania in the fall (winter, as it turned out); Mary Grew, Robert Purvis, and Edward M. Davis were appointed to make arrangements for meetings he would be asked to address. These meetings were originally planned for 16–20 November in Newtown, West Chester, Kennett Square, and Philadelphia, but had to be postponed until December.[32] Phillips was the featured speaker at the annual meeting of the Pennsylvania Anti-Slavery Society on 19 December in the Assembly Buildings of Philadelphia. Mary Grew served on the nominating committee and presented eleven resolutions, which were adopted without dissent. These resolutions called for continued vigilance on the part of abolitionists to protect the freedmen, for the impeachment and removal of Andrew Johnson, for Negro suffrage and officeholding, for a suffrage amendment to the Constitution, for equal rights for "all men without distinction of race or color," for congratulations on the Republican victory in the election of 1868, for continued support for "free speech, free schools, and a free government" in the South, for congratulations to Spain for taking antislavery measures, for support for the *Standard,* for thanks to the newspaper press for supporting Negro rights, and for tribute to the work of James Mott as the society's president. Mary Grew addressed the convention, advocating the necessity of a Constitutional amendment guaranteeing Negro suffrage. The female society's festival was held that evening.[33]

In the *Thirty-Fifth Annual Report of the Philadelphia Female Anti-Slavery Society* (February 1869), Mary Grew took note as usual of signs of progress for the cause. In "the fierce struggle between the opposing principles of Liberty and Despotism," which had convulsed the nation and threatened its existence, there had been "glorious victories" and a "marvellous deliverance." In the preceding year a black man (P. B. S. Pinchback) had been elected lieutenant governor of Louisiana and another had been elected to Congress. In the city of Washington a national convention of black men had assembled to debate the nation's problems and had received respectful treatment in the press. For the first time in the nation's history, black men in the South had voted in a presidential election. In the District of Columbia, in federal territories, and in nineteen states, colored men were legally in possession of the ballot. In Louisiana racial discrimination had been prohibited again on public conveyances and places of entertainment and public resort. The triumph of the Republican party in the 1868 elections had been hailed by "every liberty-loving soul as a triumph for Humanity."[34]

If these events, which she recorded with "grateful joy," constituted a fair representation of her review of the year, she thought abolitionists might congratulate one another upon the consummation of their work, close the records of their society, and depart to other fields of labor. "But the most cursory examination shows us that the hour of the slave's *complete* enfranchisement has not yet come."[35] In the Southern states, the spirit of slavery "still lives and rages." Assassinations of loyal men, white and colored, took place frequently by night and day. Preachers were shot in their pulpits or followed to their homes and "brutally murdered." Innocent men were dragged from their beds at midnight and tortured to death. Women were driven from their schoolhouses and allowed only the alternatives of scourging or flight. Homes were burned. The legislature of Georgia had expelled twenty-nine black members. Hundreds of persons were still being held in slavery. Black men had to walk to the polls "through fire and blood." Southern newspapers openly opposed Negro suffrage. Andrew Johnson "aids with sympathetic heart and liberal hands the enemies of liberty." Surprisingly, in this catalog of outrages, Mary Grew did not mention the Ku Klux Klan.[36]

With all these forces arrayed against the freedmen, she accounted it a grand triumph that they had won the legal right to the ballot. "We are frequently asked," she said, "what more we demand of the Government on behalf of the colored race of the South. . . . *Our reply is that we demand the Nation's bond of security for all this.*"[37] What was needed was a provision of the federal Constitution making the colored man politically equal with the white man throughout the nation. The enactments of one legislature could be repealed by the next one or rendered nugatory by the courts. The Republican party could be replaced in power by the Democratic party. It had enjoyed a majority of only three hundred thousand among four million votes in the presidential election. The Democratic party had declared the Reconstruction Acts "unconstitutional, revolutionary, and void." It was easy to foresee what would be the fate of the colored man should the Democratic party take control of the government before his rights were secured by the federal constitution. Besides, even the Republican party had not proved itself worthy to be trusted with the keeping of those rights; even in their hands the black man was not safe without specific Constitutional protection. It had not dared to include in its platform an article asserting the equal political rights of all men, without distinction of color. Once the Southern states were readmitted to the Union, they would again have exclusive control over suffrage within their borders.[38]

The same spirit of compromise between justice and expediency that had produced the Republican platform had produced its candidate for the president. General Ulysses S. Grant was chosen to represent the party "when scarcely a man in the whole nation knew whether he held its principles or not; when many of the leaders really believed that he would accept a nomination from either party."[39] This kind of trimming was also reflected in the exclusion of black veterans from the grand procession of the nation's soldiers and sailors held in Philadelphia during the past fall. Was the party afraid openly to honor the colored hero "lest by so doing they should endanger the election in Pennsylvania?"[40]

Nevertheless, a great victory had just been won. On 30 January 1869 the House of Representatives passed a proposed amendment to the Constitution providing that the right of any citizen of the United States to vote should not be denied or abridged by the United States or any state by reason of race, color, or previous condition of slavery (later changed to *servitude*). On 9 February the Senate had followed suit, adding a provision (later dropped) protecting the right to hold office. The Philadelphia abolitionists welcomed this action "with unutterable gratitude" to God. Mary Grew also expressed their gratitude to Radical Republicans such as Charles Sumner, William D. Kelley, and George W. Julian, who had fought for the measure in Congress. "Every consideration of justice to the colored man, and of national safety and prosperity, urge the ratification of this Amendment."[41] Mary Grew looked for success in this case. She noted that much of the Northern press, including several Philadelphia daily papers, was supporting the amendment. Leaders of the Republican party were becoming aware that Negro suffrage was essential to their success in the next presidential election. The Philadelphia Female Anti-Slavery Society would work with all its might for the success of this measure. They would continue to support the *National Anti-Slavery Standard,* which was the only paper in the country "especially devoted to the advocacy of the colored man's claim to all the rights of citizenship."[42] Far beyond the circle of its own subscribers, its influence was carried by other journals that reprinted its editorials. The female abolitionists would continue to do their part in "creating a public sentiment which shall compel the Legislatures of at least three-fourths of the States to ratify a Constitutional Amendment securing the colored man in all a citizen's rights."[43] At the end of her report Mary Grew took note of the death of several of the Female Society's members and of Thaddeus

Stevens, whose name would long be remembered by colored people "with benediction." She concluded:

> The path before us is brightly illumined with promise of the speedy consummation of our enterprise. We go forth upon it, inspired and strengthened by gratitude and joy for victories won; by hope that the year which we commence to-day will be the last year of our work, and by a solemn purpose that, with the help of Him who has been our pillar of cloud by day and of fire by night, we will walk steadfastly unto the end.[44]

On 14 January 1869, at a meeting of the Philadelphia Female Anti-Slavery Society, several weeks before Congress acted, Mary Grew offered petitions to Congress and the Pennsylvania legislature for a Constitutional amendment providing for suffrage "without distinction of color." They were adopted, signed by the officers, and forwarded. At the same meeting she reported that the Festival of the Friends of Freedom had yielded approximately seven hundred dollars. On 11 February it was decided to continue the same officers, with Lucretia Mott as president and Mary Grew as corresponding secretary. On 8 April 1869 Mary Grew announced that the Pennsylvania assembly had ratified the Fifteenth Amendment. On 10 June she reported on her attendance at the annual meeting of the American Anti-Slavery Society in New York and at an antislavery meeting in Boston addressed by Wendell Phillips. On 14 October 1869 it was announced that the annual meeting of the state society would be held 15 November, but there would be no festival. On 10 February 1870 Mary Grew noted that the Fifteenth Amendment had been ratified. However, the State Department did not declare it in effect until 30 March. On 10 March the society decided that the remaining money in the treasury would be used to circulate the *Standard* in the South. Plans were made for the society's final meeting. Mary Grew moved that Elizabeth Gay, Sarah A. McKim, and other former members now out of town be invited to attend this meeting.[45]

Mary Grew wrote to Elizabeth Neall Gay, urging her to come. "I trust your reverent & tender associations with 'The Old Female' are sufficiently strong to inspire a wish to be in at her death. If you can't come in person, write." Mary Grew noted that she was busy writing her final annual report, which Margaret Burleigh called "the obituary." "When I consider the number of this Report, & remember that I have written all the series excepting the first two, I have a sense of my own venerableness."[46]

The final meeting of the Philadelphia Female Anti-Slavery Society was held on 24 March 1870. Lucretia Mott presided and spoke. Other speakers included Robert Purvis, Edward M. Davis, and Aaron M. Powell. Mrs. Mott recalled the early days of the society. The names of the charter members were read. The organization adopted a resolution of thanks to Mary Grew for her "efficient and unremitting service" to the society for almost the entire period of its existence, attested to by the thirty-four annual reports that she had so "faithfully and succinctly written, marking the annual progress of the antislavery movement."[47]

Responding to this resolution, Mary Grew delivered her valedictory:

> It is now my turn, friends, to thank you; and I do it most heartily. I thank you that when I came from New England, young, beginning the work of mature life, you took me by the hand; that by the kindly imposition of your hands you ordained me to this work which I have found it most pleasant and profitable to pursue during all these years. If it had been proper for me to take part in the discussion of that resolution, I should have asked you to omit one word, simply for the reason that it is not true. I know of no self-sacrifice which clings to my anti-slavery history. My work may have been done well or ill; yet certain it is, it has not been a self-sacrificing work. It has brought me so rich a return of spiritual culture and strength; it has so fitted me for the true enjoyment of life, for all the work of life which I have done in other fields, that when I say I have received an abundant recompense of reward, the language is too weak to express my feeling. I thank you for the influences which I have derived from this Society; I thank our President here to-day for the influences which have flowed from her words and her life into my own, and which have helped to fit me for any work which I have done. I account it one of the great blessings of my life that, though born in New England, I was brought here, where women had a broader field of labor than was then permitted there; and thus I have been taught to do a work which, otherwise, I might not have been taught. I say this in reverent humility, for it is very little that I or any of us can do; but for what I have been able to do, with all my heart I thank you, for you have helped me. And for you and for myself, I thank the Providence of God which called us to this anti-slavery work in the early days, and has led us by His own way up to this hour, to this glorious result which we scarcely dared to hope our eyes should see. We are thankful for this discipline which has educated us for better service in other fields."
>
> If we put off our armour here to-day, it is but for a moment's breathing-space, to be resumed for other conflicts. However much we may feel to-day, as we close this meeting and disband our Society, that we should like to depart in peace, our eyes having seen *this* salvation, we are willing to remain and work elsewhere, as we may be called to work till we shall hear our Father's summons, "Come up higher!"[48]

Margaretta Forten, a black (daughter of James Forten, the sail maker) and one of the society's founders, presented resolutions to the effect that on account of the adoption of the Thirteenth, Fourteenth, and Fifteenth Amendments to the Constitution, "The object for which this Society was organized is thus accomplished." Therefore, it was resolved "That the Philadelphia Female Anti-Slavery Society, grateful for the part allotted to it in this great work, and rejoicing in the victory which has concluded the long conflict between Slavery and Freedom in America, does now and hereby disband."[49] It was decided to donate the society's books and records, including the minute books, to the Historical Society of Pennsylvania.

"It would have been an enjoyment to thee," Sarah Pugh wrote to one of her cousins, "to be present at the 'Euthanasia' of the Female Anti-Slavery So. The President's face was perfectly radiant, a 'visible halo of sanctity' was around her; and the Secretary read her admirable report with those exquisite intonations of voice so fitting the words. I wished all interested could *hear* her. What pleasant memories will linger around an old organization with those who were a part of it! For myself, it has been a great privilege and happiness."[50]

The Pennsylvania Anti-Slavery Society was also preparing for disbanding, though it lingered a little longer than the women's group. On 3 February 1869 Mary Grew reported that the society would employ an agent to hold meetings in Pennsylvania in order to promote ratification of the Fifteenth Amendment. On 29 September she made a statement of the funds needed for support of the *Standard* for the rest of the year. At the same meeting she and Edward M. Davis were appointed to make arrangements for the annual meeting. This meeting was held on 17 November in the Assembly Buildings, Tenth and Chestnut Streets, Philadelphia. Mary Grew served on the business committee and was one of the speakers. She "alluded to the past years of labor, and spoke of the demands of the present hour, the work of which, she doubted not, every one present was ready to perform his or her share."[51] On behalf of the business committee, she presented seven resolutions, which were adopted without dissent. The first one declared the condition of Southern blacks to be still precarious. The second one demanded full rights of citizenship for them. The third emphasized the importance of continuing to support the *Standard*. The fourth rejoiced in "the improved tone of the newspaper press of the city and of the Commonwealth" on racial issues; the fifth singled out the *Philadelphia Morning Post* for special praise in this connection. The sixth rejoiced in the progress of the states toward ratification of the Fifteenth Amendment, and the seventh, and last, deplored the continuance of race prejudice in the United States. Mary Grew took part in the discussion of these resolutions, which occupied most of the morning session. At the afternoon session she reviewed the hardships abolitionists had undergone in past years and expressed satisfaction in their kinder reception today.[52]

She continued to be active on the executive committee of the Pennsylvania Anti-Slavery Society (as corresponding secretary) until its dissolution on 5 May 1870. On 1 December 1869 she noted that the old Pennsylvania Abolition Society had contributed two hundred dollars to the work of the Anti-Slavery Society. On 5 February she reported that Wendell Phillips had proposed a meeting of the American Anti-Slavery Society to celebrate ratification of the Fifteenth Amendment. The Pennsylvania group decided that it would support this proposal, suggesting that the meeting be held in Philadelphia, "inasmuch as the American Society was formed in this city." On 2 April 1870 the committee, with Mary Grew in the chair, discussed plans for a final public meeting of the society. On 3 May it was announced that this meeting would be held in the large hall of the Assembly Buildings on the afternoon and evening of 5 May. Robert Purvis presided and made an address, saying that "the object of the Society having been at last accomplished, it ought not to be so painful to separate."[53] Letters were read from Congressmen Julian and Kelley, Senator Sumner, Colonel John W. Forney, John G. Whittier, and Benjamin C. Bacon. Mary Grew spoke at the afternoon session. At the evening session addresses were delivered by Robert B. Purvis, William Still (on the underground railroad), Frances E. W. Harper, Charles C. Burleigh, and Lucretia Mott. "A resolution that the Society do now disband was then adopted, and the meeting adjourned."[54]

Margaret J. Burleigh later added a note in the minute book of the executive committee of the Pennsylvania Anti-Slavery Society: "The members of the Ex. Com. were so fully occupied with the final meeting of the Pa. A.S. Society, held May 5th, 1870, that no opportunity was then afforded for a meeting of the Com. As the Society disbanded on that occasion the Com. was consequently dissolved."[55] The society's minute books were given to the Historical Society of Pennsylvania.

Mary Grew waited until after the final meeting of the Philadelphia Female Anti-Slavery Society to prepare its *Thirty-Sixth and Final Annual Report*, published in April 1870. "The Amended Constitution of the United States," she began, "which in the year 1865 declared that slavery should no more exist in the Nation, to-day declares that, among the conditions of American citizenship, color shall be, forevermore, unknown. Beneath that broad banner of civil and political liberty the white man and black man stand, side by side. Master and slave have become equal fellow citizens. Thus is accomplished the work for which the Anti-Slavery Societies of this country were organized."[56] As it turned out, of course, this was a grossly overoptimistic assessment of the black man's situation. Mary Grew recognized this and in subsequent paragraphs pointed out some of the problems that black people still faced. "In the capital of the Nation," for instance, "as in the large cities of even the Northern States, colored persons seeking admission to places of amusement, or of instruction, are frequently met with refusal and insult." Northern churches, with few exceptions, were not yet "sufficiently christianized to open their pew doors to black and white men alike," and the colored people of Philadelphia were still taxed for the support of schools that their children were forbidden to enter.[57] Nor was the spirit that had invoked the rebellion "wholly exorcised, as the records of persecution and suffering in the South clearly show."[58]

The bulk of Mary Grew's final report dealt with the history of the Philadelphia Female Anti-Slavery Society. It had been organized on 9 December 1833, one of the earliest of the associations based on the Garrisonian principle of immediate emancipation. It was formed by eighteen women meeting in Catherine McDermott's schoolroom. Esther Moore was its first president. The object of the society was "the dissemination of truth and the knowledge of facts relative to the subject, by the ordinary medium of books, tracts, newspapers, and lectures."[59] The annual reports of the first two years were not extant, but from the third report it could be determined that the society had begun petitioning Congress for the abolition of slavery in the District of Columbia and the territories of the United States. In the second year a standing committee was appointed for the purpose of visiting and aiding colored schools. In its third year the society sponsored a course of scientific lectures to which colored persons were invited. Throughout its history the society was racially integrated. In the same year, the organization published An *Address to the Women of Pennsylvania* to support the antislavery cause. About the same time, a member of the society, Angelina E. Grimké, who had come to Philadelphia from South Carolina with her sister Sarah, accepted a commission to labor as an agent of the American Anti-Slavery Society.[60]

In 1837 the first Anti-Slavery Convention of American Women was held in New York City, the nation's first national convention of women. The 1838 convention was held in Philadelphia's Pennsylvania Hall, which was burned to the ground by a racist and sexist mob. The women had sponsored a meeting at which men and women, black and white, had met together to discuss the slavery question. The women finished their sessions in Sarah Pugh's schoolroom. They had been promised the use of Temperance Hall, but found the doors closed against them and made their way "assailed by the insults of the populace" to their proffered refuge. The third and last of the Anti-Slavery Conventions of American Women was held in the hall of Philadelphia's Riding School in 1839.[61] By 1840 women had been integrated into the sessions of the American Anti-Slavery Society.

In the year 1840 the society sent delegates to the gathering called the World's Anti-Slavery Convention, which met in London in May. That body refused to admit any female delegates, though the original invitation had not been thus limited. Consequently, the society was not represented there.

In her history of the society, Mary Grew skipped over the bitter disputes within the antislavery movement over the role of women, political action, and the notorious Garrisonian slogan "No Union with Slaveholders." She moved on to discuss the "guilt and disgrace of the Nation" brought on by the "infamous" Fugitive Slave Act of 1850, which she said was "the signal for an extensive and cruel raid upon the colored people of the North. . . . Probably no statute was ever written, in the code of a civilized nation so carefully and cunningly devised for the purpose of depriving men of liberty."[62] She recalled some of the more notorious fugitive slave cases of the 1850s, most notably that of Jane Johnson and her sons, who were informed by Passmore Williamson of their right to freedom under Pennsylvania law. Mary Grew had written an account of this case.

She wrote of the annual fairs that the women had held from 1836 to 1861. They had yielded net profits of more than twenty-eight thousand dollars. They had not only raised money, they had inspired abolitionists with new zeal. "Hither our tribes came up to take counsel together, to recount our victories won, to be refreshed by social communion, and to renew our pledges of fidelity to the slave."[63] While there was constant fear of mob attack, only one of the fairs had actually been disrupted. In 1859, fearing disorder, the city authorities ordered the women to remove their property within three hours. Fortunately, they were able to move on such short notice to the Assembly Buildings, where they held their last meeting in 1870. After the Civil War three annual Festivals of the Friends of Freedom were held with modest success.

During its thirty-six years in existence, the Philadelphia Female Anti-Slavery Society had raised a total of almost thirty-five thousand dollars. The bulk of this revenue had been expended in disseminating the society's principles by means of the printed word and public lectures and discussions. In the early years of the society, a school for colored children, established and taught by Sarah M. Douglass, had been partially sustained from the society's treasury. The society had also contributed small sums to the Philadelphia Vigilance Committee, an agency of the Underground Railroad. "But these enterprises were always regarded as of secondary importance to our great work of direct appeal to the conscience of the Nation, in behalf of the Slave's claim to immediate, unconditional emancipation."[64] To this end, a large number of tracts and pamphlets had been circulated by the society. But its chief agencies had been the antislavery newspapers, most notably the *Liberator,* the *Pennsylvania Freeman,* and the *National Anti-Slavery Standard.* "Our largest appropriations of money have been made to the treasuries of the Pennsylvania and American Anti-Slavery Societies, and by those Societies, to the support of their organs and lecturing agents."[65]

The financial statistics of the society, she wrote, were easily recorded. Certain "great and thrilling events" that had marked its history were readily told. But the life that it had lived through all its thirty-six years, the influence that flowed from it, directly and indirectly, "to the Nation's heart," the work quietly done by its members, individually, "through the word spoken in season," "the brave, self-sacrificing deed," "the example of fidelity in a critical hour," "the calm endurance unto the end," "these can be written in no earthly book of remembrance."[66]

"Its life is lived; its work is done; its memorial is sealed," she wrote in conclusion. "It assembles, to-day, to take one parting look across its years; to breathe in silence its unutterable thanksgiving; to disband its membership and cease to be." The work of the society was "a service whose reward was in itself." The members had been permitted to take part in a work that was really accomplished by God. With "one heart and one voice" the women of the society cried, "Not unto us, O Lord: not unto us, but unto thy name be the glory; for thy right hand and thy holy arm 'hath gotten the victory.'"[67]

The American Anti-Slavery Society held its final meeting in New York City on 9 April 1870. As the time approached, Mary Grew broke five years of silence toward William Lloyd Garrison and begged him to attend.

> As the time for the Commemorative Meeting; the last meeting of the American Anti-Slavery Society, draws nigh, I cannot forbear writing to you, to say that I, and many others among your friends and fellow-workers in the grand old cause, earnestly desire your presence there. We have hoped that you would feel inclined to respond to the invitation to all friends of the cause, by coming to the Meeting and mingling with us in the exercises. . . .[68] How sadly I have missed you from all our Meetings, since 1865; how painfully I shall feel your absence at our Meeting on next Saturday, if you are, at that time, absent, I cannot tell you; nor is it important that I should.[69]

Whatever differences there may have been, or may be, among us, there is so much that we hold in common, that for one, I earnestly wish that we might all forget, for a day at least, those differences; and unite our hearts and voices in rejoicing and thanksgiving over the enfranchisement of the colored man, now made politically equal with the white man.

The letter was signed, "Cordially, Your friend, Mary Grew."[70]

7

The Campaign for Woman Suffrage
(1869–1873)

EVEN before the antislavery societies had been disbanded, Mary Grew had plunged into a new crusade—woman suffrage—that was to occupy her from 1869 to 1892.

Feminism had a long history in Pennsylvania. The Quakers had been accustomed to equality of the sexes in meetings for worship and for business and in coeducational schools. Tom Paine had described and condemned discrimination against women in the *Pennsylvania Magazine* of August 1775. Dr. Benjamin Rush had advocated equal educational opportunity for women in his *Thoughts on Female Education* (Philadelphia, 1787).[1] The first American periodical directed exclusively to women, *The Lady's Magazine and Repository of Entertaining Knowledge,* published in Philadelphia during 1792 and 1793, had included a long and enthusiastic review of Mary Wollstonecraft's classic *Vindication of the Rights of Woman.* This article may possibly have been written by Charles Brockden Brown, the pioneer American novelist, who was a native of Philadelphia and who devoted his first book, *Alcuin* (1798), to the theme of woman's rights.[2]

The immediate matrix of organized feminism was the antislavery movement. Here again, Pennsylvania had played an important role. The American Anti-Slavery Society, the national voice of radical abolitionism, was founded in Philadelphia in December 1833. Among those in attendance was Lucretia Mott, who was permitted to speak but not to sign the society's declaration of sentiments. Shortly thereafter, the Philadelphia Female Anti-Slavery Society was organized. Through this agency, women like Lucretia Mott, Sarah Pugh, and Mary Grew gained invaluable political experience, conducting meetings and circulating antislavery petitions for submission to Congress. This organization also served as host of the second and third annual conventions of antislavery women, a landmark in the national organization of women. The assembly of an interracial and mixed audience of men and women precipitated the burning of Pennsylvania Hall by a racist and sexist mob on 17 May 1838, just three days after its opening as a center for free discussion of controversial questions.[3]

The Philadelphia Female Anti-Slavery Society sent five women, one of whom was Mary Grew, as delegates to the World's Anti-Slavery Convention held in London in June 1840. There were also three women delegates from Massachusetts. All eight were denied seats in the convention and forced to withdraw to the visitors' gallery. William Lloyd Garrison, the most noteworthy of the American delegates, sat with the ladies in the gallery as a protest against this illiberal decision of the convention. It was at this time that Lucretia Mott and Elizabeth Cady Stanton became acquainted and arrived at the conclusion that women would have to fight for their own emancipation as well as emancipation of the slaves.[4]

Meeting again the following year in Boston, the two women resolved to hold a woman's rights convention.[5] Perhaps because Mrs. Stanton was so busy having children, this gathering was not held until 1848. The place was Seneca Falls, New York, Mrs. Stanton's home, and the dates were 19 and 20 July. Sessions were held in the Wesleyan Chapel, with about three hundred persons in attendance. "We hold these truths to be self-evident," the reformers declared in a document modeled on the Declaration of Independence: "that all men and women are created equal; that they are endowed by their Creator with certain inalienable rights; that among these are life, liberty, and the pursuit of happiness."[6] Included among the "repeated injuries and usurpations" that they alleged had been inflicted by men on women were discrimination against their right to hold property and to keep the wages they earned, unjust laws regarding marriage, divorce, and the guardianship of children, denial of equal educational opportunities and entrance to the professions, "scanty remuneration" for such few employments as women were permitted to undertake, and denial of the right to vote.[7]

The first significant victory for the woman's rights movement in Pennsylvania took place shortly before the Seneca Falls Convention. This was the passage of a married woman's property law, an action that had already been taken in a number of other states, beginning with Mississippi in 1839. Lucretia Mott, Mary Grew, and other Philadelphia women who had been active in the antislavery movement circulated petitions on behalf of this reform, and Mrs. Jane Grey Swisshelm, editor of the Pittsburgh *Saturday Visiter (sic)* agitated the matter in western Pennsylvania.[8] The law received the governor's signature on 11 April 1848. It provided that all property held by a single woman would continue to be her own after marriage, that she might acquire additional property during marriage, that her property was not to be sold to pay her husband's debts, and that she might dispose of her property as she saw fit.[9] Court rulings weakened this enactment to some extent, and more rigorous and comprehensive codes on the subject were passed in later years.[10]

"I am now trying to awaken sufficient interest to hold a woman's rights meeting in this city [Philadelphia]," Mrs. Mott wrote to Mrs. Stanton on 3 October 1848, a few months after the Seneca Falls Convention.[11] This was more easily said than done. Public opinion was generally hostile, especially to resolutions on behalf of political participation by women. Who was to keep house and care for the children if women got involved in politics? the *Public Ledger* asked in an editorial on 26 September 1848. "A woman is nobody. A wife is everything," it declared. The ladies of Philadelphia, it suggested, should fight to maintain their rights as "Wives, Belles, Virgins, and Mothers, and not as Women."[12] In other words, woman's place was in the home.

The Seneca Falls meeting was a local one. Shortly thereafter, a regional one was held at Rochester. The first national woman's rights convention was held at Worcester, Massachusetts, 23–24 October 1850. Mary Grew was among those signing the call for the convention, and her name appears on the convention's "Committee on Social Relations," but she is not listed among those in actual attendance.[13] Perhaps she was too ill to make the trip. She also missed the regional convention held at West Chester, Pennsylvania, on 2 June 1852. But she attended the fifth national convention held in Philadelphia on 18 October 1854, serving on the business committee.[14] She was also present at the Tenth National Woman's Rights Convention, which met at Cooper Union in New York, 10–11 May 1860, where she served on the business committee and gave the closing speech. "The word I would impress upon you all, as you go hence," she said, "is this—it is always safe to do right."[15]

During the war years the feminists set aside their own interests in order to work for emancipation of the slaves. No woman's rights conventions were held between 1861 and 1866. The National Woman's Loyal League, organized in 1864, conducted an immense petition campaign directed toward congressional passage of the Thirteenth Amendment. Four hundred thousand signatures were collected. Elizabeth Cady Stanton served as president of the league and Susan B. Anthony as secretary. This work convinced women of the importance of organization as a means of accomplishing their ends.[16] The Eleventh National Woman's Rights Convention, the first one after the war, was held in the Church of the Puritans, New York, 10 May 1866. Out of it grew the American Equal Rights Association, an organization formed to advance the interests of both blacks and women. Its main goal was the elimination of both race and sex restrictions on the right to vote. Lucretia Mott was chosen president and Elizabeth Cady Stanton first vice president.[17] Their objective proved an impossible one. The majority of abolitionists and Radical Republicans were convinced that Negro suffrage was a more pressing need than woman suffrage and that both could not be obtained at the same time. As they commonly put it, this was "the negro's hour."[18]

The feminists suffered a terrible setback in 1866 when Congress passed the Fourteenth Amendment. The second section of this momentous enactment provided that a state's representation in Congress should be reduced in proportion to the number of *male* citizens over the age of twenty-one who were denied the right to vote. The crowning blow came in 1869 with the Fifteenth Amendment, which stated explicitly that the right to vote should not be denied by any state "on account of race, color, or previous condition of servitude" but made no reference to discrimination on grounds of sex.

The American Equal Rights Association collapsed in 1869. In that year the feminists at last formed national organizations purely in their own interests—not one, however, but two, the National Woman Suffrage Association and the American Woman Suffrage Association.[19] The National Association was led by Elizabeth Cady Stanton and Susan B. Anthony, while the American Association was led by Lucy Stone and Julia Ward Howe. The National opposed ratification of the Fifteenth Amendment, while the American supported it. In the beginning, the National refused to allow men as officers, while the American welcomed them. The National favored federal action for woman suffrage, while the American worked for state enactments. The National had its headquarters in New York, the American in Boston. The National was interested in a variety of reforms, including more liberal divorce laws; the American concentrated on the suffrage issue. The National sponsored a short-lived journal called the *Revolution;* the American published the *Woman's Journal,* which lasted for many years. As the years passed, the lines of distinction between the two groups became blurred, but they were not united until 1890.[20]

The Pennsylvania Woman Suffrage Association, an auxiliary of the American Association, was organized on 22 December 1869 in Mercantile Library Hall, Philadelphia. The meeting was called together by John K. Wildman, who was to be a key figure in the organization for many years. Edward M. Davis proposed the appointment of Judge William S. Pierce as chairman of the meeting. This was done, and Pierce appointed a committee of five to prepare a constitution. Mary Grew spoke "at length in her earnest and impressive manner, presenting forcibly those familiar yet solid arguments in favor of woman suffrage which form the basis of the discussion, and which should irrevocably settle the question."[21] She was elected president of the association and held this position until her retirement in 1892, at the age of seventy-nine. Other speakers included Sojourner Truth.

The association's constitution declared its purpose to be to secure for women "the exercise of the right of suffrage and to effect such changes in the laws as shall recognize the equal rights of women with men."[22]

The work of the association consisted mainly of holding meetings, printing and circulating pamphlets and documents, petitioning the state legislature and Congress, employing a lecturing agent (Matilda Hindman), and supporting suffrage movements in other states.[23] The association also supported the *Woman's Journal,* a weekly newspaper which was begun on 8 January 1870 and was published every Saturday in Boston and Chicago, "devoted to the interests of Woman, to her educational, industrial, legal and political Equality, and especially to her right of Suffrage."[24] The first board of editors included Mary A. Livermore, Julia Ward Howe, Lucy Stone, William Lloyd Garrison, and Thomas Wentworth Higginson. The *Woman's Journal* carried regular reports of the activities of the Pennsylvania Woman Suffrage Association.

"During the month of December," the *Woman's Journal* noted on 8 January 1870, "a large amount of work was done in the interest of the cause. A Pennsylvania State Woman Suffrage Association was organized at Philadelphia, auxiliary to the American Woman Suffrage Association, with Mary Grew as President."[25] In addition, conventions had been held at Newark, New Jersey, Concord, New Hampshire, and at Worcester and other cities in Massachusetts. Suffrage organizations had been formed in Rochester, Minnesota; Cuyahoga County, Ohio; Columbus, Ohio; Ann Arbor, Michigan; and other cities. The constitution of the American Association provided for state auxiliaries. The Reverend Henry Ward Beecher had been chosen president and Lucy Stone chairman of the executive committee, of which Mary Grew was a member. Officers of the Pennsylvania Association included Edward M. Davis, Mrs. C. Farrington, and M. K. Williamson as vice presidents, Annie Heacock as recording secretary, Eliza Sprout Turner as corresponding secretary, and G. M. S. P. Jones as treasurer. Additional members of the executive committee were J. K. Wildman, Ellen M. Child, Annie Shoemaker, Charlotte L. Pierce, and Dr. H. T. Child.[26]

After the disbandment of the American Anti-Slavery Society, of which he was the last president, Wendell Phillips found himself without a job. He was persuaded to accept the nominations of the Labor

Reform and Temperance parties to run for the position of governor of Massachusetts in 1870. Mary Grew wrote him on 12 August 1870 to protest against this decision. "I confidently trust that you are aware that God has called you to higher services than that of a Massachusetts Governor, or United States President," she chided him. "I was much surprised, almost startled, last evening by the receipt of a letter from Mrs. [John T.] Sargent, expressing Mr. Sargent's and her sympathy in the purpose of the Temperance & Labor men to make you Governor of Massachusetts. I confess I do not understand it."[27]

She did not wonder that the two parties desired him for their candidate, since they could not be expected to see how much more he could do for the causes that they served while working outside of political parties than he could within them.

But Mr. and Mrs. Sargent comprehend the superiority of your prophetic mission to this Nation; and I need to be enlightened as to the reasons which can induce such persons to wish you to hold a political office. To me it seems a deplorable descent from a high moral vantage ground for you to step into such a post.

You know as well as I do, and it is no flattery, nor much praise to say it, for God has placed you there & that you occupy, as no other man does, the office of prophet and moral teacher to the Nation unfettered by sect or party. Standing thus, it is impossible that your influence should be marred by the slightest breath of suspicion that personal political advancement is one of your aims. Disinterested political service is so rare a thing that scarcely any one (but a few reformers), believe in it these days.

What you could do as Gov. of Mass. is better known to yourself than to me. What you are doing for the education of this People, I know something of; enough to make me very unwilling that you should 'come down' from your 'great work' for any purpose. We the people cannot spare you, Preacher and Prophet! to do the Gubernatorial work of Massachusetts.[28]

The report that such work was proposed to Phillips would have made little impression on Mary Grew had it not been accompanied by "the expressed sympathy of our excellent and judicious friends & fellow laborers, Mr. and Mrs. Sargent." In that connection it alarmed her sufficiently at least to prompt the foregoing expression of her sentiments, "which I trust may find favor in your sight."[29]

This letter was written from Clark's Island in Cape Cod Bay, off Plymouth, where Mary Grew and Margaret Burleigh had sought relief from the summer heat of Philadelphia. "Margaret sends her love," she concluded, "and wants to know if you think it would be a good plan to take the light from Minot's Ledge, and put it into the Parker House kitchen that the cooks might better see to do work."[30]

Lucy Stone consulted Mary Grew as to where the second annual meeting of the American Woman Suffrage Association should be held. Mary Grew replied that she thought Cleveland the "most eligible place" because it would have a larger and more enthusiastic gathering there, where the society was "so auspiciously organized." "How good the Journal is!" she added. "It should be extensively circulated."[31] She also noted that she was looking forward with much pleasure to Lucy Stone's presence at the upcoming Pennsylvania annual meeting.

The first anniversary session of the Pennsylvania Woman Suffrage Association was held in the Assembly Buildings at Tenth and Chestnut, Philadelphia, on the afternoon and evening of Thursday, 10 November 1870. President Mary Grew called the meeting to order at 3:00 P.M. and made some opening remarks.

> We are not well known in this community, as this is our first public meeting. . . . We appeal to the American nation merely to carry out their own principles of government, and to put into practice the political doctrines they hold, those doctrines which every American especially and particularly glories in, that "just government derives its power from the consent of the governed," that "taxation without representation is tyranny." . . . As in the year just closed we asked that these principles be applied to a man without distinction of color, so now we ask that it be applied to man without distinction of sex.[32]

Mary Grew continued, "In other countries, friends, we might not be able to urge these arguments, but here to-day, in the land of freedom and independence, where every man holds the ballot as the sign of citizenship, we may labor. Our effort is solely to put the ballot into the hands of women." Doubtless there were many other things that woman needed to strive to obtain, and doubtless the ballot would enable her to do much in these directions, so that she might enlarge her sphere of usefulness and "be better able to gain an honest livelihood. . . . We know that woman has the same right and the same need of the ballot that man has." Mary Grew ended with an appeal to young men and women to enlist in this cause. "We need your labor. . . . We know victory is certain, simply because our cause is just."[33]

After the president's opening remarks, committees on resolutions, nominations, and finances were announced. Then Eliza Sproat Turner, corresponding secretary, gave her report. She recalled the organization of the association on 22 December 1869 and declared that according to article 2 of its constitution its chief object was to promote the cause of woman suffrage and, "with this end in view, to procure and distribute tracts, documents, and other printed matter; to prepare and circulate petitions to the Legislature and to Congress; to employ lecturers and agents, hold meetings, and take any other steps that may be deemed proper by the Executive Committee." This committee was to include one representative from each county in the state. So far, within less than a year, delegates from twenty-two counties had been obtained—including the Honorable John M. Broomall, Mrs. Jane Grey Swisshelm, Dr. Hiram Corson, and "many others whose names reflect honor on our cause." The organization's aims were not limited to suffrage; it would work to elevate the status of women in all aspects of life. Mrs. Turner expressed her satisfaction at the progress of women in medicine. Students at the Woman's Medical College of Philadelphia were now being admitted to clinical training on an equal basis with men. Mrs. Turner also noted that women were needed to help end corruption in politics; this was the era of "the Grant scandals".[34]

The treasurer reported receipts of $103.50 and expenditures of $78.25. The resolutions committee proposed a statement that was adopted demanding "for the women of this Commonwealth freedom to exercise their right of suffrage, on the same conditions as that right is exercised by male citizens." Officers were elected for the ensuing year: Mary Grew as president, Eliza Sproat Turner as corresponding secretary. Julia Ward Howe, Henry B. Blackwell, and Lucretia Mott spoke, the latter taking as her theme "the legal status of women." At the evening session Mary Grew spoke again, stating that through "a recent reform" a woman could retain her own property after marriage, but was still not able to control her earnings after marriage. The closing speech was made by Lucy Stone.[35]

In January 1871 Mary Grew journeyed to Boston to address the Radical Club of Chestnut Street. This was an organization of religious liberals, chiefly Unitarians, who felt a need for "larger liberty of faith, fellowship, and communion." Founded in the spring of 1867, it was designed to meet a demand for "the freest investigation of all forms of religious thought and inquiry."[36] The club was led by the Reverend John T. Sargent, a radical Unitarian who had lost his pulpit. Its meetings were held in the Sargents' home. Its speakers included such luminaries as Emerson, Whittier, Julia Ward Howe, Francis Ellingwood Abbot, Henry James, Octavius B. Frothingham, Thomas Wentworth Higginson, John Fiske, and Oliver Wendell Holmes. In its earlier years, the papers were chiefly concerned with religious questions but later they dealt largely with scientific matters. "The conversations," Mrs. Sargent wrote, "were not less interesting than the essays." The meetings were characterized by "rare thoughtfulness, deep human tenderness, and profound earnestness."[37]

Mary Grew took for her theme "Essential Christianity," and in her address gave the fullest expression of her mature religious views. "The question, What is Christianity?" she said, "is but asking, What were the main ideas in the teachings of Christ?" "Surely these two,—" she answered, "—the fatherhood of God and the brotherhood of man." The ideal of God that Christ presented was that of a father, "loving and tender beyond human conception; tenderest to those who most needed him." The duty to God which Christ enjoined was "reverent love and trust and obedience; the duty toward man, brotherly love and brotherly service." The religion of Jesus was preached to "the humble, uncultured souls of his time, and the common people heard him gladly." But no philosopher or metaphysician had ever evolved a system of ethics equal to that which he taught, or given to the world a rule of life so profound and so simple as his precept "Whatsoever ye would that men should do to you, do ye even so unto them." Jesus would have men show love to God "by love to man; by feeding the hungry, clothing the naked, ministering to the sick, and comforting the afflicted."[38]

Later in her address Mary Grew declared that Christianity consisted of three principles: faith in God, "not belief in a creed but confidence in a Father; consciousness of the soul's intimate filial relation to God; and love to God and the neighbor, co-existing with the first two primciples."[39]

Christianity was not to be confused with the church, she insisted. The churches had piled on men's shoulders "burdens grievous to be borne." They had constructed various systems of doctrine and ritual, which they had presented to men as the embodiment of that religion, and had taught that belief and observance of these were necessary conditions of Christian character, while their standard of morals had always been little higher than that of the government under which they had lived. The antislavery struggle of the preceding generation in America had revealed clearly the character of the American church. The Church had not only upheld the evil system of slavery, "but the negro and his defenders were alike the objects of the church's scorn." The Church had fallen into "the grave error of thinking creed more important than character."[40] Mary Grew's lecture was followed by an animated discussion.

John Greenleaf Whittier, who was unable to attend the meeting, sent an apology for his absence and a poetic tribute to Mary Grew, which was read at the meeting:

How Mary Grew

With wisdom far beyond her years,
And graver than her wondering peers,

So strong, so mild, combining still
The tender heart and queenly will,
To conscience and to duty true,
So, up from childhood, Mary Grew!

Then in her gracious womanhood
She gave her days to doing good.
She dared the scornful laugh of men,
The hounding mob, the slanderer's pen.
She did the work she found to do,—
A Christian heroine, Mary Grew!

The freed slave thanks her; blessing comes
To her from women's weary homes;
The wronged and erring find in her
Their censor mild and comforter.
The world were safe if but a few
Could grow in grace as Mary Grew!

So, New Year's Eve, I sit and say,
By this low wood-fire, ashen gray;
Just wishing, as the night shuts down,
That I could hear in Boston town,
In pleasant Chestnut Avenue,
From her own lips, how Mary Grew!

And hear her graceful hostess tell
The silver-voiced oracle
Who lately through her parlors spoke
As through Dodona's sacred oak,
A wiser truth than any told
By Sappho's lips of ruddy gold,—
The way to make the world anew,
Is just to grow—as Mary Grew![41]

Shortly after her return from Boston, Mary Grew addressed a letter to Ann Phillips. "If I had not been so thoroughly fatigued, after my return from New England," she wrote, "I should have found time, amidst the numerous business matters that had accumulated in my absence, to write to you before this. . . . Now, I can add to the interest of my letter by telling you how much pleasure we have all derived from Wendell's visit." Ann's husband had recently lectured in Philadelphia. "Seth Terry, writing to me once of a short visit his family had had from Wendell, said, 'What a benediction he is!' 'So say *we* all of us.'"[42] Mary Grew spoke of introducing a young friend of hers, one Miss Brown, to Phillips; the young lady had spoken very earnestly of the "new stimulus, new strength" that she had derived from the short interview with him, for which she was very grateful.[43]

In the same letter, Mary Grew spoke of calling on Charles Greene, a few days before Phillips's visit to Philadelphia. "I was too tired, to go sooner; but when I did go, I made a long visit." She thought the Greenes should have a person in the house who could cook for them and otherwise help them, but she was afraid they could not be persuaded to accept this kind of assistance, and she was not sure that the experiment would be successful, if tried. The work actually done in the household could not be great or burdensome (the washing was sent out to be done), "but if they were willing to allow it, their comfort might be promoted by the introduction of more work, & a person to do it." If any avenue should open by which they could be made more comfortable, she would let Ann Phillips know. "They were very glad to hear from you, and express their gratitude to you for your thoughtful care for them."

"My New England trip," Mary Grew went on, "which I enjoyed so much, I live over again in pleasant recollections. One of its very bright spots is your chamber, where I saw so much more of you than I can in my summer visits to the North. I cannot tell you how much I enjoyed my interviews with you. Well, I'll try not to envy Mrs. Sargent who can run in, on any day, & have a chat with you; but rather rejoice in her good fortune. . . . I trust that Wendell will return to you in good health," she wrote. "I should think he would be worn out, with his continuous lecturing, only he isn't."[44]

On 23 March 1871 Mary Grew wrote Elizabeth Neall Gay regarding the death of Abby Kimber. It will be recalled that the delegates of the Philadelphia Female Anti-Slavery Society to the World's Anti-Slavery Convention in London in 1840 were Lucretia Mott, Mary Grew, Sarah Pugh, Abby Kimber, and Elizabeth Neall. With the female delegates from Massachusetts, they had been denied seats in the convention. "Abby Kimber has passed away," Mary Grew reported. "I do not like to use the word death in connection with one who had so much vitality, and whose life, today, is fuller & richer than ever before. The death & the pain, & the loss, belong to those whom she has left, who will surely feel her absence."[45]

On 10 May 1871 Mary Grew attended and spoke at the semiannual meeting of the American Woman Suffrage Association at Steinway Hall in New York City. Almost a thousand delegates were present.

When I am asked to give arguments for the cause of woman suffrage, it seems like the old times when we were asked to give arguments for the freedom of the slave. It is enough for me to know that the charter of our

Nation states that "taxation without representation is tyranny," and that all just government is founded on the consent of the governed. . . . You, my brother, claim the right to vote because you are taxed, because you are one of the governed; and you know if an attempt was made to touch your right to vote, you would sacrifice everything to defend it. What would money be worth to you without it? You call it the symbol of your citizenship; and without it you would be slaves—not free. Listen, then, when a woman tells you that her freedom is but nominal without it.[46]

On 3 June 1871 Mary Grew wrote to Lucy Stone and her husband, Henry Blackwell, regarding the policy of Horace Greeley's *New York Tribune* toward the American Woman Suffrage Association. "I agree with you," she wrote, "that it is a good thing for our Cause The Tribune has published the main points of difference between the two societies; but I wish it had a better spirit towards our Cause. I have not much more faith in that journal than I have in the N.Y. Nation, which is none at all."[47]

As if the National and the American Woman Suffrage Associations did not already have sufficiently serious sources of disagreement, in 1871 they became involved in a dispute over the usefulness of the notorious "free lover" Victoria Woodhull to the suffrage cause. The executive committee of the Pennsylvania Woman Suffrage Association published a notice in two of Philadelphia's daily papers repudiating the social theories of *Woodhull and Claflin's Weekly.* "It surprises me," Mary Grew wrote, "that any of our friends can sympathize with Mrs. W's theories of marriage, however much they may sympathize with her as a suffering woman, who was the victim of a bad husband. In my short interview with her in N.Y. she impressed me as a woman better than her theories. But I do not know her well."[48]

In October 1871 New York City was swept by a terrible fire. Mary Grew collected clothing and funds for relief of its victims, which she channeled through Sydney and Elizabeth Gay. Fortunately, the Gays' house was spared.

The second annual meeting of the Pennsylvania Woman Suffrage Association was held in the lecture room of the Mercantile Library, 22 November 1871, with Mary Grew presiding and about one hundred persons present. Lucy Stone and Julia Ward Howe were among the speakers. The association adopted a resolution declaring that the calling of a state constitutional convention "offers us the opportunity and lays on us the urgent duty of demanding and earnestly working for the exclusion of the word *male* from the provision defining the qualifications for the elective franchise."[49] Henry Blackwell wrote an editorial for the *Woman's Journal* (published 9 December 1871) commenting on this meeting and remarking that "the calm and decisive ability which the President, Miss Mary Grew, manifested as chairman, was a practical illustration of woman's ability to govern."[50]

In February 1872 the Pennsylvania Woman Suffrage Association established headquarters at No. 700 Arch Street, Philadelphia. "As we have recently 'set up' our tabernacle, we feel rather grand about it; and naturally wish to make as much display as possible," Mary Grew wrote to Elizabeth Gay. She thought this achievement owed much to "Sally Hallowell's real enthusiasm and perseverance." She was determined to "wrest our Soc. out of every clutch of 'Woodhullism.'" Passmore Williamson had offered the use of a room rent free. Members of the executive committee were dividing office duty among six volunteers, each person taking one day per week, performing the duties of office agent from 10:00 A.M. to 1:00 P.M. "I am not one of the six volunteers," she wrote, "being too far advanced in years, and too much dilapidated to enter into such an engagement; but I hold myself ready as an occasional substitute." Mary Grew observed, "We think we are gaining strength and influence here. Several of our daily papers almost advocate our cause; and they, generally, speak respectfully of it."[51] The assembly had considered their petition for women to be allowed to vote in the next presidential election, but the measure had lost by a vote of 38–31.

Mary Grew and Margaret Burleigh visited Lucretia Mott on the afternoon of 20 February 1872 and discussed "the Woodhull problem." Mrs. Mott and Maria Davis, she reported to Elizabeth Neall Gay, thought that Victoria Woodhull was "an injured woman, pure in her life; and unfortunate in her use of language, which causes her to be misunderstood. They both would admit (I think) that she holds theories in which they do not believe; but they evidently think her a person qualified to instruct the public; *which I do not.*"[52]

In March 1872 Mary Grew and Margaret Burleigh "rushed down South, rather suddenly," in the hope that Margaret might find relief from a troublesome affliction of her throat. Writing to Ann Phillips from Charleston, on 21 April 1872, she asked, "Did I ever expect to write to you from South Carolina? Did I ever expect to be here, and talk freely to the colored population?"[53] Everything was "so strange" and "so unlike our northern life, that it seems a little dream-like." She could scarcely realize that in the city of Charleston, "the pride & glory of the 'proud Palmetto State,'" she had addressed a large congregation of colored persons, nearly all of them once slaves, and had congratulated them on "their freedom and citizenship."[54]

"Bad as the political condition of South Carolina is today, & is likely to be for a year or two to come; there is much to be hoped for the future of these colored children." Already they were making their school instruction of practical benefit to their parents. There was the case of a woman who told her employer that he had not paid her all the wages due her. He asked, indignantly, how she knew his calculation of the amount was wrong. She replied that she could not have told, but her boy went to school and had learned arithmetic, and he told her it was wrong. The man cursed the "nigger schools" but rectified the error, and the mother went home saying, "He may cuss, but my boy's got 'the larnin.'"[55]

Mary Grew thought the black children were showing a good deal of proficiency in grammar as well as in arithmetic. This was especially true in their school exercises; they found much more difficulty in applying the rules of grammar to their daily conversation. She found their recitations sometimes amusing. When, for instance, a class was asked by the teacher the gender of the word "sister," an eager little girl quickly responded, "He's feminine; him's a gal."[56] "There is a wonderful element of poetry & pathos mingled with the simplicity & ignorance of this people," she concluded. "I should like to spend an hour in your room, telling you & Wendell of some of our southern experience, comical and pathetic."[57]

On 8 October 1872 Mary Grew wrote a letter to Lucy Stone regarding the affairs of the *Woman's Journal* and the American Woman Suffrage Association. With regard to the *Journal,* she would be very glad to do something in aid of it if she could. Possibly some special effort on its behalf might be made at the annual meeting of the Pennsylvania Association. She would like to talk to Lucy Stone about mutual help for the American meeting and the Pennsylvania meeting. "You know that Penna. is very weak compared with Massachusetts, in material for Woman Suffrage Meetings, or work." There was a possibility she might have the opportunity of talking with Lucy Stone in person later in the month. She might go to Boston as a delegate to the National Unitarian Conference, which was to be held on 22 October and following. "If I should go, I shall see you, I trust; & we can talk over matters." However, she added, "Don't say that I am going to the conference, or to Boston, for I may not go."[58] She could never be sure that her health would permit her to go to conventions.

At a meeting of the executive committee of the Pennsylvania Woman Suffrage Association in October 1872, resolutions were adopted commending the announcement of the Republican party of Massachusetts for their support of woman suffrage and calling upon the Republican party of Pennsylvania "to prove themselves equally true to the principles of just government." A Republican newspaper in Philadelphia had recently declared that under the laws of the United

States and Pennsylvania, women, though not granted the right of suffrage, were conceded "nearly everything else that they can possibly desire." The Suffrage Association passed resolutions declaring that women wanted the right to control their own earnings, to be secure in the guardianship of their children, and to be accorded more equal rights in the inheritance of property.[59]

The annual meeting of the Pennsylvania Woman Suffrage Association was held in the lecture room of Horticultural Hall on 6 December 1872 at 3:00 P.M., with Mary Grew presiding. It was a rainy day, and there was only "a moderate attendance." "After a few remarks from Miss Grew and the reading of the constitution," committee appointments were announced. The report of the executive committee was read by its chairman, John K. Wildman. It had sent a petition to the legislature asking for representation of women in the coming state constitutional convention. The petition had been denied. It had also asked for a law giving married women the right to control their own earnings. Such a law had been passed but was "so hampered with obnoxious provisions that it seemed to be little more than a mockery of justice."[60] The association had distributed hundreds of tracts and numerous copies of the *Woman's Journal*.

At its annual meeting the association adopted a petition to the constitutional convention of the State of Pennsylvania:

> As one half of the adult citizens of Pennsylvania are now deprived of the ballot, who, being thus disfranchised, are governed as an inferior class, compelled to obey laws in the making of which they have no voice, and their property taxed without any representation in the government, The Pennsylvania Woman Suffrage Association respectfully petitions your honorable body to amend section one of article three of the present Constitution, so as to secure perfect equality of citizenship without distinction of sex. We also ask to be heard by you in support of this petition, at such time and place as shall be deemed proper.[61]

Accompanying this petition were the following resolutions:

> *Whereas,* The American People have asserted, as the basis of their National Government, that "governments derive their just powers from the consent of the governed," and that "taxation without representation is tyranny"; therefore,
>
> *Resolved,* That this Association claim for the women of this nation the right of suffrage and the power to exercise that right upon the same terms upon which it is exercised by men.
>
> *Resolved,* That whatever arguments for this claim may be derived from the favorable influence of woman upon the moral atmosphere of politics,

or upon legislation in behalf of moral reforms, we base our claim upon simple justice to every citizen.[62]

In connection with the petition to the constitutional convention, the suffrage association passed a resolution expressing appreciation to the Honorable John M. Broomall for presenting to the convention, "at an early day, a resolution in favor of this act of justice." Another resolution expressed encouragement that woman suffrage had been adopted in the territory of Wyoming, that the Republican party of Massachusetts was supporting the cause, and that numerous journals were advocating woman suffrage. Some of the daily papers in Philadelphia were supporting the reform and giving women a "respectful hearing." John K. Wildman reported that there was "much excellent speaking" at the annual meeting. "The speeches of Charles C. Burleigh, Rev. Charles G. Ames, and Mary Grew, were especially valuable. . . . A good spirit prevailed," and there was "hope of ultimate success."[63] It was announced that two thousand copies of the message of the governor of Wyoming Territory on woman suffrage had been printed for circulation—"the first tract published by the Association." The executive committee had sent a request to three hundred Pennsylvania newspapers asking them to publish a notice that all supporters of woman suffrage throughout the state should send their names and addresses to the office of the Pennsylvania Woman Suffrage Association at 700 Arch Street, Philadelphia. "The response has been most gratifying."[64]

The culmination of the nineteenth-century woman suffrage campaign in Pennsylvania came with the debates on the issue conducted by the constitutional convention of 1872–73. This body met in Harrisburg from 12 November to 27 November 1872, reconvened in Philadelphia on 7 January 1873, and adjourned on 3 November 1873.[65] There were 133 delegates, the majority of whom were Republicans.

The Pennsylvania Woman Suffrage Association was granted a respectful hearing before members of the constitutional convention. The executive committee of the association appointed a committee to present its suffrage petition—Mary Grew, Sarah C. Hallowell, and Passmore Williamson. The committee on suffrage and elections received the petition and offered a resolution asking for use of the hall in which the convention was meeting (in Philadelphia) for the evenings of 15 and 16 January. The resolution was adopted. Wednesday evening, the fifteenth, was assigned to Matilda Hindman, representing the Pittsburgh Society, and to Mary Grew, Sarah C. Hallowell, Fanny B. Ames, and the Reverend Charles G. Ames, representing the state association. Thursday evening, the sixteenth, was assigned to representatives of the Citizens' Suffrage Association, the Radical Club, and the Internationals. At 7:30 P.M. on the fifteenth, Hugh N. McAllister, chairman of the committee on suffrage, elections, and representation, took a seat at the clerk's desk, immediately below the speaker's chair, and announced that Miss Hindman would address the committee, whose members were seated in a semicircle immediately in front of the platform. About half the members of the convention were present, many of them accompanied by their wives or "lady friends," and nearly all the seats on the floor of the hall were occupied. The gallery was also filled with visitors, observers, and friends of the cause. Among them, "appearing remarkably bright and cheerful, was that earnest pioneer in this good work, LUCRETIA MOTT, now past her eightieth year."[66]

Mary Grew was the third speaker, following Hindman (who spoke about forty-five minutes) and Hallowell. "Her remarks largely derived their force from her thorough conviction of the justice of Woman's claim to the ballot. She would base all the arguments in its behalf, as an axiomatic sum, on the well-founded principle 'that all just governments derive their powers from the consent of the governed.' That begins and ends the argument." She went on to call attention to the injustices done to women because they had no say in the use of their tax monies, no share in the control of schools, and no rights in respect to the guardianship of their children. She also demanded equal pay for equal work, as in schoolteaching. Her address was "eloquent, forcible, and impressive, and was frequently interrupted by applause."[67] She was followed by Mrs. Fanny B. Ames and then, finally, by the Reverend Charles G. Ames. At the conclusion a member of the committee on suffrage presented their thanks to the Pennsylvania Woman Suffrage Association for "the able and intelligent manner in which the question had been presented."[68] The meeting was then adjourned. It was too early to tell what the results of the hearings would be, according to John K. Wildman, "but we do not mean to indulge the delusive hope that any startling triumph is at our doors."[69]

On 1 February 1873 Hugh N. McAllister of Bellefonte, on behalf of the committee on suffrage, elections and representation, reported a suffrage article that limited the voting privilege to male citizens over the age of twenty-one who could meet specified citizenship and residence requirements. Three members of the committee presented a minority report, which recommended that the question of admitting women to the suffrage be referred to a popular referendum. John M. Broomall of Media, who had served in Congress from 1863 to 1869, moved an amendment to the majority report striking out the word *male*.[70] The convention had received a number of petitions asking the enfranchisement of women, and it spent most of a week (3–7 February) debating this issue in committee of the whole. It also permitted Bishop Matthew Simpson of the Methodist Episcopal Church to appear in the convention hall for an evening address supporting woman suffrage.[71]

Opponents of woman suffrage, led by McAllister, argued that woman's place was in the home, that women were represented at the polls by their male relatives, that woman suffrage would produce family discord, and that participation in politics would be degrading to women. They also maintained that the vast majority of women did not want the right to vote and would not take advantage of it if it were granted. Advocates of the reform, led by Broomall, maintained that suffrage was a natural right, that many women had no men to represent their interests, that woman suffrage would elevate the tone of politics, that it was working well in Wyoming Territory, and that it would make possible effective control of the liquor evil. They also emphasized the innate capacity of women for participating equally with men in the affairs of the world. Supporters of woman suffrage came forward from both political parties, but it was obvious that they did not have enough strength to carry through this innovation, and in the end Broomall withdrew his amendment.[72] The proposal for a popular referendum on the issue was eventually defeated by a vote of 75 to 25, with 33 absent.[73] The feminists emerged from the convention with one small victory. Article 10, section 3 of the Constitution provided that women twenty-one years of age and older were to be eligible to any office or control or management under the school laws of the state.

Reporting on the convention for the *Woman's Journal,* Mary Grew noted that she had been invited to attend its sessions and had heard much of the debate on suffrage. She had been given a seat on the main floor, "a dangerous innovation upon 'time-honored custom'" (recall the London convention of 1840). She was impressed by the fact that nearly every opponent of woman suffrage had begun his speech "with an apologetic tone, and a repudiation of any want of loyalty to Womanhood." She thought many of the arguments were silly, like the one that women would soil their long skirts on the way to the polls. Two speakers had expressed themselves in "coarse and indecent speech," and another had "deliberately insulted the women present, and all women who ask for suffrage." On one point all opponents of woman suffrage agreed, namely that politics was "a sink of corruption, that its atmosphere is defiling; that womanly refinement would be forever lost, if permitted to come within its influence." She thought men ought to want women to help them improve the tone of politics. Writing at the time of the suffrage debate, before Broomall withdrew his amendment, Mary Grew remarked that the outcome was not easy to predict. Members of the convention "may recklessly throw away this rare opportunity of doing a great deal of justice; but we can bide our time."[74]

Writing after the defeat of the suffrage amendment, John K. Wildman expressed his belief that the effect of the debates on this issue had been "more positive and advantageous than was looked for." He had not really expected the suffragists to win. The debates had awakened interest among the people at large and had developed a "friendly feeling" on behalf of the cause. In the same letter Wildman reported that Matilda Hindman, who had already done outstanding work in Pittsburgh, had been appointed state agent, and that a campaign had been launched to raise $1,000 to support her work; $156 had already been collected. The association had issued a circular signed by Mary Grew and four other women asking that donations be sent to "the Woman Suffrage Room, 700 Arch Street, Philadelphia." The association's object was to take the issue to every county and legislative district in the state.[75]

Writing to Lucy Stone on 20 February 1873, Mary Grew expressed her opinion that the Pennsylvania constitutional convention was helping the cause of woman suffrage, "although many of its members have no idea of doing so; and would be very much astonished if they should be told of it." Now was a particularly good time for pressing their claims in the state, and if they had money enough to put three or four good agents into the field, most effective work might be done during the next six months. Though they could not do this, they would use diligently "all the means we have of agitating the subject in the community." There was certainly "great reason for encouragement in the rapid progress which our cause is making in nearly every part of the country."[76] Writing to Henry Blackwell on 11 March, she noted that the constitutional convention had brought the subject of woman suffrage into the newspapers and before the people in an unusual degree, "in which we rejoice."[77]

A struggle lasting almost fifty years lay ahead before Mary Grew and her successors were able to win the battle for woman suffrage. And when the battle was won, it was through federal action, not state, as had been the case with blacks. Mary Grew labored in that cause for nearly twenty years more before she retired.

8

Keeping the Faith (1873–1896)

A terrible business depression descended on the United States in 1873. "The great panic has affected many things by its withering touch, both directly and indirectly," wrote John K. Wildman, "and even our State Woman Suffrage Association has consciously felt its blighting influence."[1] It seemed impossible to have a large-scale annual meeting in an expensive hall, so the officers decided to hold the meeting in the association's rooms at No. 700 Arch Street. It convened on Wednesday, 10 December, at 3:00 P.M. "The plan was justified in the result, and although the meeting was small, its main object of electing officers for the ensuing year, was probably as well accomplished as if the display had been greater, and the expense in proportion."[2]

Mary Grew occupied the chair. After calling the meeting to order, she made "such remarks as the occasion called for" and reviewed the activities of the society during the past year, of which the most important endeavors concerned the effort to get woman suffrage written into the state's new constitution. She called special attention to the provision in the fundamental law that made women eligible to any office of control or management under the school laws of the state. "That is one step, although it be a small and very timid one, in the right path. Women placed here and there in any public position, will make men acquainted with their fitness and capacity, and they will become so accustomed to the novelty as to be reconciled to other advances. The experiment will do good."[3]

The association had also circulated a large number of tracts and had sent broadcast ten thousand flyers showing "the alacrity of Congressmen" in largely augmenting their own salaries ("the Salary Grab") but declining to make a small addition to the pay of women clerks in the government departments. The association had employed Matilda Hindman as traveling agent for several months—"an indefatigable and useful worker." The association's constitution had been amended to make the executive committee consist of eight members instead of five. Mary Grew was reelected president.[4]

153

Matilda Hindman spoke at the sixth annual convention of the American Woman Suffrage Association, which met in Detroit on 13–14 October 1874. She also read the report of the Pennsylvania Association. Eliza Sproat Turner, another Pennsylvania representative, was appointed to the committee on resolutions and nominations. During the year, the Pennsylvania group had held several public meetings at its headquarters and distributed numerous tracts and papers. "By the judicious manner in which the work has been conducted, prejudice, in a great measure, has been removed, opposition, in the form of ridicule, burlesque, and mis-statement, does not now present itself."[5]

The annual meeting of the state society was held at West Chester on Wednesday, 18 November, morning, afternoon, and evening. The change from Philadelphia was "a good one, as it brought the subject of Woman Suffrage before a new audience, and gave freshness to the undertaking by encompassing it with new surroundings. . . . The meeting in every way seemed to be successful," wrote Vice President John K. Wildman. Mary Grew opened the morning session and spoke concerning the inconsistency between political theory and practice in the United States. The problem of financing the movement was discussed. At the afternoon session officers were elected. The association passed a resolution declaring that by depriving one-half of the population of the right to vote, the nation and the states stood self-convicted of injustice and tyranny. However, it also passed a resolution hailing the improvement of public education and the opening of colleges to young women as signs of progress. At the close of the evening meeting, Mary Grew spoke "a few impressive words, which went directly to the souls of the hearers."[6]

Mary Grew was ill much of 1875. Belatedly acknowledging receipt of a letter and a photograph from William Lloyd Garrison, she wrote on 17 March 1875, "I have been sick, and unfit for the effort of writing a letter. . . . I wish I were able to send you a letter worthy to be a response to yours, but I am scarcely well enough to write at all, yet I am not willing to wait any longer, lest you should think me neglectful of your thoughtful kindness."[7] On 5 April 1875, she wrote in a similar vein to Lucy Stone:

I will thank you to say to Mr. Blackwell that ever since I received his letter, in Feb., I have been hoping to be able to comply with his request, to furnish him some account of our Suffrage Meetings, for the Journal. I have been so miserably out of health, that I could not attempt it; I have asked one or two others to do it. Yet it has not been done; & I suppose I shall make a desperate attempt at it soon, if no one else does it. There is so much to be done that one cannot help wishing for vigorous health, to enable the hand to keep pace with the will.[8]

The *Woman's Journal*, indeed, carried an account by Mary Grew of the meetings and other activities of Pennsylvania suffragists in its 17 April issue. Again in December the *Woman's Journal* reported that Mary Grew had been too sick to attend the Pennsylvania society's annual meeting.[9]

When 1876 arrived, the question arose as to how the woman suffrage groups were to celebrate the nation's centennial. The National Association requested permission to present a declaration of rights for women at the Fourth of July celebration at Independence Hall. Denied this privilege, Susan B. Anthony and four other women went up on the platform and presented their declaration on parchment to the chairman, scattering printed copies of it broadside as they left. They then occupied a bandstand in Independence Square, where Miss Anthony read the declaration "in a clear voice that carried far out across the listening throng." The American Association did not associate itself with the declaration, much less with the manner of its presentation, and after being refused a place on the program, requested exhibition space. Eventually the women got wall space to display some printed matter, but "so high that few could see it."[10]

The American Association gathered in Horticultural Hall, Philadelphia, to celebrte the centennial of the granting of woman suffrage by the constitutional convention of New Jersey on 2 July 1776. Lucy Stone and Henry Blackwell spoke, and the Hutchinson Family sang.[11]

The Pennsylvania Woman Suffrage Association held its annual meeting on 18 October in Saint George's Hall. Mary Grew presided and made the opening remarks, which "breathed a spirit of hope and encouragement." The association adopted eight resolutions. The first two declared that the nation had made much progress in respect for human rights and that women had made gains in education, employment, the professions, and property rights. However, taxation without representation was tyranny. There was reason to hope that the suffrage goal would be reached. The fifth resolution demanded the equality of all persons before the law. The next one charged that women's indifference was contributing to the failure to achieve woman suffrage. The seventh urged young people to get the best education they could to prepare for suffrage. The last one noted with satisfaction the assembly of a Congress of Women in Philadelphia in connection with the Centennial Exposition.[12]

Early in 1877 Mary Grew took part in the founding of one of the nation's first general woman's clubs, Philadelphia's New Century Club. On 8 February a small group of ladies met in the parlor of Mrs. J. P. Lesley to organize a club "where all questions of the day could be discussed without prejudice." They took their name from a newspaper that women had published at the Centennial Exposition entitled the

New Century for Women. Mary Grew was the club's first vice president. The club took an interest in education, charities, literature, legislation, prisons, art, music, employment of women, science, household arts, and entertainment, among other topics reflected in its committee structure.[13] One of the club's most notable achievments in its early years was the success of Mary Grew and Lucretia L. Blankenburg in getting the station houses to employ police matrons to care for women prisoners and lost children, beginning in 1886.[14] In 1879 the club rented a house at 1112 Girard Street to accommodate its varied activities. In 1881 the club granted the use of its rooms to a committee set up to establish evening classes for working women, under the leadership of Eliza Sproat Turner. Out of this grew the New Century Guild for Working Women, an important vehicle for adult education. The guild offered courses in dressmaking, cooking, millinery, laundry work, telegraphy, and bookkeeping. Later it became a working girls' club with recreational facilities as well as study groups. Its vocational classes were taken over in 1892 by the newly founded Drexel Institute, but the guild continued active through later years.[15]

Mary Grew was disgusted by the surrender of the Radical Republicans to the South's master class in "the Compromise of 1877," under which Northern troops were withdrawn from the South in return for Southern acceptance of Hayes's election as president. "With all my heart & soul," she wrote William Lloyd Garison on 2 April 1877, "I thank you for your protest against the miserable policy of 'conciliation & compromise' with the oppression of the colored race in the South. . . . I am almost sick with disappointment of the high hopes which Hayes' election inspired," she continued, "so weakly does he *seem* to be on the point of yielding to the dictation of those southern aristocrats whose tone is so well understood by us. . . . The trumpet-blasts which you and Wendell Phillips, from time to time sound in the ears of this nation, are most cheering and encouraging to your fellow-soldiers in the anti-slavery host, and will *help,* if anything will, to complete the salvation of the Republic."[16]

The ninth annual meeting of the Pennsylvania Woman Suffrage Association was held at Kennett Square on 19 November 1878. After calling the meeting to order, Mary Grew spoke on the progress of the cause, urging continued work and material support. She also made the closing speech that evening, appealing to young people to join the suffrage crusade.[17]

Some time in 1879 Mary Grew sent a note to Lucy Stone, enclosing a clipping regarding a woman in Raleigh, North Carolina, who had succeeded her husband as president of a national bank. "I think it is the first instance of the kind," she wrote, and "as such is another encouraging sign of the times. . . . How abundant, & how constantly increasing such signs are!" She also reported that she had been sick for weeks and was still "quite feeble."[18]

The 1879 meeting of the Pennsylvania Woman Suffrage Association was held in Philadelphia on 4 November. John K. Wildman reported that the woman suffrage constituency was not only undiminished but "palpably increasing." A letter of regret was read from Representative William D. Kelley, giving qualified support for the movement but stating that he was too busy to attend the meeting. As usual, Mary Grew spoke. The convention adopted resolutions hailing "improving public sentiment," rejoicing in the decision of Massachusetts and New Hampshire to permit women to vote for school directors, urging women to work for the election of female school directors in Pennsylvania and to circulate petitions to the state General Assembly on behalf of giving women the right to vote for school directors. Other resolutions thanked the legislature for authorizing the appointment of women as prison inspectors and urged the establishment of a prison for women administered by women. One recommended to Pennsylvanians the favorable reports by territorial officials regarding the beneficial results of woman suffrage in Wyoming. The eighth hailed the new facilities for higher education of women and more lucrative employment opportunities. The ninth mourned the recent death of William Lloyd Garrison, "an able advocate" of woman suffrage. The tenth, and last, reaffirmed the suffragists' belief that since "all just government derives its power from the consent of the governed" and since "taxation without representation is tyranny," women should be given the right to vote.[19]

In September 1880 Mary Grew was vacationing at Mountain View House in Whitefield, New Hampshire. She endorsed the hotel and the scenery. She was also pleased with the local Free-Will Baptist Church and its liberalism. "Slowly and steadily the unsightly partition walls, political, social, and ecclesiastical, which have so long divided and marred the prosperity of God's human family, are bending and crumbling. Blessed will they be who lived to see them utterly fall." She noted that the church's hymnbook included antislavery hymns, that it recognized that "in Christ Jesus there is neither male nor female," and that its pulpit was open to Unitarian preachers.[20]

While in New Hampshire, Mary Grew received a letter from Sarah Pugh notifying her that Lucretia Mott was gravely ill. She promptly addressed a note to Mrs. Mott.

My Beloved & Revered Friend,
    It may be that I shall no more see your face and hear your voice, before you enter the celestial city and I meet you there. Therefore I want to thank you, before you go, for all that you have been to me: for all the blessedness

which has flowed from your soul into my soul, from your life into my life.

I can offer you only my gratitude and love, and my earnest wish that your remaining days on earth may be serene, and hallowed with blessed memories and glorious hopes.

Thy affectionate friend
of many years,
Mary Grew[21]

Mrs. Mott died on 11 November 1880. Mary Grew wrote a tribute to her for the *Philadelphia Public Ledger*. "The name of Lucretia Mott is a synonym for a rare combination of Christian graces," she wrote. The most prominent element of her character was her "constant loyalty to Righteousness and Truth, as interpreted by her conscience." The highest law she acknowledged was "the voice of God within the soul."[22]

Mary Grew's sister Susan died in Providence, Rhode Island, 9 January 1881, at the age of 76.[23] She had shared Mary's reform interests and, like Mary, had never married.

The eleventh annual meeting of the Pennsylvania Woman Suffrage Association was held on 14 December 1880 at the Academy Hall, Spring Garden Street, Philadelphia, under unfavorable weather conditions. Mary Grew "fulfilled the duties of her position from the beginning to the end of the meeting with ability and satisfaction," according to John K. Wildman's report. "Long experience enables her to conduct the affairs of a meeting with readiness, skill and dispatch."[24] Lucy Stone and Henry Blackwell were present and spoke. A memorial testimony to Lucretia Mott, prepared by Mary Grew, was read and adopted.

The 1881 annual meeting was held in Media, the home of John M. Broomall, who had led the fight for woman suffrage in the constitutional convention of 1872–73. He was the featured speaker at this meeting. Mary Grew called the meeting to order and spoke. The chief item of business was the report of the executive committee giving a history of the association from its founding in 1869.[25]

On 29 July 1882 the *Woman's Journal* carried an article by Mary Grew about women preaching. She noted that one Unitarian church in New England had been served by two successive women pastors and that many Unitarian pulpits were open to women. She also stated that women were holding office in the American Unitarian Association. "No religious organization exists, I believe," she said, "in which men and women stand in perfect equality, but some are far in advance of others in this respect. We give honor where honor is due, and look for further progress."[26]

The 1882 annual suffrage meeting was held 15 November in the

Spring Garden Unitarian Church. It was called to order by Mary Grew, who made a brief opening address. She spoke "with her usual fervor, hopefulness and reverent earnestness," and her words were "wise and fitting."[27] Lucy Stone and Antoinette Brown Blackwell also were among the speakers. Among the resolutions was one asking the admission of women to the University of Pennsylvania.

Mary Grew and Margaret Burleigh spent a large part of the summer of 1883 at Norwood's, a "charming retreat" in York, Maine, "wh. is no less attractive to us in this, our fifth season, than it was in the first. . . . I hope to see you as I pass through Boston on my return," Mary Grew wrote Lucy Stone, "wh. will probably be about the middle of September." With this letter she sent two clippings from the *Philadelphia Public Ledger,* a paper that she said was "in the main, friendly to woman suffrage & equality of rights."[28]

On 4 December 1883 surviving abolitionists met at Horticultural Hall in Philadelphia to celebrate the fiftieth anniversary of the founding of the American Anti-Slavery Society. The presiding officer was Robert Purvis. John Greenleaf Whittier gave his recollections of the founding convention of 1833. Mary Grew was included among the other speakers. She was introduced as "a life-long abolitionist." The founders of the society, she declared, had from the beginning demanded "absolute justice for the slave. . . . And by that faith in Right they conquered." She recalled the "Martyr Age" that the early abolitionists had gone through. They did not know how difficult the task would be. "Least of all did we anticipate the opposition which we encountered from churches and other religious organizations." There were two exceptions—the Covenanters and the Free-Will Baptists. Now the specific work of the American Anti-Slavery Society had been accomplished. "Its lessons remain for instruction to the generations to come. God grant that these lessons may be heeded; that man may learn the great truth, that injustice cannot prosper; that he who fastens a chain upon his brother fetters himself thereby; that though the footsteps of Nemesis may be slow, they are sure, because the Lord God Omnipotent reigneth."[29]

"For decades the method of state referenda on woman suffrage" (the method followed by the American Woman Suffrage Association), Eleanor Flexner has written, "produced meager results in return for exhausting labors."[30] In 1884, it produced a victory in Oregon. Mary Grew contributed through her influence with Pennsylvanians to raise money to support this effort. "Your letter with Lucy's appended words, came to me this morning," she wrote Henry Blackwell. "I am very glad that it was not a day later; for I leave home tomorrow, to be absent a week or more. I have just written Passmore Williamson &

John K. Wildman, & shall write to two or three other persons, urging immediate attention to this matter of the money for Oregon." Wildman would send to Blackwell at once such sums as he had in his possession for this object. She would send Wildman her contribution and several donations she had obtained. She was working to get new subscriptions to *Woman's Journal,* which she thought would boost contributions. "But raising money for suffrage, here, is hard work." She had introduced the subject at the New Century Club at its last meeting, reading a statement from Lucy Stone on the matter. "It was an innovation, no doubt, a startling one; but Mrs. Turner approved it; & we both know that the Club has been unconsciously growing in the direction of Woman Suffrage, for some time. A little money was given to me, not much, but it was an important step to have the subject squarely brought before that body." If Mr. Blackwell needed to reach her during the next ten days, he should communicate with Mr. Wildman. "I have really no strength to spare for such work, but this is an unusually important crisis," she wrote. "When I return home I will see what has been, & what further can be done."[31]

On 1 August 1884 died Sarah Pugh, with whom Mary Grew had worked closely for half a century in the cause of reform. Mary Grew wrote an obituary tribute to her for the *Woman's Journal.* As president of the Philadelphia Female Anti-Slavery Society throughout most of its history, "her faith and courage were unshaken." She "serenely confronted the violence of mobs, and the more quiet, but not more Christian, opposition of social circles." When the second Anti-Slavery Convention of American Women was driven from Pennsylvania Hall by arson, Sarah Pugh offered the use of her schoolroom, with the owner's consent, for the women's meeting. When the emancipation of the slaves had been achieved, she had devoted herself to the cause of "impartial suffrage for man and woman; in which she was faithful to the end of her earthly life."[32]

The annual meeting of the Pennsylvania Woman Suffrage Association was held in Spring Garden Unitarian Church on 11 December 1884, with Mary Grew presiding. "She always takes a cheerful and confident view," the reporter noted. Among the resolutions adopted was one declaring "our most important work" to be removal of the word *male* from the provisions of the Constitution concerning voter qualifications. Another one rejoiced in the opening of Dickinson College to women. The featured speaker was John M. Broomall, who told members of the audience that they should be encouraged that woman suffrage was no longer ridiculed by the press as it was a few years back. "People are beginning to see that it must come sooner or later."[33]

Writing to Elizabeth Neall Gay on 23 February 1885, Mary Grew made an interesting observation on the election of 1884: "I wanted to talk with you & Sydney, during that horrid Presidential campaign. I would not quite say, as did the woman watching a fight between her husband & a bear, that I did not care which beat, of the two great parties' candidates; but I felt that the elevation of either to the Presidency was disgraceful to the nation."[34] Blaine's public ethics had been impugned and Cleveland's private morality had been questioned.

Mary Grew and Margaret Burleigh summered again in 1885 at Norwood's in York, Maine. "We are revelling in the beauty & freshness of this charming place," Mary wrote. She and Margaret belonged to a group of five ladies who spent an hour each morning reading a life of George Eliot.[35] "We came home on the 18th of Sept.," she reported, "and found the weather here (in Philadelphia) pleasantly cool." The summer had passed enjoyably, but she feared that Margaret had gained no strength; "she is quite feeble; but she was better in the atmosphere of York than she would have been in Phila."[36]

Henry Blackwell was the featured speaker at the sixteenth annual meeting of the Pennsylvania Woman Suffrage Association in December 1885. It convened in the Spring Garden Unitarian Church with Mary Grew in the chair. There was "not a large attendance" at either the afternoon or evening session. In his address, Blackwell argued that woman suffrage was not only a matter of "simple justice," inherently right, but had an important relation to education, morality, women's work and wages, and was "imperatively required to establish the success of the temperance movement."[37]

In 1886 the association's executive committee was meeting monthly in the parlor of the New Century Club, 1112 Girard Street. At the 26 May meeting it was announced that nine hundred leaflets had been distributed during the past month and that the association had received a legacy of one thousand dollars from the estate of the late Mary H. Newbold.[38]

The annual meeting for 1886 was held in Association Hall, Fifteenth and Chestnut Streets, on the afternoon and evening of 27 October. John K. Wildman reported that Mary Grew was in the chair and spoke, displaying "serene confidence in the ultimate triumph of impartial suffrage." A resolution was passed that in order to reform "the evils which afflict society" and to promote the cause of "temperance, purity, and peace," woman suffrage was necessary. The association also declared that the United States was not a true democracy as long as half the population was deprived of political rights. Robert Purvis, the well-known black leader, spoke at the evening session. The executive committee reported that a number of "new and enthusiastic members" had joined, that fifteen hundred leaflets had been distributed to colleges, and that subscriptions to the *Woman's Journal* had been given to schools, libraries, and colleges. The association had corresponded with other similar groups, had heard and discussed a paper on "The Legal Status of Women in Pennsylvania," and had petitioned Congress for a suffrage amendment to the Constitution.[39]

On 1 April 1887 Mary Grew and two other officers of the Pennsylvania branch wrote to Lucy Stone expressing their hope that the American Woman Suffrage Association would decide to hold its next annual meeting in Philadelphia. "Our cause needs help in this State, where laborers & money are not so abundant as in some other parts of our country; & such a Meeting will, doubtless, be an inspiration for good among us, & in neighboring communities."[40]

The American Association did indeed meet in Philadelphia on 31 October 1887. However, Mary Grew was too ill to attend. On behalf of the Pennsylvania Association, she sent a message of welcome. "Our State Association heartily congratulates you on the work which you have accomplished," she wrote, "and shares with you the confident faith in the complete triumph of our just enterprise. . . . We welcome you to Philadelphia in the hopes that from this meeting will flow inspiration which shall be a mighty impetus to the cause of impartial suffrage in Pennsylvania, and thereby hasten the hour when this Republic shall establish what the world has never seen, 'a government of the people, by the people, for the people.' "[41]

In the spring of 1888 Mary Grew traveled to Washington to attend a meeting of the International Council of Women. This occasion brought together representatives from missionary societies, literary clubs, labor leagues, temperance groups, social purity organizations, and professional associations, as well as local, state, and national suffrage associations. It was planned as a commemoration of the fortieth anniversary of the 1848 Seneca Falls Convention. Mary Grew spoke at a session called "The Conference of Pioneers." While she rejoiced at the progress women had made, she could not forget that the work was not done. "Some of us very aged ones," she said, "may not live to see the completion of this work; may not join in the jubilee which shall celebrate the emancipation of women." They would bequeath the task to their young friends "with all its glorious opportunities, its solemn responsibilities, and with our parting word, 'Be faithful unto death or victory.' "[42]

On 19 May 1886 John K. Wildman reported that the Pennsylvania Woman Suffrage Association had secured the services of Mrs. S. S. Fessenden for a period of three months to promote the related causes of woman suffrage and temperance. She would speak to temperance societies on behalf of suffrage. The *Woman's Journal* carried a report of her Pennsylvania work in its issue of 15 June 1888. As a result of her work, woman suffrage associations were organized in Montgomery and Delaware Counties.[43] On 20 October 1888 the newspaper reported that Matilda Hindman had persuaded the Pittsburgh Conference of the Methodist Episcopal Church to accept a resolution favoring woman suffrage. She had been allowed *one minute* to present her views at the annual meeting of the Pennsylvania State Woman's Christian Temperance Union in Pittsburgh and had persuaded them to adopt a resolution appealing to the state legislature for a suffrage amendment to the state constitution. The nineteenth annual meeting of the Pennsylvania Woman Suffrage Association was held 26 December 1888 at 1112 Girard Street, with Mary Grew presiding. The executive committee reported on Mrs. Fessenden's work and on the society's finances, which were in good condition, with a balance of $882.89 in the treasury.[44]

The twentieth annual meeting was held on the evening of 24 October 1889 and the following morning in Association Hall, Mary Grew presiding. In her opening remarks she referred to comments in Lord Bryce's *American Commonwealth* concerning the American affirmation of the equality of all citizens before the law. She said this contention was not supported by the evidence. "We are here to-night to make them [Bryce's comments] true." Mary Grew was again nominated for the presidency but "at first declined, saying that she had now been a long time in the work, and some younger woman ought to take her place." A number of delegates protested, and she accepted reelection for another year. The association adopted a resolution declaring, "we address ourselves to future work with hope, courage, and unfaltering faith in the final triumph of the eternal principles of justice and righteousness."[45] Lucy Stone was the featured speaker.

After three years of negotiations, the two major suffrage organizations united under the title National American Woman Suffrage Association, in February 1890. Mary Grew was too ill to attend the convention where the union took place. "If a wearisome illness had not drawn largely upon my strength," she wrote Lucy Stone on 28 March, "I should have written before this, to congratulate you & Mr. [Henry] and Miss [Alice Stone] Blackwell upon the grand success of the first Meeting of the National-American W. Suff. Ass'n. I had no expectation of being able to attend it, & was not, therefore, disappointed, though I could not help regretting my enforced absence." She rejoiced that henceforth there was not to be two sides or parties but "all one in a grand cause." But she was still afraid that some members of the old National faction might attempt to introduce "extraneous matters," such as divorce law. In the same letter, Mary Grew expressed her satisfaction over the admission of Wyoming to statehood, with full suffrage for women. She also reported that Pennsylvania's suffragists were working to collect money for the suffrage battle in South Dakota, which was won in 1890. Incidentally, she remarked that "it is astonishing that Prohibitionists cannot see that Woman Suffrage is their shortest, safest way to the end they propose."[46]

Mary Grew and Margaret Burleigh again spent the summer of 1890 at York, Maine. Soon after their arrival, Mary contracted a severe cough, "which proved very obstinate, baffling, for a long time [resistant to?] physicians' efforts." At last it had yielded, but it returned from time to time and had depleted her strength. On their way to Maine they had called on John Greenleaf Whittier and had "a delightful interview with him, as our interviews with him always are."[47]

By 26 November 1890 Mary Grew was well enough to preside over the twenty-first annual meeting, held afternoon and evening. In her opening remarks she hailed the opening up of new occupations for women. Other speakers included the Honorable William Dudley Foulke, Julia Ward Howe, and the Reverend Anna Howard Shaw. The meeting was concluded with a recital of "The Battle Hymn of the Republic" by Mrs. Howe. In her speech Mary Grew had asserted, "The soundest and safest base for any claim to rest upon is that of abstract justice and right, and suffrage for women has long been claimed upon that ground."[48]

On 21 April 1891 Mary Grew published a letter to the editor of the *Woman's Journal* concerning married women's property rights in Pennsylvania. She commented on the act passed by the state legislature and signed by Governor James A. Beaver in 1887, which she thought was adequate. She denied a report that had appeared in the *Woman's Journal* stating that the House committee had reported adversely on the bill. Now there was a bill authorizing married women to organize corporations and to serve as officers thereof. The New Century Club had sent a committee to Harrisburg to lobby for it, and she thought there was a good chance of its being passed. "Probably many married women in this State," she wrote, "are not cognizant of the extent of their legal property rights. I shall be much obliged if you will give to this article a place in the *Journal*, for their enlightenment, and also for the credit of Pennsylvania."[49]

The first meeting of the Pennsylvania Woman Suffrage Association after the summer vacation was held at 1520 Chestnut Street, Philadelphia, on 30 September. There were about fifty members and guests present, and Mary Grew presided. She opened the meeting with "a brief address of welcome and some remarks on the bright hopes the future held forth, and on the steady advancement of women."[50] The twenty-second annual meeting was held 4–5 November in Association Hall. Again Mary Grew opened the convention with "a few remarks concerning the suffrage movement and its advance." Reports of auxiliary societies were presented. The report of the Delaware County Society was "especially noteworthy."[51] Chester County, Montgomery County, and Lackawanna County had also sent delegates. By this time the state association had a network of county auxiliaries.

Mary Grew's dear friend and housemate, Margaret Burleigh, with whom she had been associated almost fifty years, died early in 1892. In her reply to a letter of sympathy from Isabel Howland, she made some interesting comments on their relationship:

> Your words respecting my beloved friend touch me deeply. Evidently, you understood her fine character; & you comprehend & appreciate, as few persons do, the nature of the relation which existed, which exists, between her & myself. Her only surviving niece, Miss Ella Jones, also does. To me it seems to have been a closer union than that of most marriages. We know there have been other such between two men, & also between two women. And why should there not be? Love is spiritual; only passion is sexual.[52]

Mary Grew seems to have believed that she would meet Margaret Burleigh in another life. "Why do we speak of those who have 'gone up higher,' as though they were of the past? They live more really, more fully, than ever before; and they love us with a purer, tenderer, nobler love." Mary Grew felt that her own life was nearing its end; she was seventy-eight years old. "I try to wait patiently. I do not feel wholly separated from her who was so large a part of my life."[53]

Writing to Maria Mott Davis a little later, she said, "It seems strange, & sometimes half unreal, that after nearly fifty years of close union with another soul, I should be alone. Yes, you know what it is; & how it seems as if half of one's self is gone." Friends had reminded her that it was her "earnest desire" that she should live long enough to care for Margaret to the end; "and it was. . . . And I am constantly thankful that not upon her fell the sorrow of survivorship. I always desired this for her, & especially as she became more feeble."[54] Then her own health gave way again. "When Margaret went away my strength seemed to follow her; & it has been very slow in returning. Sometimes I think it never will return." She was spending June and July with Eliza Sproat Turner and her husband "in their beautiful summer home" at Chadd's Ford. "It is quiet and restful."[55]

Mrs. Davis had alluded in her letter of sympathy to the disparity between the New Century Club house and the gathering places of "our old Female." This had recalled to Mary Grew's memory many recollections of "the blessed Anti-Slavery days. . . . You and I have reason to be thankful that we lived in them. How fast the band of our fellow-workers is passing onward & upward! How few are left!" Whittier had written to her, "I don't see why I stay." "Some of us can reply that he stays to bless us a while longer."[56] Whittier died later that year.

In the same letter replying to Mrs. Davis, Mary Grew commented on "the wonderful progress in the emancipation of women from old-time fetters." She sometimes thought that people only half realized it. "Certainly younger women who cannot look back to the experience of their sisters in the early decades of this century, do not realise it." On the suffrage matter, she wrote, "You & I cannot expect to see with mortal eyes, woman's full enfranchisement; but your grandchildren doubtless will."[57]

The year 1892 was Mary Grew's last as president of the Pennsylvania Woman Suffrage Association. She presided over the twenty-third annual meeting, at the Grand Opera House at Chester, Pennsylvania, on 30 November 1892. She spoke of the progress of women in the past generation. Women held the ballot in municipal or school elections in twenty-one states. They were voting for president in one state. They were standing in the pulpits of churches and serving as college professors. Woman's rights advocates should "feel inspired with reverent gratitude."[58] Miss Jane Campbell gave a report on the year's work of the association. It had held regular bimonthly meetings. It had distributed literature "with a lavish hand" throughout the state. It had circulated copies of *Woman's Journal*. It had received a bequest from a Mrs. Myers, who was a friend of Mary Grew's. The association and its five auxiliaries had a total of 370 members and was entitled to send six delegates to the National American convention in Washington. Allegheny County had its own separate association, under the presidency of Matilda Hindman. Jane Campbell commented that the association's greatest need was for better cooperation between the Philadelphia and Pittsburgh groups.[59] The featured speaker at this meeting was Henry Blackwell. When Mary Grew retired as president, she was succeeded by Lucretia Longshore Blankenburg.[60]

Mary Grew's health gave way again in January 1893. "I am really not fit for much effort," she wrote, "& spend a great deal of time on a sofa."[61] On 19 January she wrote, "I am rather more than usually miserable today; unfortunately, because I have said that I will address The Unitarian Club of this city, tonight, on my recollections of J. G.

Whittier."[62] She was well enough to speak at a meeting of the New Century Club on 19 February, "where reminiscences of Anti-Slavery days were told to a large audience by Dr. Furness, Harriet Purvis & myself. How new & strange & exciting it was to most of them! A very few of 'the old guard,' who survive unto this day, were there."[63] In July she was in Chadd's Ford again with her friends the Turners, whose summer home was "a beautiful place on a high hill, near the Brandywine River." In the winter the Turners lived very near her in Philadelphia, "only two houses between our residences. . . . They are a brother & sister to me; & they minister most kindly to my comfort, & sympathize with my loneliness."[64]

In the same letter where she spoke of her relationship with the Turners, written to Elizabeth Neall Gay on 3 July 1893, Mary Grew gave her opinion of Elizabeth Cady Stanton and the more radical wing of the woman suffrage movement. She quoted Wendell Phillips to the effect that if suffragists allowed Mrs. Stanton's theories of divorce to be advocated in their meetings, the time would soon come when respectable men and women would not sit on their platforms. "Free divorce was, & probably is, a favorite theory of Mrs. Stanton's; but I think that Susan Anthony did not hold it, & I believe she has resisted efforts of Mrs. S. to promulgate, in Suffrage Meetings, her opinions respecting the Bible."[65]

Mary Grew celebrated her eightieth birthday on 1 September 1893. Friends gave her a "birthday book" with more than a hundred tributes. Her delay in acknowledging these letters, she said by way of apology to one of these friends, "has been caused by my frequent illness & consequent feebleness. . . . How precious they are to me it would be difficult to say; or to tell of my surprise when the beautiful book was presented to me. . . . It is one of the greatest joys of my life that I was permitted to be a worker in the great Anti-Slavery Enterprise. And how good it is to greet, from time to time the few of 'The Old Guard' who still remain on earth!"[66]

Elizabeth Gay lost her brother Daniel Neall early in 1894. Neall had been president of the association that erected Pennsylvania Hall, which was destroyed by a mob in 1838. Mary Grew was able to attend the funeral and to pay tribute to his "fidelity to the Anti-Slavery cause, & to the cause of righteousness generally."[67] I feel that, in your brother's departure," she wrote Elizabeth, "I have lost a tried & true friend. My friends are fast passing beyond my sight. There is comfort in the thought, 'a little while.' "[68]

In April Mary Grew wrote that an attack of laryngitis had left her "quite feeble for a long time; & that was followed by other ailments which keep me on the sofa many hours of the day; (sometimes) while all my plans of active work are disrupted." The little work that she was able to do was chiefly in the cause of woman suffrage. The Philadelphia County society was "very active & earnest. . . . We have more than 500 members, & have sent $100 to Kansas for campaign work." The Pennsylvanians were "encouraged & delighted with the movement in New York city."[69]

In June she went to Providence, Rhode Island, to visit a niece and her family, "doubting my fitness to take the journey. . . . I was not fit for it, & I learned by it that my strength has been much reduced during the last year." She was "scarcely able to move about" for several days after her arrival.[70]

In July she was at Chadd's Ford with the Turners, in the hope of "recruiting some strength in this airy retreat." "My dear Mr. & Mrs. Turner take very good care of me," she wrote Elizabeth Gay. "I wish you were here to see them in their beautiful summer home. Mrs. T. is far from vigorous, but very busy caring for 'The Working-Women's Guild,' in which she seems to live & move & have her being." In August Mary Grew wrote Mrs. Gay that she had had a severe cough. She had been trying to write short letters and turn her eyes from "the formidable pile of unanswered ones." "And now I *must* lie down," she concluded.[71]

In September she reported that she hoped to visit Elizabeth Gay the following month. On 14 September she wrote, "This morning I met my friends, Gen. & Mrs. Saxton, & had a pleasant interview with them."[72] Two days later she announced her decision to run down to Atlantic City for a few days or a week, hoping to rid herself of the remains of the cough that had attended her during the greater part of the summer. "Sea air usually benefits me." She continued by way of justification for the trip, "I want to go to you in as good physical condition as possible."[73] On 28 September she wrote that she had returned from Atlantic City "somewhat stronger. . . . A Convention of Factory Inspectors is in session here; and I must look in on it tomorrow." Mary Grew was deeply concerned about the plight of women working in factories. She thought it was heartrending to hear or read the terrible reports of the inspectors of "the condition of some of our working women, yes, saleswomen or seamstresses employed by the great commercial & manufacturing Institutions of the city." But she was doubtful as to what could be done about it. "I do not see how legislation is to correct the evil." Then she added, as an afterthought, "American slavery was abolished; so we will not despair. . . Don't you, sometimes," she concluded, "wish to live in Howells' Altruria?"[74]

In October she spent two weeks with Elizabeth Gay in New York

City. After returning to Philadelphia, however, she found herself "not well enough to attend the Annual Meeting of our Suffrage Soc'y, on Wednesday eve'g, wh. was a disappointment to me." This was probably the Philadelphia County meeting. She hoped to attend the annual meeting of the state association at West Chester. The special interest in woman suffrage at that time centered around the vote on a constitutional amendment in Kansas. In December she wrote Elizabeth Gay that she had had a serious cold, and then "collapsed from overwork."[75]

Despite recurrent illness, Mary Grew pressed forward with her work for woman's rights. "Our Suffrage Soc'y," she wrote, "is trying to influence the Finance Com. of our City Council to increase appropriations for our Public Schools, in order that women may be paid equally with men for equal service; & also to prevent unjust discrimination on account of sex, in appointments to the best positions." If the municipal committee granted the suffrage society a hearing, she would have to be a member of the society's committee to meet the city officials, "as soon as I shall be well enough to do so. . . . A large amount of time I spend on my sofa."[76]

"If you knew how miserable I am and have been for some time past," Mary Grew wrote to Elizabeth Gay early in 1895, "you would not wonder that I neglect my correspondents." Nevertheless, she made a point of going out frequently, "for if I stay indoors two or three days consecutively, I am more unwell than ever. And there are Meetings & Meetings!" She had just been to a meeting of the Health Protective Society, an offspring of "our Club" devoted to persuading the municipal authorities to do a better job of keeping the city clean. She had not attended the last suffrage meeting, but she understood that a few members had tried to open it to discussion of extraneous issues such as prohibition and the single tax, which she thought would weaken the force of the suffrage movement. "It seems to me," she mused, "that I have lived a very long time on this planet. I wonder how much longer I am to stay."[77]

She spent the summer again with the Turners in Chadd's Ford— "this place of rest and quietness." She had been reading Samuel T. Pickard's biography of Whittier. She did not know that Whittier was "quite so thorough and zealous a politician as he is there revealed." She had found errors in the book. She did not agree with Pickard's treatment of the antislavery schism of 1840 and of the World's Anti-Slavery Convention, particularly on the issue of women's participation. She spoke of the beauties of the Turners' home: "The trees surround us, but are not permitted to keep the sunshine from the house. . . . The wide porches, entwined by thick vines, are nice places to sit in & write, as I am doing now, in one of them, or to lie at rest in a hammock, as I shall do soon."[78]

"The summer has passed very quietly with me, in this beautiful place," she wrote on 25 August, "& I am, probably as well as I should expect to be at nearly 82 years old."[79] She would return to the city in September and then go to Hartford to visit a niece. The state suffrage society would hold a fair in October. Each county society would have one or more tables. However, her days of working for or in fairs had ended with the last antislavery fair, "of blessed memory." She would make a gift of money to this fair and would visit it.

On Monday 12 October 1896, the Philadelphia *Public Ledger* carried the following obituary notice with a portrait:

A FAMOUS ABOLITIONIST

Death of Miss Mary Grew,
a Prominent Anti-Slavery Worker
After Sixty-five Years of Unceasing
Effort in Many Philanthropic Movements
She Passed Away at the Age of 83 Years

She had died on Saturday morning, 10 October, at her residence, 2044 Mount Vernon Street. She had maintained her activity right up to the close of her life. On the previous Wednesday she had attended a meeting of the New Century Guild. On Friday afternoon she had been able to read and to write letters. But she had been showing signs of failing health. Her death was attributed to "old age rather than any particular ailment."[80] The city records give the cause of her death as "General Debility." Her will provided that most of her property would go to her nieces and nephews after her death. The will does not enable one to calculate the extent of her estate.[81]

The funeral service took place on the morning of 13 October at the First Unitarian Church of Philadelphia. At an early hour the church was filled with men and women who had been associated with her or admired her work in the antislavery and woman suffrage crusades. The Reverend Dr. Joseph May conducted the service and paid tribute to her character—"her strength of purpose, unfaltering courage, her aggression toward the wrong and strong defence of the right." The service closed with a prayer and the singing of "Nearer, My God to Thee" by the choir. The floral offerings were "numerous and beautiful." Interment was in Philadelphia's Woodland Cemetery.[82]

John K. Wildman of Bristol, Pennsylvania, who had served with her as an officer of the Pennsylvania Woman Suffrage Association, wrote an obituary tribute for *Woman's Journal*. "One more prominent figure that graced the faithful band of anti-slavery apostles has passed away; one more eminent champion of impartial suffrage has been called to the land of silence. The lips of Mary Grew are sealed; her pen rests." The liberty of the slave and the rights of women had been dear to her heart. "Both claimed her energy, engrossed her vigilance and roused her zeal." From beginning to end, she had been "faithful, energetic, zealous and unceasing. . . . Her lips were eloquent; her pen was ready, diligent and felicitous. She had a gifted mind and a resolute will."[83]

Henry Blackwell also wrote a tribute for the *Woman's Journal:*

One of the most faithful and devoted of the anti-slavery leaders is no more; one of the most earnest and influential woman suffrage workers has passed away. . . . She was a woman quiet and unpretentious, of singular gentleness and simplicity. Calm, candid, earnest and sincere, she enlisted friends, disarmed opponents, and never made a personal enemy. Her New England birth and training, as in the case of Benjamin Franklin, seemed to give her special energy and mental alertness, while the Quaker atmosphere which environed her in later life added an element of judicial deliberation and a certain background of repose.[84]

In Retrospect

MARY Grew might well have said in the famous words of Paul: "I have fought a good fight, I have finished my course, I have kept the faith."[1] For fifty-eight years, despite frequent periods of illness, she devoted her life largely to social reform. From 1834 to 1870 she had poured out her energies in the antislavery movement in Philadelphia. From 1870 to 1892 she had headed the woman suffrage movement in Pennsylvania. She had ample reason to be satisfied with her life as she had lived it. Writing to her in 1893, Emily Howland, one of her protégés and a reformer in her own right, said, "The largess of life is yours dowered with a brain alive to the issues of your time and heart aglow with service for truth, blessed with a friendship [with Margaret Jones Burleigh] as rare as the friend is noble—your joy is all immortal."[2]

Born in Hartford, Connecticut, in 1813, she was the daughter of the Reverend Henry Grew, a Baptist minister who had migrated as a youth from England to New England. He was a man of independent means, and Mary Grew never lacked for the amenities of life and never had to worry about earning her own living. She had the advantages of a first-rate education at Catharine Beecher's Hartford Female Seminary. Throughout her life, she wrote easily and spoke well. Settling with her parents in Philadelphia in 1834, she promptly joined the recently organized Philadelphia Female Anti-Slavery Society, an auxiliary of the American Anti-Slavery Sociedty, the national agency of radical abolitionism. Both of these societies had been founded in 1833.

In 1836 she was chosen corresponding secretary of the Philadelphia women's group, a position she held until it disbanded in 1870. In this capacity she wrote its annual reports, which were published in pamphlet form. They sometimes ran as long as one hundred pages and were, perhaps, Mary Grew's greatest accomplishment. In these reports she reviewed each year the problem of slavery in the United States and chronicled the progress of the antislavery movement, not only in Philadelphia but throughout the North.

Mary Grew also often served as chairwoman or a member of the committee that held the annual Christmas bazaars that were so important in raising money for and publicizing the antislavery movement. Week after week, the women got together and sewed items, many of them adorned with antislavery mottoes, for sale at these fairs. The Philadelphia Female Anti-Slavery Society contributed a large share of the funds that supported the Pennsylvania Anti-Slavery Society, which was established in 1837 and continued until 1870. This organization soon admitted women as well as men, and Mary Grew became active in it, serving for many years on its executive committee. For several years she served as editor of the (Philadelphia) *Pennsylvania Freeman,* the weekly newspaper sponsored by the state society from 1838 to 1854. After the *Freeman* merged with the (New York) *National Anti-Slavery Standard* in 1854, she served as a correspondent for the *Standard,* which was the organ of the American Anti-Slavery Society from 1840 to 1870. Thus she established credentials as a pioneer woman journalist.

The Philadelphia women and the state society bombarded Congress and the legislature in Harrisburg with antislavery petitions, thereby thrusting themselves into politics. This experience served the women well when they fought for their own rights a little later. Mary Grew wrote many of these petitions, went from door to door soliciting signatures for them, and sent them to the state's representatives and senators. The abolitionists called on Congress to abolish slavery in the District of Columbia and other federal territories and to refuse to admit any new slave states. They asked for the prohibition of the interstate slave trade and the repeal of fugitive slave legislation. Congress put a "gag rule" on these petitions, and the abolitionists had to fight for the right of petition itself, an effort in which they were helped in the House of Representatives by former President John Quincy Adams. They petitioned the state legislature to take measures to prevent Pennsylvanians from cooperating in the return of fugitive slaves to the South.

In 1837 Mary Grew attended the first Anti-Slavery Convention of American Women, held in New York City. This was probably the first national convention of women. It was interracial.[3] The second meeting of this group was held in Philadelphia in 1838. There Mary Grew introduced a resolution asking churches to refuse fellowship with slaveholders. This convention sponsored a public meeting devoted to the antislavery cause in Pennsylvania Hall, a handsome new auditorium built with abolitionist contributions. It was attended by blacks as well as whites, women as well as men, and was addressed by William Lloyd Garrison, Lucretia Mott, and Angelina Grimké Weld. Heralded as a "Temple of Freedom," the hall was ransacked and burned to the ground the next evening by a racist and sexist mob, amid cries that it was a "Temple of Amalgamation" (i.e., miscegenation). At that time it was not considered proper for women to address mixed audiences. Mary Grew was one of the hardy band of pioneer women orators.[4] Despite the calamity that had befallen it in Philadelphia in 1838, the Anti-Slavery Convention of American Women again met there in 1839, using building of the Pennsylvania Riding School. Mary Grew again took part. This was the last of the separate female conventions. Elizabeth Cady Stanton thought that these gatherings laid the groundwork for the woman's rights movement.

In 1840 women were given full equality in the American Anti-Slavery Society, including the right to serve as officers. In the same year eight American women were appointed as delegates to the World's Anti-Slavery Convention in London. Mary Grew was selected as a delegate from the Philadelphia Female Anti-Slavery Society. After arrival, she and the other female representatives were denied the right to participate and were asked to observe proceedings from the gallery. The Reverend Henry Grew was among those opposing the seating of women. It was at this time that Elizabeth Cady Stanton and Lucretia Mott became acquainted and resolved to fight for the rights of women when they returned to the United States. In 1848 they organized the Seneca Falls, New York, Convention, which adopted a Women's Declaration of Independence.

Though not present at Seneca Falls, Mary Grew began her direct work for woman's rights in 1848, when she circulated petitions on behalf of a Pennsylvania law to protect the property rights of married women. In later years she worked for legislation to give married women control of their own earnings. The assembly took action to accomplish this in 1872.

In the 1850s, as the sectional conflict intensified, Mary Grew took a keen interest in the fugitive slave issue, writing accounts of several cases involving it. She sponsored petitions to the state legislature to take stronger measures to prevent the return of fugitives. While she had earlier opposed the use of force to free the slaves, she rejoiced in the outbreak of the Civil War, seeing it as a guarantee of abolition. She hailed President Lincoln's Emancipation Proclamation as marking "The Day of Jubilee" and the Thirteenth Amendment as vindicating a generation's worth of abolitionist agitation. She thought the abolitionists could take the lion's share of the credit for the radical change in Northern public opinion on slavery during the period from 1831 to 1865.

Professor Lawrence J. Friedman has referred to the abolitionists as "gregarious saints."[5] They loved to get together in conventions, and they felt they were God's agents. He speaks of "the Boston Clique," led by William Lloyd Garrison, Wendell Phillips, and Maria Weston

Chapman. There was a Philadelphia clique, led by James and Lucretia Mott, Sarah Pugh, Mary Grew, Miller McKim, and Robert Purvis. It was allied with the Boston group. Mary Grew found much of her satisfaction in life from the weekly, monthly, and annual meetings of the Philadelphia Female Anti-Slavery Society and the Pennsylvania Anti-Slavery Society. She was also strongly influenced by religion, though her main interest was in its social rather than its devotional aspects. A guiding principle of her life was the admonition of Paul, "Remember them that are in bonds, as bound with them."[6] Brought up a Baptist, she was influenced by Lucretia Mott and the Hicksite Quakers, and in later life she became a Unitarian. She sometimes preached in liberal pulpits.

The abolitionists claimed credit not only for the freeing of the slaves but also for giving the freedmen civil rights and the suffrage. Mary Grew supported the Civil Rights Bill of 1866 and the protections for blacks in the Fourteenth Amendment. She thought it was especially important that blacks be given the right to vote, and she stood with Wendell Phillips and others who held that the antislavery societies should continue their work until Negro suffrage was guaranteed by the Constitution, as it was thought to be in the Fifteenth Amendment. Mary Grew was an advocate of racial equality. The Philadelphia Female Anti-Slavery Society included black women and took an interest in the welfare of free blacks. Robert Purvis, a black man, played a major role in the Pennsylvania Anti-Slavery Society. Mary Grew served with him on this organization's executive committee. The Philadelphia abolitionists worked for almost ten years to get blacks admitted to the city's streetcars, a goal finally achieved through the passage of state law in 1867.

In 1869 Mary Grew became the president of the newly established Pennsylvania Woman Suffrage Association. Believing that the vote was more desperately needed by black men than white women, she sided with the American Woman Suffrage Association headed by Lucy Stone rather than the more radical National Woman Suffrage Association led by Elizabeth Cady Stanton and Susan B. Anthony. She continued as head of the Pennsylvania group until 1892, when she retired at the age of seventy-nine. She supported this reform on grounds of simple justice rather than on the possibility of its improving the moral tone of politics. It was needed to achieve government by consent of the governed. The highlight of the campaign for woman suffrage in nineteenth-century Pennsylvania was the effort to get it written into the new constitution of 1873, a move which was unsuccessful. Woman suffrage in this state had to wait until the Nineteenth Amendment was added to the federal Constitution in 1920.

Mary Grew was one of the founders of the New Century Club of

Philadelphia, an important early woman's club with broad interests and activities, established in 1877. She devoted much of her later life to its work.

In almost sixty years of effort, Mary Grew had helped achieve freedom for the slaves and civil rights for the freedmen. She had also helped lay the foundation for measures to protect the economic rights of women and for woman suffrage. In both reforms she had greatly enlarged the traditional sphere of women. John Greenleaf Whittier summed up her career in the last two lines of a poetic tribute written in 1871:

> The way to make the world anew
> Is just to grow—as Mary Grew![7]

Notes

Preface

1. The fullest treatment of this subject is in Blanche Glassman Hersh, *The Slavery of Sex: Feminist-Abolitionists in America* (Urbana: University of Illinois Press, 1978), which includes a list of fifty-one women who were both abolitionists and feminists. However, the text has only one incidental reference to Mary Grew. Also useful on this relationship is Keith E. Melder, *Beginnings of Sisterhood: The American Woman's Rights Movement, 1800–1850* (New York: Schocken Books, 1977), 56–76.

2. There are two modern biographies: Margaret Hope Bacon, *Valiant Friend: The Life of Lucretia Mott* (New York: Walker and Co., 1980); and Otelia Cromwell, *Lucretia Mott* (Cambridge: Harvard University Press, 1958).

3. A brief sketch of her life by Ira V. Brown was published in Edward T. James, Janet Wilson James, and Paul S. Boyer, eds., *Notable American Women, 1607–1950*, 3 vols. (Cambridge: Harvard University Press, Belknap Press, 1971), 2:91–92.

Chapter 1. An Antislavery Apprenticeship (1813–1840)

1. Theodore A. Bingham, comp. *Genealogy of the Bingham Family in the United States* (Harrisburg, Pa.: Harrisburg Publishing Co., 1898), 220.

2. Francis Jackson Garrison, *Ann Phillips, Wife of Wendell Phillips: A Memorial Sketch* (Boston: Privately printed, 1886), 3.

3. *Centennial Memorial of the First Baptist Church of Hartford, Connecticut* (Hartford: Privately printed, 1890), 192–94.

4. William G. McLoughlin, *New England Dissent, 1630–1833: The Baptists and the Separation of Church and State*, 2 vols., (Cambridge: Harvard University Press, 1971), 2:1013–15.

5. Henry Grew to Wendell and Ann Phillips, 15 November 1843, in Crawford Blagden Collection, Houghton Library, Harvard University. This collection, comprising approximately seven thousand pieces, chiefly letters written to Wendell Phillips, was given to Harvard in 1978. It includes sixty-seven letters written from Mary Grew to Wendell and Ann Phillips.

6. A copy of Henry Grew's will, dated 19 January 1861, was supplied to the author by John E. Walsh, Jr., register of wills for the County of Philadelphia, on 17 August 1961.

7. Bingham, *Genealogy*, 219–20.

8. On this school see Mae Elizabeth Harveson, *Catharine Esther Beecher: Pioneer Educator* (Philadelphia: Privately printed, 1932), 34–62; and Kathryn Kish Sklar, *Catharine Beecher: A Study in American Domesticity* (New Haven: Yale University Press, 1973), 59–101.

9. Records of the Hartford Female Seminary, Connecticut Historical Society, Hartford. Information kindly supplied by staff of the society.

10. Sklar, *Catharine Beecher*, 72.

11. Ibid., 101. See also Catharine Esther Beecher, *Suggestions Respecting Improvements in Education, Presented to the Trustees of the Hartford Female Seminary and Published at Their Request* (Hartford, Conn.: Packard and Butler, 1829). Bound with this essay is the *Catalogue of the Officers, Teachers, and Pupils of the Hartford Female Seminary for the Two Terms of 1829*. Both of these items are available in the microfilm *History of Women* (New Haven, Conn.: Research Publications, Inc., 1975), reel 126, no. 820.

12. Sklar, *Catharine Beecher*, 76.

13. Obituary, *Philadelphia Public Ledger*, 12 October 1896, 3.

14. Walter M. Merrill, ed., *The Letters of William Lloyd Garrison*, vol. 1, *I Will Be Heard: 1822–1835* (Cambridge: Harvard University Press, Belknap Press, 1971), 291–92.

15. Philadelphia Female Anti-Slavery Society, Minute Book, 1833–38), 14 December 1833, Historical Society of Pennsylvania. Standard histories of the antislavery movement include Dwight Lowell Dumond, *Antislavery: The Crusade for Freedom in America* (Ann Arbor: University of Michigan Press, 1961); and Louis Filler, *Crusade against Slavery: Friends, Foes, and Reforms, 1820–1860* (Algonac, Mich.: Reference Publications, 1986), originally written for the *New American Nation Series* (New York: Harper and Brothers, 1960). There are good shorter histories of abolitionism by Merton L. Dillon, Gerald Sorin, James Brewer Stewart, and Ronald G. Walters. The standard history of female abolitionism is Alma Lutz, *Crusade for Freedom: Women of the Antislavery Movement* (Boston: Beacon Press, 1968). On the Pennsylvania women see Ira V. Brown, "Cradle of Feminism: The Philadelphia Female Anti-Slavery Society, 1833–1840," *Pennsylvania Magazine of History and Biography* 102 (April 1978): 143–66.

16. Minute Book of the Philadelphia Female Anti-Slavery Society, 14 December 1833.

17. Board of Managers of the Philadelphia Female Anti-Slavery Society, Minute Book, 1833–36), 1 December 1834; 2 April 1836; 7 May 1835, Historical Society of Pennsylvania.

18. "Third Annual Report of the Philadelphia Female Anti-Slavery Society," 12 January 1837, in Minute Book, 1833–38).

19. *Fourth Annual Report of the Philadelphia Female Anti-Slavery Society, January 11, 1838* (Philadelphia: Printed by Merrihew and Gunn, 1838), 6.

20. Samuel McKean to Mary Grew, 26 January 1836, in correspondence of the Philadelphia Female Anti-Slavery Society, Historical Society of Pennsylvania.

21. James Harper to Mary Grew, 15 February 1836, ibid.

22. Samuel Flagg Bemis, *John Quincy Adams and the Union* (New York: Alfred A. Knopf, 1956), 337, 340.

23. Philadelphia Female Anti-Slavery Society, *Address of the Female Anti-Slavery Society of Philadelphia, to the Women of Pennsylvania, with the Form of a Petition to the Congress of the U. States* (Philadelphia: Merrihew and Gunn, Printers, 1836), 1–8.

24. Jean Fagan Yellin, *Women and Sisters: The Antislavery Feminists in American Culture* (New Haven: Yale University Press, 1989), esp. chap. 1.

25. Mary Grew to Maria Weston Chapman, 9 September 1836, Antislavery Collection, Boston Public Library.

26. Printed in the *National Enquirer, and Constitutional Advocate of Universal Liberty* (Phiadelphia), 18 February 1837.

27. Ibid., 25 February 1837.

28. *Proceedings of the Anti-Slavery Convention of American Women, Held in the City*

of New-York, May 9th, 10th, 11th, and 12th, 1837 (New York: Printed by William S. Dorr, 1837), 3–16.

29. Ibid., 9. On Sarah and Angelina Grimké, see Gerda Lerner, *The Grimké Sisters from South Carolina: Rebels against Slavery* (Boston: Houghton Mifflin Co., 1967).

30. Philadelphia Female Anti-Slavery Society, Minute Book, 1833–38), 18 May 1837.

31. Ibid., 14 June 1837.

32. Minute Book of the Philadelphia Female Anti-Slavery Society, 1833–38), 12 October 1837.

33. Gerda Lerner, *The Majority Finds Its Past: Placing Women in History* (New York: Oxford University Press, 1979), 120, 128. Hundreds of antislavery petitions are preserved in the National Archives.

34. *Fourth Annual Report,* 6.

35. Ibid., 4.

36. Ibid., 8–9.

37. Minute Book of the Philadelphia Female Anti-Slavery Society (1833–38), 14 December 1837.

38. *National Enquirer,* 22 February 1838.

39. *History of Pennsylvania Hall, Which Was Destroyed by a Mob, on the 17th of May, 1838* (Philadelphia: Merrihew and Gunn, Printers, 1838), 5. This work is attributed to Samuel Webb. See also William F. Lloyd, "The Roots of Fear: A History of Pennsylvania Hall," M.A. thesis, Pennsylvania State University, 1963.

40. Board of Managers of the Pennsylvania Hall Association, Minute Book, 13 March 1837, Historical Society of Pennsylvania.

41. *History of Pennsylvania Hall,* 3.

42. *Proceedings of the Anti-Slavery Convention of American Women, Held in Philadelphia, May 15th, 16th, 17th, and 18th, 1838* (Philadelphia: Printed by Merrihew and Gunn, 1838), 5.

43. [Laura H. Lovell], *Report of a Delegate to the Anti-Slavery Convention of American Women, Held in Philadelphia, May, 1838* (Boston: I. Knapp, 1838), 9–10.

44. See Ira V. Brown, "Racism and Sexism: The Case of Pennsylvania Hall," *Phylon* 37 (June 1976): 126–36.

45. Lorman Ratner, *Powder Keg: Northern Opposition to the Antislavery Movement, 1831–1840* (New York: Basic Books, 1968), 82–83.

46. Quoted in *History of Pennsylvania Hall,* 170.

47. Quoted in the *Liberator,* 25 May 1838.

48. *Proceedings* (1838), 8.

49. Ibid., 10.

50. Philadelphia Female Anti-Slavery Society Minute Book, 1838–39, 14 June 1838.

51. *Fifth Annual Report of the Philadelphia Female Anti-Slavery Society, January 10, 1839* (Philadelphia: Merrihew and Thompson, Printers, 1839), 7.

52. Mary Grew to Anne Warren Weston, 25 December 1838, Weston Papers, Boston Public Library.

53. *Proceedings of the Third Anti-Slavery Convention of American Women, Held in Philadelphia, May 1st, 2d, and 3d, 1839* (Philadelphia: Printed by Merrihew and Thompson, 1839), 3–4, 13. On these three national conventions of antislavery women see Ira V. Brown, "'Am I Not a Woman and a Sister?': The Anti-Slavery Convention of American Women, 1837–1839," *Pennsylvania History* 50 (January 1983): 1–19.

54. Elizabeth Cady Stanton, Susan B. Anthony, and Matilda Joslyn Gage, eds.,

History of Woman Suffrage, vol. 1, *1848–1861* (1881–1922; reprint, New York: Arno Press, 1969), 342.

55. Melder, *Beginnings of Sisterhood,* 107.

56. *Sixth Annual Report of the Philadelphia Female Anti-Slavery Society, January 9, 1840* (Philadelphia: Merrihew and Thompson, Printers, 1840), 10, 16.

57. Ibid., 15.

58. Philaelphia Female Anti-Slavery Society, Minute Book, 1830–44), 10 October 1839, 14 October 1841; Ruth K. Nuermberger, *The Free Produce Movement: A Quaker Protest against Slavery* (Durham, N.C.: Duke University Press, 1942), 26.

59. *Sixth Annual Report,* 11.

60. Ibid., 18.

61. *Sixth Annual Report of the Executive Committee of the American Anti-Slavery Society* (New York: William S. Dorr, 1839), 28.

62. *Liberator* (Boston), 22 May 1840, 82.

63. Walter M. Merrill, *Against Wind and Tide: A Biography of William Lloyd Garrison* (Cambridge: Harvard University Press, 1963), 159. See also Aileen S. Kraditor, *Means and Ends in American Abolitionism: Garrison and His Critics on Strategy and Tactics, 1834–1850* (New York: Vintage Books, 1970).

64. William Cohen, "The Pennsylvania Anti-Slavery Society," M.A. thesis, Columbia University, 1960, pp. 30, 32. Also very useful is the same author's Ph.D. thesis, "James Miller McKim: Pennsylvania Abolitionist," New York, University, 1968. For a briefer account see Ira V. Brown, "Miller McKim and Pennsylvania Abolitionism," *Pennsylvania History* 30 (January 1963): 56–72.

65. *Seventh Annual Report of the Philadelphia Female Anti-Slavery Society. January 14, 1841.* (Philadelphia: Merrihew and Thompson, Printers, 1841), 16–17.

66. Douglas H. Maynard, "The World's Anti-Slavery Convention of 1840," *Mississippi Valley Historical Review* 47 (December 1960): 56.

67. British and Foreign Anti-Slavery Society, *Invitation to the London General Conference to Commence on June 12, 1840* (London, 1839?), 2.

68. Howard Temperley, *British Antislavery, 1833–1870* (Columbia: University of South Carolina Press, 1972), 87.

69. Maynard, "World's Anti-Slavery Convention," 456–57.

70. Frederick B. Tolles, ed., *Slavery and "The Woman Question": Lucretia Mott's Diary of Her Visit to Great Britain to Attend the World's Anti-Slavery Convention of 1840,* supplement no. 23 to the *Journal of the Friends' Historical Society* (London, 1952), 13.

71. Ibid., 14.

72. Mary Grew's Diary, 7 May 1840, 1. Typewritten copy supplied by the Schlesinger Library, Radcliffe College.

73. Ibid., 19 May 1840, 5.

74. Ibid., 26 May 1840, 7.

75. Ibid., 27 May 1840, 7.

76. Ibid., 28 May 1840, 8.

77. Ibid., 9, 11.

78. Ibid., 31 May 1840, 12, 13.

79. Ibid., 13.

80. Ibid., 13–14.

81. Ibid., 12 June 1840, 27.

82. Ibid.

83. Tolles, *Slavery and "The Woman Question,"* 21–22.

84. Ibid., 23–23.

85. Ibid., 28.
86. Mary Grew's Diary, 15 June 1840, 31–32.
87. Garrison, *Ann Phillips*, 7.
88. *Proceedings of the General Anti-Slavery Convention, Called by the Committee of the British and Foreign Anti-Slavery Society, and Held in London from Friday, June 12th, to Tuesday, June 23rd, 1840* (London, 1841), 23.
89. Ibid., 27.
90. Ibid., 35–36.
91. Ibid., 45.
92. Wendell Phillips Garrison and Francis Jackson Garrison, *William Lloyd Garrison, 1805–1879: The Story of His Life Told by His Children* 4 vols. (1885–89; reprint, New York: Negro Universities Press, 1969), 2:373–74.
93. Betty Fladeland, *Men and Brothers: Anglo-American Antislavery Cooperation* (Urbana: University of Illinois Press, 1972), 265.
94. Mary Grew's Diary, 16 June 1840, 33.
95. Stanton, Anthony, and Gage, *History of Woman Suffrage* 1:420–21. See also Elizabeth Cady Stanton, *Eighty Years and More: Reminiscences, 1815–1897* (reprint ed., New York: Shocken Books, 1971), 82–83.
96. Mary Grew's Diary, 23 June 1840, 38.
97. Ibid., 28 July 1840, 58.
98. Ibid., 12 Sept. 1840, 77.

Chapter 2. Broadening Fields of Service (1840–1850)

1. *Seventh Annual Report*, 9.
2. Ibid., 10–11.
3. *National Enquirer*, 11 February 1837, 86.
4. Ibid., 87.
5. Ibid., 18 February 1837, 87, 89.
6. Cohen, "Pennsylvania Anti-Slavery Society," is a very good piece of work.
7. Philadelphia Female Anti-Slavery Society, Minute Book, 1839–44), 8 April 1841.
8. *Pennsylvania Freeman* (Philadelphia), 12 May 1841. "Report of Fourth Annual Meeting of the Anti-Slavery Society of Eastern Pennsylvania." Pages not numbered. This was the organ of the Pennsylvania Anti-Slavery Society from 1838 to 1854. It represented a continuation of Benjamin Lundy's *National Enquirer* under a new name.
9. Ibid.
10. Ibid.
11. Ibid.
12. See above, p. 19.
13. Philadelphia Female Anti-Slavery Society, Minute Book, 1839–44, 3 May 1841.
14.. Ibid., 10 June 1841.
15. Ibid.
16. Joseph A. Boromé, "The Vigilant Committee of Philadelphia," *Pennsylvania Magazine of History and Biography* 92 (July 1968): 320–351. See also Larry Gara, *Liberty Line: The Legend of the Underground Railroad* (Lexington: University of Kentucky Press, 1961).

17. Philadelphia Female Anti-Slavery Society, Minute Book, 1839–44, 19 April 1842.

18. Ibid., 8 September 1842, 13 October 1842.

19. Ibid., 9 February 1843.

20. Ibid., 8 December 1842.

21. Henry Grew to Wendell and Ann Phillips, 15 November 1843, Crawford Blagden Collection.

22. Mary Grew to Wendell and Ann Phillips, 15 November 1843, ibid.

23. See Julie Winch, *Philadelphia's Black Elite: Activism, Accommodation, and the Struggle for Autonomy, 1787–1848* (Philadelphia: Temple University Press, 1988).

24. *National Anti-Slavery Standard* (New York), 14 December 1843, 110.

25. Ibid., 110–11.

26. Ibid., 111.

27. Ibid.

28. Mary Grew to Wendell and Ann Phillips, 14 December 1843, Crawford Blagden Collection.

29. *National Anti-Slavery Standard,* 22 August 1844.

30. Ibid. Charles Dexter Cleveland, principal of a female academy in Philadelphia, had taught classics at Dickinson College and New York University. He was the compiler of several literary "compendiums."

31. *Pennsylvania Freeman,* 22 August 1844.

32. *Eleventh Annual Report of the Philadelphia Female Anti-Slavery Society, January 9, 1845* (Philadelphia: Merrihew and Thompson, Printers, 1845), 7.

33. Ibid., 6.

34. Sister M. Theophane Geary, *A History of Third Parties in Pennsylvania, 1840–1860* (Washington, D.C.: Catholic University of America, 1938), 43, 110.

35. Mary Grew to Wendell Phillips, 24 November 1844, Crawford Blagden Collection.

36. *Eleventh Annual Report,* 4.

37. Ibid., 11–12.

38. *Pennsylvania Freeman,* 28 August 1845.

39. Ibid., 9 October 1845; 6 November 1845.

40. C. D. Cleveland, Samuel Porter, and T. S. Cavender to Edward M. Davis, Mary Grew, and James Miller McKim, 30 November 1845, Edward M. Davis Papers, Houghton Library, Harvard University.

41. Henry Grew to Wendell Phillips, 29 July 1845, ibid.

42. Mary Grew to Elizabeth Neall Gay, 7 November 1845, Sydney Howard Gay Collection, Columbia University.

43. *National Enquirer,* 8 March 1838.

44. The history of this paper has been carefully traced in Robert Stephen Hochreiter, "The *Pennsylvania Freeman,* 1836–1854," Ph.D. thesis, Pennsylvania State University, 1980.

45. Edward M. Davis to Maria Weston Chapman, 21 November 1845, Weston Papers, Boston Public Library.

46. Mary Grew to Wendell Phillips, 12 May 1847, Crawford Blagden Collection. See A. John Alexander, "The Ideas of Lysander Spooner," *New England Quarterly* 23 (June 1950): 204–7.

47. Hochreiter, *Pennsylvania Freman,*" 197–98.

48. Ibid., 199–200.

49. Ibid., 200.

50. Ibid., 191–92.

51. Mary Grew to James Miller McKim, 29 May 1846, printed in the *Pennsylvania Freeman*, 4 June 1846.

52. Mary Grew to James Miller McKim, 10 June 1846, printed in the *Pennsylvania Freeman*, 18 June 1846.

53. *Thirteenth Annual Report of the Philadelphia Female Anti-Slavery Society* (Philadelphia: Merrihew and Thompson, 1847), 6.

54. Hochreiter, *"Pennsylvania Freeman,"* 187–89.

55. Mary Grew to Wendell Phillips, 12 May 1847, Crawford Blagden Collection.

56. Rosine Association of Philadelphia, *Reports and Realities from the Sketch-Book of a Manager of the Rosine Association, December, 1855* (Philadephia: J. Duross, Printers, 1855), 7–49. I am indebted to Dr. Lori D. Ginzberg of the Pennsylvania State University for this citation. See her article, "'Moral Suasion Is Moral Balderdash': Women, Politics, and Social Activism in the 1850s," *Journal of American History* 73 (December 1986): 601–22.

57. Hochreiter, *"Pennsylvania Freeman,"* 188–89.

58. Charles W. Dahlinger, "The Dawn of the Woman's Movement: An Account of the Origin and History of the Pennsylvania Married Woman's Property Law of 1848," *Western Pennsylvania Historical Magazine* 1 (1918): 77.

59. Hochreiter, *"Pennsylvania Freeman,"* 207–8.

60. Ibid., 209–10.

61. *Pennsylvania Freeman*, 15 November 1849.

62. Ibid., 22 November 1849.

63. Ibid., 13 December 1849.

64. Ibid., 20 December 1849.

65. Ibid., 7 February 1850.

66. Ibid., 14 February 1850.

67. Ibid., 14 March 1850.

68. Ibid., 21 March 1850.

69. Ibid., 9 May 1850.

Chapter 3. Toward Civil War (1850–1861)

1. *Sixteenth Annual Report of the Philadephia Female Anti-Slavery Society* (Philadelphia: Merrihew and Thompson, Printers, 1850), 3–6.

2. Ibid., 7–10.

3. Ibid., 12.

4. Philadelphia Female Anti-Slavery Society, Minute Book, 1848–62, 14 March 1850.

5. Ibid., 13 June 1850.

6. Mary Grew to Elizabeth Neall Gay, 25 September 1850, Sydney Howard Gay Collection, Columbia University.

7. Executive Committee of the Pennsylvania Anti-Slavery Society, Minute Book, 1846–56, 22 October 1850; 19 November 1850, 26 November 1850, 18 February 1851.

8. Philadelphia Female Anti-Slavery Society, Minute Book, 1848–62, 13 March 1851.

9. Stanley W. Campbell, *The Slave Catchers: Enforcement of the Fugitive Slave Law, 1850–1860* (Chapel Hill: University of North Carolina Press, 1968), 99–100.

10. Mary Grew to Wendell Phillips, 19 May 1851, Crawford Blagden Collection.

11. Mary Grew to Wendell Phillips, 15 October 1851, ibid.

12. A good, brief account of this episode may be found in Roderick W. Nash, "William Parker and the Christiana Riot," *Journal of Negro History* 46 (January 1961): 24–31. For fuller information see William U. Hensel, *The Christiana Riot and the Treason Trials of 1851* (Lancaster, Pa.: New Era Printing Co., 1911).

13. *Pennsylvania Freeman,* 18 September 1851.

14. Albert J. Wahl, "The Pennsylvania Yearly Meeting of Progressive Friends," *Pennsylvania History* 25 (April 1958): 132.

15. *Pennsylvania Freeman,* 18 December 1851.

16. George W. Hart (state representative) and William A. Crabb (state senator) to Mary Grew, 28 February 1852, Correspondence of the Philadelphia Female Anti-Slavery Society, Historical Society of Pennsylvania.

17. Hochreiter, *"Pennsylvania Freeman,"* 228.

18. Mary Grew to Bristol and Clifton Ladies Anti-Slavery Society, October 1852, Gay Collection.

19. Ibid. See also *Nineteenth Annual Report of the Philadelphia Female Anti-Slavery Society* (Philadelphia: Merrihew & Thompson, Printers, 1853), 7–9.

20. *Nineteenth Annual Report,* 5.

21. Executive Committee of the Pennsylvania Anti-Slavery Society, Minute Book, 1846–56, 28 December 1852.

22. Mary Grew to Elizabeth Neall Gay, 16 March 1852, Gay Collection.

23. Mary Grew to Elizabeth Neall Gay, 10 August 1852, ibid.

24. Mary Grew to Sydney Howard Gay, 28 November 1852, ibid.

25. *Nineteenth Annual Report;,* 18–20.

26. Ibid., 17.

27. *Pennsylvania Freeman,* 19 May 1853.

28. Executive Committee of the Pennsylvania Anti-Slavery Society, Minute Book, 1846–56, 22 March 1853.

29. Mary Grew to Elizabeth Neall Gay, 16 June 1853, Gay Collection.

30. Mary Grew to Elizabeth Neall Gay, 3 July 1853, ibid.

31. Mary Grew to Elizabeth Neall Gay, 14 October 1853, ibid.

32. Philadelphia Female Anti-Slavery Society, Minute Book, 1848–62, 10 November 1853.

33. *Proceedings of the American Anti-Slavery Society, at Its Second Decade, Held in the City of Philadelphia, Dec. 3d, 4th, & 5th, 1853* (New York: American Anti-Slavery Society, 1854), 4.

34. Ibid., 147.

35. Ibid., 17.

36. Executive Committee of the Pennsylvania Anti-Slavery Society, Minute Book, 1846–56, 7 February 1854.

37. Philadelphia Female Anti-Slavery Society, Minute Book, 1848–62, 9 February 1854.

38. Pennsylvania Anti-Slavery Society, Minute Book, 1846–56, 21 February 1854.

39. Philadelphia Female Anti-Slavery Society, Minute Book, 1848–62, 11 May 1854.

40. *Pennsylvania Freeman,* 8 June 1854.

41. Mary Grew to Elizabeth Neall Gay, 24 September 1854, Gay Collection.

42. *Twenty-first Annual Report of the Philadelphia Female Anti-Slavery Society* (Philadelphia: Merrihew and Thompson, 1855), 3.

43. Ibid., 4.

44. Ibid., 5, 6.

45. Ibid., 6.
46. Ibid., 7–8.
47. Ibid., 10.
48. Ibid., 15.
49. Ibid., 17–18.
50. Stanton, Anthony, Gage, *History of Woman Suffrage* 1:379–80.
51. Ibid., 380.
52. Ibid., 382.
53. Ibid., 383.
54. Ibid.
55. Ibid.
56. Mary Grew to Sydney and Elizabeth Gay, 13 January 1855, Gay Collection.
57. Executive Committee of the Pennsylvania Anti-Slavery Society, Minute Book, 15 March 1855.
58. Margaret Burleigh and Mary Grew to William Lloyd and Helen Benson Garrison, 5 August 1855, William Lloyd Garrison Correspondence, Boston Public Library.
59. Ralph Lowell Eckert, "Antislavery Martyrdom: The Ordeal of Passmore Williamson," *Pennsylvania Magazine of History and Biography* 100 (October 1976): 521.
60. Ibid., 522–27, 531–32.
61. Executive Committee of the Pennsylvania Anti-Slavery Society, Minutes, 2 October 1855, 23 October 1855.
62. [Mary Grew], *Narrative of Facts in the Case of Passmore Williamson* (Philadelphia: Pennsylvania Anti-Slavery Society, 1855), 21.
63. Ibid., 21–22.
64. Philadelphia Female Anti-Slavery Society, Minute Book, 1848–62, 13 September 1855.
65. Ibid.
66. Ibid. The full text of the resolutions may be found in the *Twenty-Second Annual Report of the Philadelphia Female Anti-Slavery Society* (Philadelphia: Marrihew and Thompson, Printers, 1856), 23–24.
67. Eckert, "Antislavery Martyrdom," 529.
68. [Grew], *Narrative of Facts,* 16.
69. Ibid. See also Larry Gara, "William Still and the Underground Railroad," *Pennsylvania History* 28 (January 1961): 33–44.
70. Eckert, "Antislavery Martyrdom," 531–32.
71. Ibid., 538.
72. Allan Nevins, *Ordeal of the Union,* vol. 2, *A House Dividing, 1852–1857* (New York: Charles Scribner's Sons, 1947): 413–15.
73. *Twenty-Second Annual Report,* 40.
74. Philadelphia Female Anti-Slavery Society, Minute Book, 1848–62, 10 April 1856.
75. Ibid., 12 June 1856.
76. Mary Grew to Charles Sumner, 18 June 1856, Houghton Library, Sumner Papers, Harvard University.
77. Mary Grew to Wendell Phillips, 23 June 1856, Crawford Blagden Collection.
78. Mary Grew to Elizabeth Neall Gay, 11 September 1856, Gay Collection.
79. Mary Grew to Wendell Phillips, 10 September 1856, Crawford Blagden Collection.
80. Mary Grew to Wendell Phillips, 13 November 1856, ibid.

81. Ibid. On Martha Griffith see Walter Merrill and Louis Ruchames, eds., *The Letters of William Lloyd Garrison*, vol. 4, *From Disunionism to the Brink of War, 1850–1860* (Cambridge: Harvard University Press, Belknap Press, 1975): 417. The Griffith book was first published by J. S. Redfield of New York in 1857 (copyright 1856) and was reprinted by the Negro History Press (Detroit) in 1969 and, in a paperbook edition, by Mnemosyne Publishing Co. (Miami), also in 1969. Unfortunately none of these editions contains biographical data on the author or critical comment on the book.

82. Mary Grew to Wendell Phillips, 28 December 1856, Crawford Blagden Collection.

83. *Twenty-Third Annual Report of the Philadelphia Female Anti-Slavery Society* (Philadelphia: Merrihew and Thompson, Printers, 1857), 5–6.

84. Ibid., 12.

85. Ibid., 14.

86. Mary Grew to Wendell Phillips, 27 January 1857, Crawford Blagden Collection.

87. Mary Grew to Wendell and Ann Phillips, 27 April 1857, ibid.

88. William Lloyd Garrison to Helen E. Garrison, 18 May 1857, in Merrill and Ruchames, *Letters of William Lloyd Garrison* 4:441.

89. Mary Grew to Wendell and Ann Phillips, 9 July 1857, Crawford Blagden Collection.

90. Mary Grew to Elizabeth Neall Gay, 31 July 1857, Gay Collection.

91. Mary Grew to Wendell Phillips, 11 September 1857, Crawford Blagden Collection.

92. Mary Grew to Elizabeth Neall Gay, 21 September 1857, Gay Collection.

93. Ibid.

94. Mary Grew to William Lloyd Garrison, 4 October 1857, Garrison Correspondence, Boston Public Library; *National Anti-Slavery Standard*, 31 October 1857.

95. Mary Grew to Elizabeth Neall Gay, 6 December 1857, Gay Collection.

96. Mary Grew to Elizabeth Neall Gay, 10 March 1858, ibid.

97. Lucretia Mott to ?, 16 May 1858, Lucretia Mott Papers, Friends Historical Library, Swarthmore College.

98. Mary Grew to Wendell Phillips, 3 June 1858, Crawford Blagden Collection.

99. Ibid.

100. Ibid.

101. Merrill and Ruchames, *Letters of William Lloyd Garrison* 4:558.

102. Pennsylvania Anti-Slavery Society Executive Committee, Minute Book, 1856–70, 3 November 1858.

103. Cromwell, *Lucretia Mott*, 168.

104. *Twenty-Sixth Annual Report of the Philadelphia Female Anti-Slavery Society* (Philadelphia: Merrihew and Thompson, Printers, 1860), 7.

105. Ibid., 8–9.

106. Mary Grew to Wendell Phillips, 14 October 1859, Crawford Blagden Collection.

107. James M. McPherson, *Ordeal by Fire: The Civil War and Reconstruction* (New York: Alfred A. Knopf, 1982), 115–16.

108. *Philadelphia Public Ledger*, 3 December 1859, 1.

109. *Twenty-Sixth Annual*, 16.

110. Ibid., 13–14.

111. Philadelphia Female Anti-Slavery Society, Minute Book, 1848–62, 16 November 1859.

112. Ibid., 8 December 1859.
113. *Twenty-Seventh Annual Report of the Philadelphia Female Anti-Slavery Society* (Philadelphia: Merrihew and Thompson, Printers, 1861), 17–18.
114. Ibid., 18–19, 25.
115. Ibid., 23.
116. Executive Committee of the Pennsylvania Anti-Slavery Society, Minutes, 18 January 1860.
117. Mary Grew to Wendell Phillips, 14 February 1860, Crawford Blagden Collection.
118. Mary Grew to Wendell Phillips, 20 April 1860, ibid.
119. Stanton, Anthony, and Gage, *History of Woman Suffrage* 1:688–737.
120. Ibid., 737.
121. Mary Grew to Elizabeth Neall Gay, 12 June 1860, Gay Collection.
122. Ibid.
123. Mary Grew to Wendell Phillips, 15 October 1860, Crawford Blagden Collection.
124. Ibid.
125. Ibid.
126. Mary Grew to Wendell Phillips, 23 October 1860, Crawford Blagden Collection.
127. Mary Grew to Wendell Phillips, 2 December 1860, Crawford Blagden Collection.
128. Mary Grew to Ann Phillips, 18 December 1860, ibid.
129. *Twenty-Seventh Annual Report,* 11, 23.
130. Ibid., 3, 5, 11, 20, 22.

Chapter 4. "The Day of Jubilee" (1861–1865)

1. Executive Committee of the Pennsylvania Anti-Slavery Society, 1856–70, 2 January 1861.
2. Philadelphia Female Anti-Slavery Society, Minute Book, 1848–62, 10 January 1861.
3. Mary Grew to Helen Benson Garrison, 13 and 15 January 1861, Garrison Papers.
4. Ibid.
5. Mary Grew to William Lloyd Garrison, 25 January 1861, ibid.
6. Ibid.
7. Mary Grew to Wendell Phillips, 15 March 1861, Crawford Blagden Collection.
8. Giraud Chester, *Embattled Maiden: The Life of Anna Dickinson* (New York: Putnam, 1951), 10–25.
9. Mary Grew to Wendell Phillips, 15 March 1861. Crawford Blagden Collection.
10. Ibid.
11. Mary Grew to Elizabeth Gay, 12 April 1861, Gay Collection.
12. Executive Committee of the Pennsylvania Anti-Slavery Society, Minute Book, 1856–70, 17 April 1861.
13. Philadelphia Female Anti-Slavery Society, 1848–62, 13 June 1861.
14. William Lloyd Garrison to James Miller McKim, 11 September 1858, in

Merrill and Ruchames, *Letters of William Lloyd Garrison*, vol. 4, *From Disunionism to the Brink of War, 1850–1860,* 553.

15. Mary Grew to William Lloyd and Helen E. Garrison, 12 April 1861, Garrison Papers.

16. Mary Grew to William Lloyd Garrison, Jr., 9 August 1861, Sophia Smith Collection, Smith College.

17. Philadelphia Female Anti-Slavery Society, Minute Book, 1848–62, 12 September 1861.

18. *National Anti-Slavery Standard,* 2 November 1861.

19. William Lloyd Garrison to Helen E. Garrison, 29 October 1861, in Merrill and Ruchames, *Letters of William Lloyd Garrison,* vol. 5, *Let the Oppressed Go Free, 1861–1867,* 43.

20. *National Anti-Slavery Standard,* 5 October 1861.

21. Philadelphia Female Anti-Slavery Society, Minutes, 1848–62, 14 November 1861.

22. *Twenty-Eighth Annual Report of the Philadelphia Female Anti-Slavery Society* (Philadelphia: Merrihew and Thompson, Printers, 1862), 21, 22.

23. Mary Grew to Sydney Howard Gay, 22 December 1861, Gay Collection.

24. *Twenty-Eighth Annual Report,* 23.

25. Ibid., 3.

26. Ibid., 7–8.

27. Ibid., 10.

28. Ibid., 11.

29. Ibid.

30. Ibid., 12.

31. Ibid., 15.

32. Ibid., 17.

33. Ibid., 18–20.

34. Philadelphia Female Anti-Slavery Society, Minute Book, 1848–62, 9 January 1862.

35. Ibid., 13 February 1862.

36. Mary Grew to Wendell Phillips, 21 January 1862, Crawford Blagden Collection.

37. Philadelphia Female Anti-Slavery Society, Minute Book, 1848–62, 13 March 1862.

38. Ibid., 8 May 1862.

39. Ibid., 12 June 1862.

40. Executive Committee of the Pennsylvania Anti-Slavery Society, Minute Book, 1856–70, 12 and 19 February 1862.

41. Ibid., 5 March 1862.

42. Ibid., 12 March 1862. On this phase of freedman's aid work see Willie Lee Rose, *Rehearsal for Reconstruction: The Port Royal Experiment* (Indianapolis, Ind.: Bobbs-Merrill, 1964).

43. Mary Grew to Elizabeth Neall Gay, undated but, from the context, early summer 1862, Gay Collection. The Columbia staff has misdated it as 1864.

44. Ibid.

45. William Lloyd Garrison to Helen E. Garrison, 10 June 1862, in Merrill and Ruchames, eds., *The Letters of William Lloyd Garrison* 5:95.

46. *Philadelphia Public Ledger,* 11 August 1862.

47. *National Anti-Slavery Standard,* 16 August 1962.

48. Ibid.

49. *Liberator* (Boston), 15 August 1862.

50. Copy of Henry Grew's will supplied to the author by the office of the Register of Wills, Philadelphia County, 17 August 1961.

51. Philadelphia Female Anti-Slavery Society, Minute Book, 1862–67, 11 September 1862.

52. Mary Grew to William Lloyd Garrison, 2 October 1862, Garrison Papers.

53. Ibid.

54. Philadelphia Female Anti-Slavery Society, Minute Book, 1862–67, 9 October 1862.

55. Ibid.

56. Ibid., 8 January 1863. For the history and significance of this famous document see John Hope Franklin, *The Emancipation Proclamation* (Garden City, N.Y.: Doubleday, 1963).

57. Ibid.

58. *Twenty-Ninth Annual Report of the Philadelphia Female Anti-Slavery Society* (Philadelphia: Merrihew and Thompson, Printers, 1863), 3–4.

59. Ibid., 4–13.

60. Ibid., 24.

61. Philadelphia Female Anti-Slavery Society, Minutes, 1862–67, 12 February 1863.

62. Mary Grew to Elizabeth Neall Gay, 24 May 1863, Gay Collection.

63. Ibid.

64. Mary Grew to Elizabeth Neall Gay, 17 January 1864, Gay Collection.

65. Mary Grew to Wendell Phillips, 7 November 1863, Crawford Blagden Collection. See Alexander V. G. Allen, *Life and Letters of Phillips Brooks,* 2 vols. (New York: E. P. Dutton and Co., 1900), 1 : 330–597 on his years in Philadelphia.

66. Merrill and Ruchames, *Letters of William Lloyd Garrison* 5 : 175.

67. *Proceedings of the American Anti-Slavery Society at Its Third Decade, Held in the City of Philadelphia, Dec. 3d and 4th, 1863* (New York: American Anti-Slavery Society, 1864), 41.

68. Ibid., 124–28. Mary Grew's address appears at the end of the *Proceedings,* but a footnote indicated it had been given earlier. Perhaps she was late in supplying copy for the printer.

69. Ibid., 128–30.

70. *Thirtieth Annual Report of the Philadelphia Female Anti-Slavery Society* (Philadelphia: Merrihew and Thompson Printers, 1864), 4, 5.

71. Ibid., 5–6.

72. Ibid., 6.

73. Ibid., 10.

74. Ibid., 13.

75. Ibid., 17.

76. Ibid.

77. Ibid., 24.

78. Ibid., 27.

79. Ibid., 29.

80. Executive Committee of the Pennsylvania Anti-Slavery Society, Minutes, (1856–70), 1 January 1864.

81. Mary Grew to Elizabeth Neall Gay, 17 January 1864, Gay Collection.

82. Ibid.

83. Mary Grew to William Lloyd Garrison, 24 February 1864, Garrison Papers.

84. Mary Grew to William Lloyd Garrison, Jr., 28 February 1864, Sophia Smith

Collection.

85. Mary Grew to William Lloyd Garrison, Jr., 1 May 1864, ibid.

86. Mary Grew to Samuel May, Jr., 31 March 1864, Garrison Papers, quoted in James M. McPherson, *The Struggle for Equality: Abolitionists and the Negro in the Civil War and Reconstruction* (Princeton, N.J.: Princeton University Press, 1964), 267.

87. Mary Grew to Wendell Phillips, 22 April 1864, Crawford Blagden Collection.

88. William Lloyd Garrison to Helen E. Garrison, 13 May 1864, in Merrill and Ruchames, *Letters of William Lloyd Garrison* 5 : 204.

89. Executive Committee of the Pennsylvania Anti-Slavery Society, Minutes, 1856–70, 1 June 1864.

90. Mary Grew to Elizabeth Neall Gay, 9 August 1864, Gay Collection.

91. Ibid.

92. Mary Grew to Wendell Phillips Garrison, 3 August 1864, Houghton Library, Harvard University.

93. Mary Grew to Wendell Phillips, 12 October 1864, Crawford Blagden Collection.

94. *National Anti-Slavery Standard,* 19 November 1864.

95. Lucretia Mott to Martha Coffin Wright, 14 November 1864, in Anna Davis Hallowell, *James and Lucretia Mott: Life and Letters* (Boston: Houghton, Mifflin and Co., 1884), 412.

96. Philadelphia Female Anti-Slavery Society, Minute Book, 1862–67, 8 December 1864, 9 February 1865.

97. Mary Grew to Susan Grew, 1 February 1865, Houghton Library, Harvard University.

98. Mary Grew to William Lloyd Garrison, 1 February 1865, Garrison Papers.

99. *Thirty-First Annual Report of the Philadelphia Female Anti-Slavery Society February, 1865* (Philadelphia: Merrihew and Son, Printers, 1865), 10.

100. Ibid., 11–15.

101. Ibid., 22.

102. Ibid., 27.

103. Ibid., 29.

Chapter 5. Battling for Negro Suffrage (1865–1867)

1. Executive Committee of the Pennsylvania Anti-Slavery Society, Minutes, 1856–70, 1 March 1865.

2. Ibid., 26 April 1865.

3. Philadelphia Female Anti-Slavery Society, Minutes, 1862–67, 13 April 1865.

4. Ibid.

5. Mary Grew to Samuel May, Jr., 29 April 1865, Sophia Smith Collection.

6. McPherson, *Struggle for Equality,* 304–5.

7. Mary Grew to Wendell Phillips, 24 July 1865, Crawford Blagden Collection.

8. Mary Grew to Elizabeth Neall Gay, 28 July 1865, Gay Collection.

9. Mary Grew to William Lloyd Garrison, 6 August 1865, Garrison Papers.

10. Mary Grew to Elizabeth Neall Gay, 28 July 1865, Gay Collection.

11. Ibid.

12. Mary Grew to Wendell Phillips, 24 July 1865, Crawford Blagden Collection.

13. Philadelphia Female Anti-Slavery Society, Minutes, 1862–67, 14 September 1865.

14. *National Anti-Slavery Standard,* 4 November 1865.

15. Ibid.

16. Ibid., 11 November 1865.

17. Ibid.

18. Ibid., 4 November 1865.

19. Ibid., 11 November 1865.

20. Mary Grew to Ann Phillips, 7 November 1865, Crawford Blagden Collection.

21. Executive Committee of the Pennsylvania Anti-Slavery Society, Minute Book, 1856–70, 30 November 1865.

22. Mary Grew to Susan Grew, 19 December 1865, Houghton Library, Harvard University.

23. Ibid.

24. Ibid.

25. Ibid.

26. Ibid.

27. Ibid.

28. Executive Committee of the Pennsylvania Anti-Slavery Society, Minutes, 1856–70, 27 December 1865.

29. Ibid., 3 January 1866.

30. *Thirty-Second Annual Report of the Philadelphia Female Anti-Slavery Society* (Philadelphia: Merrihew and Son, Printers, 1866), 3.

31. Ibid., 4–7.

32. Ibid., 8.

33. Ibid., 15.

34. Ibid., 16.

35. Ibid., 23.

36. Ibid., 24.

37. Ibid., 25.

38. Ibid., 25–26.

39. Mary Grew to Wendell and Ann Phillips, 4 January 1866, Crawford Blagden Collection.

40. Ibid.

41. Ibid.

42. Ibid.

43. Philadelphia Female Anti-Slavery Society, Minutes, 1862–67, 11 January 1866.

44. Mary Grew to Elizabeth Neall Gay, 17 January 1866, Gay Collection.

45. Philadelphia Female Anti-Slavery Society, Minutes, 1862–67, 12 April 1866. For background see Eric Foner, *Reconstruction: America's Unfinished Revolution, 1863–1877* (New York: Harper and Row, 1988).

46. Mary Grew to Ann Phillips, 4 May 1866, Crawford Blagden Collection.

47. McPherson, *Ordeal by Fire,* 395, 508. For detailed information on Saxton's work, see Rose, *Rehearsal for Reconstruction.*

48. Mary Grew to Ann Phillips, 4 May 1866, Crawford Blagden Collection.

49. *National Anti-Slavery Standard,* 19 May 1866.

50. Ibid.

51. Ibid.

52. Ibid., 26 May 1866.

53. Ibid.

54. Mary Grew to Wendell Phillips, 7 June 1866, Crawford Blagden Collection.

55. Ibid.

56. Ibid.
57. Ibid.
58. Ibid.
59. Mary Grew to Edward M. Davis, 7 June 1866, Edward M. Davis Papers, Houghton Library, Harvard University.
60. Mary Grew to Mrs. Aaron M. Powell, 6 August 1866, Houghton Library, Harvard University.
61. *National Anti-Slavery Standard,* 18 August 1866.
62. Ibid., 25 August 1866.
63. Philadelphia Female Anti-Slavery Society, Minutes, 1862–67, 13 September 1866, 11 October 1866, 12 December 1866, and 14 February 1867.
64. Executive Committee of the Pennsylvania Anti-Slavery Society, Minutes, 1856–70, 11 October 1866, 31 October 1866.
65. Ibid., 5 December 1866.
66. *National Anti-Slavery Standard,* 1 December 1866.
67. Philadelphia Female Anti-Slavery Society, Minutes, 1862–67, 13 December 1866.
68. Ibid., 14 February 1867.
69. *Thirty-Third Annual Report of the Philadelphia Female Anti-Slavery Society* (Philadelphia: Merrihew and Son, Printers, 1867), 4.
70. Ibid., 7.
71. Ibid., 13.
72. Ibid., 14.
73. Ibid., 16.
74. Ibid., 16–17.
75. Ibid., 17.
76. Ibid., 19.
77. Ibid., 21.
78. Ibid., 22.
79. Ibid., 27, 28. On Furness, see Elizabeth M. Geffen, "William Henry Furness: Philadelphia Antislavery Preacher," *Pennsylvania Magazine of History and Biography* 82 (July 1958): 259–92.
80. *Thirty-Third Annual Report,* 29–30.

Chapter 6. Dissolving the Antislavery Societies (1867–1870)

1. *Thirty-third Annual Report of the Philadelphia Female Anti-Slavery Society* (Philadelphia: Merrihew and Son, Printers, 1867), 31.
2. Ibid., 32.
3. Ibid.
4. Mary Grew to Wendell Phillips, 22 January 1867, Crawford Blagden Collection.
5. Philadelphia Female Anti-Slavery Society, Minutes, 1862–67, 14 February 1867.
6. Executive Committee of the Pennsylvania Anti-Slavery Society, Minutes, 1856–70, 27 February 1867.
7. Philadelphia Female Anti-Slavery Society, Minutes, 1862–67, 14 March

1867; Executive Committee of the Pennsylvania Anti-Slavery Society, Minutes, 1856–70, 26 June 1867, 25 September 1867.

8. Mary Grew to Wendell Phillips, 23 July 1867, Crawford Blagden Collection.

9. Ibid.

10. Ibid.

11. Ibid.

12. *National Anti-Slavery Standard*, 16 November 1867.

13. Ibid.

14. Mary Grew to Ann Phillips, 21 November 1867, Crawford Blagden Collection.

15. Margaret Burleigh to Ann Phillips, ibid.

16. *Thirty-Fourth Annual Report of the Philadelphia Female Anti-Slavery Society* (Philadelphia Female Anti-Slavery Society (Philadelphia: Merrihew and Son, Printers, 1868), 3.

17. Ibid., 4.

18. Ibid., 5–7.

19. Ibid., 12. See Ira V. Brown, "William D. Kelley and Radical Reconstruction," *Pennsylvania Magazine of History and Biography* 85 (July 1961): 316–29, esp. 325–26.

20. *Thirty-fourth Annual Report*, 8–25.

21. Ibid., 26–29. See Joseph B. James, *The Framing of the Fourteenth Amendment* (Urbana: University of Illinois Press, 1956).

22. *Thirty-fourth Annual Report*, 29.

23. Ibid., 31–32.

24. *Memorial of Sarah Pugh: A Tribute of Respect from Her Cousins* (Philadelphia: J. B. Lippincott Co., 1888), 116.

25. Hallowell, *James and Lucretia Mott*, 433–35. Dr. William H. Furness and Robert Purvis also spoke at the funeral.

26. Executive Committee of the Pennsylvania Anti-Slavery Society, Minutes, 1856–70, 3 February 1868, 18 February 1868.

27. Philadelphia Female Anti-Slavery Society, Minutes, 1868–70, 12 March 1868.

28. Ibid., 13 February 1868.

29. Mary Grew to Wendell Phillips, 21 January 1868, Crawford Blagden Collection.

30. Mary Grew to Ann Greene Phillips, 3 May 1868, Crawford Blagden Collection.

31. Ibid.

32. Philadelphia Female Anti-Slavery Society, Minutes, 1868–70, 9 April 1868, 11 June 1868; the Executive Committee of the Pennsylvania Anti-Slavery Society, Minutes, 17 June 1868, 16 September 1868.

33. *National Anti-Slavery Standard*, 19 December 1868.

34. *Thirty-Fifth Annual Report of the Philadelphia Female Anti-Slavery Society* (Philadelphia: Merrihew and Son, Printers, 1869), 1–5.

35. Ibid., 6.

36. Ibid., 6–12.

37. Ibid., 12.

38. Ibid., 13–16.

39. Ibid., 17.

40. Ibid.

41. Ibid., 22. See William Gillette, *The Right to Vote: Politics and the Passage of the Fifteenth Amendment* (Baltimore: Johns Hopkins University Press, 1965).

42. *Thirty-fifth Annual Report*, 25.

43. Ibid., 26.

44. Ibid., 27.

45. Philadelphia Female Anti-Slavery Society, Minutes, 1868–70, 10 March 1870.

46. Mary Grew to Elizabeth Neall Gay, 15 March 1870, Gay Collection.

47. Philadelphia Female Anti-Slavery Society, Minutes, 1868–70, 24 March 1870.

48. *Thirty-Sixth and Final Annual Report of the Philadelphia Female Anti-Slavery Society* (Philadelphia: Merrihew and Son, Printers, 1970), 35–37.

49. Philadelphia Female Anti-Slavery Society, Minutes, 1868–70, 24 March 1870.

50. *Memorial of Sarah Pugh*, 118.

51. *National Anti-Slavery Standard*, 27 November 1869.

52. Ibid.

53. *Philadelphia Public Ledger*, 6 May 1870.

54. Ibid.

55. Executive Committee of the Pennsylvania Anti-Slavery Society, Minutes, 1856–70.

56. *Thirty-Sixth and Final Annual Report*, 3.

57. Ibid., 5. Pennsylvania required the maintenance of segregated schools from 1854 to 1881. See Brown, "Pennsylvania and the Rights of the Negro," 54–56.

58. *Thirty-Sixth and Final Annual Report*, 5.

59. Ibid., 9.

60. Ibid., 10.

61. Ibid., 15.

62. Ibid., 16.

63. Ibid., 23.

64. Ibid., 28.

65. Ibid.

66. Ibid.

67. Ibid., 29.

68. Mary Grew to William Lloyd Garrison, 2 April 1870, Garrison Papers.

69. Ibid.

70. Ibid. There are two excellent studies of Garrison: Merrill, *Against Wind and Tide;* and John L. Thomas, *The Liberator: William Lloyd Garrison* (Boston: Little, Brown and Co., 1963).

Chapter 7. The Campaign for Woman Suffrage (1869–1973)

1. Eleanor Flexner, *Century of Struggle: The Woman's Rights Movement in the United States* (Cambridge: Harvard University Press, Belknap Press, 1959), 14–17, 340. See also Sara M. Evans, *Born for Liberty: A History of Women in America* (New York: Free Press, 1989).

2. Bertha M. Stearns, "A Speculation Concerning Charles Brockden Brown," *Pennsylvania Magazine of History and Biography* 59 (April 1935): 99–105.

3. See above, chap. 1.

4. Maynard, "World's Anti-Slavery Convention," 452–71.

5. Cromwell, *Lucretia Mott*, 128.

6. Stanton, Anthony, and Gage, *History of Woman Suffrage* 1:67–77.

7. Ibid., 70–73.

8. Dahlinger, "Dawn of the Woman's Movement," 73–78.

9. *Laws of the General Assembly of the Commonwealth of Pennsylvania, Passed at the Session of 1848* (Harrisburg: J. M. G. Lescure, Printer to the State, 1848), 536–38.

10. Dahlinger, "Dawn of the Woman's Movement," 78–83; see also Charles W. O'Brien, "The Growth in Pennsylvania of the Property Rights of Married Women," *American Law Register* 49 (September 1901): 524–30.

11. Theodore Stanton and Harriet Stanton Blatch, eds., *Elizabeth Cady Stanton, as Revealed in Her Letters, Diary, and Reminiscences*, 2 vols. (New York: Harper and Brow., 1922), 2:22.

12. *Philadelphia Public Ledger,* 20 September 1848.

13. Stanton, Anthony, and Gage, *History of Woman Suffrage* 1:821, 824, 825.

14. See above, pp. 55–56.

15. Stanton, Anthony, and Gage, *History of Woman Suffrage* 1:737.

16. Flexner, *Century of Struggle,* 110–11.

17. Stanton, Anthony, and Gage, *History of Woman Suffrage* 2:173–74.

18. Flexner, *Century of Struggle,* 142–43.

19. Robert E. Riegel, "The Split of the Feminist Movement in 1869," *Mississippi Valley Historical Review* 49 (December 1962): 485–96. For a more recent interpretation of the events leading up to the formation of these two organizations, see Ellen Carol DuBois, *Feminism and Suffrage: The Emergence of an Independent Women's Movement in America, 1848–1869* (Ithaca: Cornell University Press, 1978).

20. Flexner, *Century of Struggle,* 152–53, 220.

21. Stanton, Anthony, and Gage, *History of Woman Suffrage* 3:457.

22. Jennie B. Roessing, "The Equal Suffrage Campaign in Pennsylvania," *Annals of the American Academy of Political and Social Science* 56 (1914): 153.

23. Stanton, Anthony, and Gage, *History of Woman Suffrage* 3:461.

24. *Woman's Journal,* 8 January 1870.

25. Ibid.

26. Ibid., 15 January 1870.

27. Mary Grew to Wendell Phillips, 12 August 1870, Crawford Blagden Collection.

28. Ibid.

29. Ibid.

30. Ibid.

31. Mary Grew to Lucy Stone, 19 October 1870, National American Woman Suffrage Association Papers, Library of Congress.

32. *Woman's Journal,* 19 November 1870.

33. Ibid.

34. Ibid.

35. Ibid.

36. Mary Elizabeth (Mrs. John T.) Sargent, ed., *Sketches and Reminiscences of the Radical Club of Chestnut Street, Boston* (Boston: James R. Osgood and Co., 1880), preface. See also Stow Persons, *Free Religion: An American Faith* (New Haven: Yale University Press, 1947), 38–39.

37. Sargent, *Sketches,* preface.

38. Ibid., 118.

39. Ibid., 121.

40. Ibid., 119.

41. John Greenleaf Whittier, *Poetical Works* 4 vols. (Boston and New York: Houghton, Mifflin and Co., 1904), 4:126–27.

42. Mary Grew to Ann Phillips, 24 February 1871, Crawford Blagden Collection.

43. Ibid.

44. Ibid.

45. Mary Grew to Elizabeth Neall Gay, 23 March 1871, Gay Collection.

46. Stanton, Anthony, and Gage, *History of Woman Suffrage* 2:814–15.

47. Mary Grew to Henry Blackwell and Lucy Stone, 3 June 1871, National American Woman Suffrage Association Papers.

48. Mary Grew to Elizabeth Neall Gay, 14 October 1871, 20 October 1871, Gay Collection. In a letter to John K. Wildman, 7 November 1871, Lucy Stone wrote, "Please say to dear good, clear eyed Mary Grew, that my one wish, in regard to Mrs. Woodhull is that, [neither] she nor her ideas, may be so much as heard of at our meeting." In Leslie Wheeler, ed., *Loving Warriors: Selected Letters of Lucy Stone and Henry B. Blackwell, 1853 to 1893* (New York: Dial Press, 1981), 240.

49. *Woman's Journal,* 2 December 1871.

50. Ibid., 9 December 1871.

51. Mary Grew to Elizabeth Neall Gay, 20 February 1872, Gay Collection.

52. Ibid., 21 February 1872.

53. Mary Grew to Ann Phillips, 21 April 1872, Crawford Blagden Collection.

54. Ibid.

55. Ibid.

56. Ibid.

57. Ibid.

58. Mary Grew to Lucy Stone, 8 October 1872, National American Woman Suffrage Association Papers.

59. *Woman's Journal,* 26 October 1872.

60. Ibid., 7 December 1872.

61. Ibid.

62. Ibid.

63. Ibid.

64. Ibid., 14 December 1872.

65. A. D. Harlan, ed., *Pennsylvania Constitutional Convention of 1872 and 1873: Its Members and Officers and the Result of Their Labors* (Philadelphia: Inquirer Book and Job Printers, 1873).

66. *Woman's Journal,* 25 January 1873.

67. Ibid. Report by John K. Wildman.

68. Ibid.

69. Ibid.

70. *Debates of the Convention to Amend the Constitution of Pennsylvania,* etc., 9 vols. (Harrisburg: Benjamin Singerly, State Printer 1873), 1:503, 523–25.

71. *Philadelphia Public Ledger,* 8 February 1873.

72. *Debates of the Convention* 1:525–38. For preliminary exploration of the woman suffrage issue in this convention, I am indebted to a seminar paper by one of my former students, Mrs. Katherine Y. Armitage.

73. Ibid. 5:186–87.

74. *Woman's Journal,* 15 February 1873.

75. Ibid., 22 March 1873.

76. Mary Grew to Lucy Stone, 20 February 1873, National American Woman Suffrage Association Papers.

77. Mary Grew to Henry Blackwell, 11 March 1873, ibid.

Chapter 8. Keeping the Faith (1873–1896)

1. *Woman's Journal,* 27 December 1873.

2. Ibid.

3. Ibid.

4. Ibid.

5. Ibid., 10 and 24 October 1874.

6. Ibid., 28 November 1874.

7. Mary Grew to William Lloyd Garrison, 17 March 1875, Garrison Papers.

8. Mary Grew to Lucy Stone, 5 April 1875, National American Woman Suffrage Association Papers.

9. *Woman's Journal,* 4 December 1875.

10. Flexner, *Century of Struggle,* 170–72.

11. *Woman's Journal,* 8 July 1876.

12. Ibid., 28 October 1876, 4 November 1876.

13. Mrs. F. C. Albrecht, comp., *Annals of the New Century Club, 1877–1935* (Philadelphia: Press of J. M. Armstrong, 1937?), 7–15.

14. Lucretia L. Blankenburg, *The Blankenburgs of Philadelphia, by One of Them* (Philadelphia: The John C. Winston Co., 1928), 120.

15. Albrecht, *Annals of the New Century Club,* 16–18. See also Claire E. Fox, "Eliza L. Sproat Randolph Turner," in James, *Notable American Women* 3:485–86.

16. Mary Grew to William Lloyd Garrison, 2 April 1877, Garrison Papers.

17. *Woman's Journal,* 30 November 1878.

18. Mary Grew to Lucy Stone, 1879, National American Woman Suffrage Papers.

19. *Woman's Journal,* 22 November 1879.

20. Ibid., 4 September 1880.

21. Mary Grew to Lucretia Mott, 8 September 1880, Mott Manuscripts, Friends Historical Library of Swarthmore College.

22. *Philadelphia Public Ledger,* 13 November 1880.

23. *Woman's Journal,* 15 January 1881.

24. Ibid.

25. *Woman's Journal,* 17 December 1881.

26. Mary Grew to *Woman's Journal,* 20 July 1882, published 29 July 1882.

27. *Woman's Journal,* 25 November 1882. Report by John K. Wildman, vice president.

28. Mary Grew to Lucy Stone, 22 August 1883, National American Woman Suffrage, Association Papers.

29. *Commemoration of the Fiftieth Anniversary of the Organization of the American Anti-Slavery Society, in Philadelphia* (Philadelphia: Thos. S. Dando and Co., 1884), 22–25.

30. Flexner, *Century of Struggle,* 175.

31. Mary Grew to Henry Blackwell, 9 April 1884, National American Woman Suffrage Association Papers.

32. Woman's Journal, 16 August 1884. There is a biographical sketch of Sarah Pugh by Larry Gara in James, *Notable American Women* 3 : 104–5.

33. *Woman's Journal*, 3 January 1885.

34. Mary Grew to Elizabeth Neall Gay, 23 February 1885, Gay Collection.

35. Ibid., 17 July 1885.

36. Ibid., 1 October 1885.

37. *Woman's Journal*, 26 December 1885.

38. Ibid., 5 June 1886.

39. Ibid., 23 October 1886, 13 November 1886.

40. Mary Grew et al. to Lucy Stone, 1 April 1887, National American Woman Suffrage Association Papers.

41. *Woman's Journal*, 12 November 1887.

42. Quoted in Elizabeth Cazden, *Antoinette Brown Blackwell: A Biography* (Old Westbury, N.Y.: Feminist Press, 1983), 221.

43. *Woman's Journal*, 19 May 1888, 16 June 1888, 8 December 1888, 29 December 1888.

44. Ibid., 5 January 1889.

45. Ibid., 9 November 1889, 16 November 1889.

46. Mary Grew to Lucy Stone, 28 March 1890, National American Woman Suffrage Association Papers.

47. Mary Grew to Elizabeth Neall Gay, 12 September 1890, Gay Collection.

48. *Woman's Journal*, 20 December 1890.

49. Ibid., 21 April 1891.

50. Ibid., 10 October 1891.

51. Ibid., 5 December 1891.

52. Mary Grew to Isabel Howland, 27 April 1892, Howland Papers, Sophia Smith Collection.

53. Ibid.

54. Mary Grew to Maria Mott Davis, 29 June 1892, Mott Manuscripts, Friends Historical Library of Swarthmore College.

55. Ibid.

56. Ibid.

57. Ibid.

58. *Woman's Journal*, 17 December 1892.

59. Ibid., 24 December 1892.

60. See sketch in James, *Notable American Women* 1 : 170–71; and Blankenburg, *Blankenburgs of Philadelphia.*

61. Mary Grew to Elizabeth Neall Gay, 16 January 1893, Gay Collection.

62. Ibid., 19 January 1893.

63. Ibid., 5 March 1893.

64. Ibid., 3 July 1893.

65. Ibid.

66. Mary Grew to "Mrs. Cheney," 10 May 1894.

67. Mary Grew to Elizabeth Neall Gay, 13 January 1894, Gay Collection.

68. Ibid., 10 January 1894.

69. Ibid., 28 April 1894.

70. Ibid., 22 June 1894.

71. Ibid., 7 August 1894.

72. Mary Grew to Elizabeth Neall Gay, 14 September 1894, Gay Collection.

73. Ibid., 16 September 1894.

74. Ibid., 28 September 1894.

75. Ibid., 24 October 1894, 2 November 1894, 11 December 1894, Gay Collection.

76. Ibid., 11 December 1894.

77. Mary Grew to Elizabeth Neall Gay, 15 January 1895, Gay Collection.

78. Ibid., 21 June 1895.

79. Ibid., 25 August 1895.

80. *Philadelphia Public Ledger,* 12 October 1896.

81. Copy of will kindly supplied by Register of Wills, Philadelphia County, 17 August 1961.

82. *Woman's Journal,* 17 October 1896.

83. Ibid.

84. Ibid.

In Retrospect

1. 2 Tim. 4:7 (KJV).

12. Quoted in Lee Virginia Chambers-Schiller, *Liberty, a Better Husband: Single Women in America, The Generations of 1780–1840* (New Haven: Yale University Press, 1984), 210.

3. *Turning the World Upside Down: The Anti-Slavery Convention of American Women, Held in New York City May 9–12, 1837,* with an introduction by Dorothy Sterling (New York: Feminist Press at the City University of New York, 1987), 3.

4. Lillian O'Connor, *Pioneer Woman Orators: Rhetoric in the Ante-Bellum Reform Movement* (New York: Columbia University Press, 1954), 73–74.

5. Lawrence J. Friedman, *Gregarious Saints: Self and Community in American Abolitionism, 1830–1870* (New York: Cambridge University Press, 1982).

6. Heb. 13:3 (KJV).

7. Whittier, *Poetical Works,* 4:127.

Bibliography

Bibliographies

Blair, Karen J. *The History of American Women's Voluntary Organizations, 1810–1960: A Guide to Sources.* Boston: G. K. Hall and Co., 1989.

Dumond, Dwight Lowell. *A Bibliography of Antislavery in America.* 1961. Ann Arbor: University of Michigan Press, 1967.

Filler, Louis. *Crusade against Slavery: Friends, Foes, and Reforms, 1820–1860.* Algonac, Mich.: Reference Publications, 1986. Has a noteworthy, up-to-date bibliography.

Freidel, Frank, ed. *Harvard Guide to American History.* Rev. ed. 2 vols. Cambridge: Harvard University Press, Belknap Press, 1974.

Trussell, John B. B., Jr. *Pennsylvania Historical Bibliography.* Additions through 1982. 5 vols. Harrisburg: Pennsylvania Historical and Museum Commission, 1979–86.

Wall, Carol, ed. *Bibliography of Pennsylvania History: A Supplement.* Harrisburg: Pennsylvania Historical and Museum Commission, 1976. Covers period 1953–67 inclusive.

Wilkinson, Norman, comp. *Bibliography of Pennsylvania History.* Harrisburg: Pennsylvania Historical and Museum Commission, 1957.

Primary Sources

MANUSCRIPTS

Garrison Family Papers. Sophia Smith Collection. Smith College.

Garrison, William Lloyd. Papers. Antislavery Collection. Boston Public Library.

Gay, Sydney Howard, and Elizabeth Neall Gay. Papers. Butler Library, Columbia University.

Grew, Henry. Will. Register of Wills, Philadelphia County.

Grew, Mary. Diary of Trip to Great Britain, 1840. Schlesinger Library, Radcliffe College.

Grew, Mary. Will. Register of Wills, Philadelphia County.

Hartford Female Seminary. Records. Connecticut Historical Society, Hartford.

Howland, Isabel. Papers. Sophia Smith Collection. Smith College.

Mott, Lucretia. Manuscripts. Friends Historical Library, Swarthmore College.

National American Woman Suffrage Association. Papers. Library of Congress.

Pennsylvania Anti-Slavery Society. Minute Books, 1838–46; Executive Committee Minute Books, 1846–56, 1856–70. Historical Society of Pennsylvania, Philadelphia. Available on reel 31 of the Microfilm Publication of the Papers of the

Pennsylvania Abolition Society at the Historical Society of Pennsylvania. University Microfilms International.

Pennsylvania Hall Association. Minute Book of the Board of Managers. Historical Society of Pennsylvania.

Philadelphia Female Anti-Slavery Society. Minute Books, 1833–38, 1838–39, 1839–44, 1845–48, 1848–62, 1862–67, 1868–70; Board of Managers. Minute Books, 1833–36, 1836–39, 1839–41; Incoming Correspondence, 1834–47, 1849–53. Historical Society of Pennsylvania. Available on reels 30 and 31 of the Microfilm Publication of the Papers of the Pennsylvania Abolition Society at the Historical Society of Pennsylvania. University Microfilms International.

Phillips, Wendell. Papers. Crawford Blagden Collection. Houghton Library, Harvard University.

Whittier, John Greenleaf. Manuscripts. Friends Historical Library, Swarthmore College.

PRINTED SOURCES

American Anti-Slavery Society. *Commemoration of the Fiftieth Anniversary of the Organization of the American Anti-Slavery Society, in Philadelphia.* Philadelphia: Thos. S. Dando and Co., 1884.

American Anti-Slavery Society. *Proceedings of the American Anti-Slavery Society, at Its Second Decade, Held in the City of Philadelphia, Dec. 3d, 4th, & 5th, 1853.* New York: American Anti-Slavery Society, 1854.

American Anti-Slavery Society. *Proceedings of the American Anti-Slavery Society at Its Third Decade, Held in the City of Philadelphia, Dec. 3d and 4th, 1863.* New York: American Anti-Slavery Society, 1864.

American Anti-Slavery Society. *Sixth Annual Report of the Executive Committee of the American Anti-Slavery Society.* New York: William S. Dorr, 1839.

Anti-Slavery Convention of American Women. *Proceedings of the Anti-Slavery Convention of American Women.* 3 vols. New York and Philadelphia, 1837–39. The 1837 proceedings have been reprinted under the title *Turning the World Upside Down.* New York: Feminist Press at the City University of New York, 1987.

Beecher, Catharine Esther. *Suggestions Respecting Improvements in Education, Presented to the Trustees of the Hartford Female Seminary and Published at Their Request.* Hartford, Conn.: Packard and Butler, 1829.

British and Foreign Anti-Slavery Society. *Invitation to the London General Conference to Commence on June 12, 1840.* London, 1839.

Debates of the Convention to Amend the Constitution of Pennsylvania, etc. 9 vols. Harrisburg, Pa.: Benjamin Singerly, State Printer, 1873.

Garrison, Wendell Phillips, and Francis Jackson Garrison. *William Lloyd Garrison: The Story of His Life Told by His Children.* 4 vols. 1885–89. Reprint. New York: Negro Universities Press, 1969.

[Grew, Mary.] *Narrative of Facts in the Case of Passmore Williamson.* Philadelphia: Pennsylvania Anti-Slavery Society, 1855.

Harlan, A. D., ed. *Pennsylvania Constitutional Convention of 1872 and 1873: Its Members and Officers and the Result of Their Labors.* Philadelphia: Inquirer Book and Job Printers, 1873.

Hartford Female Seminary. *Catalogue of the Officers, Teachers, and Pupils of the Hartford Female Seminary, for the Two Terms of 1829.* Bound with Beecher, *Suggestions.* Both of these items are available in the microfilm *History of Women.* Reel 126, no. 820. New Haven, Conn.: Research Publications, 1975.

Lasser, Carol, and Marlene Deahl Merrill, eds. *Friends and Sisters: Letters between Lucy Stone and Antoinette Brown Blackwell, 1846–1893.* Urbana: University of Illinois Press, 1987.

[Lovell, Laura H.]. *Report of a Delegate to the Anti-Slavery Convention of American Women, Held in Philadelphia, May, 1838.* Boston: I. Knapp, 1838.

Memorial of Sarah Pugh: A Tribute of Respect from Her Cousins. Philadelphia: J. B. Lippincott Co., 1888.

Merrill, Walter M., and Louis Ruchames, eds. *The Letters of William Lloyd Garrison.* 6 vols. Cambridge: Harvard University Press, Belknap Press, 1971–81.

Philadelphia Female Anti-Slavery Society. *Address of the Female Anti-Slavery Society of Philadelphia, to the Women of Pennsylvania, with the Form of a Petition to the Congress of the U. States.* Philadelphia: Merrihew and Gunn, Printers, 1836.

Philadelphia Female Anti-Slavery Society. *Annual Reports,* 1834–70.

Rosine Association of Philadelphia. *Reports and Realities from the Sketch-Book of a Manager of the Rosine Association, December 1855.* Philadelphia: J. Duress, Printers, 1855.

Sargent, Mary Elizabeth (Mrs. John T.), ed. *Sketches and Reminiscences of the Radical Club of Chestnut Street, Boston.* Boston: James R. Osgood and Co., 1880.

Stanton, Elizabeth Cady, *History of Woman Suffrage.* Edited by Susan B. Anthony and Matilda Joslyn Gage, 6 vols. 1881–1922. Reprint. New York: Arno Press, 1969.

Stanton, Theodore, and Harriet Stanton Blatch, eds. *Elizabeth Cady Stanton, as Revealed in Her Letters, Diary, and Reminiscences.* 2 vols. New York: Harper and Bros., 1922.

Tolles, Frederick B., ed. *Slavery and "The Woman Question": Lucretia Mott's Diary of Her Visit to Great Britain to Attend the World's Anti-Slavery Convention of 1840.* Supplement no. 23 to the *Journal of the Friends' Historical Society* (London, 1952).

[Webb, Samuel.] *History of Pennsylvania Hall, Which Was Destroyed by a Mob, on the 17th of May, 1838.* Philadelphia: Merrihew and Gunn, Printers, 1838.

Wheeler, Leslie, ed. *Loving Warriors: Selected Letters of Lucy Stone and Henry B. Blackwell, 1853 to 1893.* New York: Dial Press, 1981.

Whittier, John Greenleaf. *Poetical Works.* 4 vols. Houghton, Mifflin and Co., 1904.

World's Anti-Slavery Convention. *Proceedings of the General Anti-Slavery Convention Called by the Committee of the British and Foreign Anti-Slavery Society, and Held in London from Friday, June 12th, to Tuesday, June 23rd, 1840.* London, 1841.

NEWSPAPERS

The Liberator (Boston), 1831–65.

Pennsylvania Freeman (Philadelphia), 1836–54. Originally called the *National Enquirer* (1836–38).

National Anti-Slavery Standard (New York), 1854–70.

The Woman's Journal (Boston), 1870–96.
Philadelphia Public Ledger. Scattered issues.

Secondary Works

BOOKS

Albrecht, Mrs. F. C., comp. *Annals of the New Century Club, 1877–1935.* Philadelphia: Press of J. M. Armstrong, 1937?

Bacon, Margaret Hope. *Mothers of Feminism: The Story of Quaker Women in America.* San Francisco: Harper and Row, Publishers, 1986.

———. *Valiant Friend: The Life of Lucretia Mott.* New York: Walker and Co., 1980.

Barry, Kathleen. *Susan B. Anthony: A Biography of a Singular Feminist.* New York and London: New York University Press, 1988.

Bemis, Samuel Flagg. *John Quincy Adams and the Union.* New York: Alfred A. Knopf, 1956.

Biddle, Gertrude B., and Sarah D. Lowrie, eds. *Notable Women of Pennsylvania.* Philadelphia: University of Pennsylvania Press, 1942.

Bingham, Theodore A., comp. *Genealogy of the Bingham Family in the United States.* Harrisburg, Pa.: Harrisburg Publishing Co., 1898.

Blackwell, Alice Stone. *Lucy Stone: Pioneer of Woman's Rights.* Boston: Little, Brown and Co., 1930.

Blankenburg, Lucretia L. *The Blankenburgs of Philadelphia, by One of Them.* Philadelphia: The John C. Winston Co., 1928.

Boydston, Jeanne, Mary Kelley, and Anne Margolis. *The Limits of Sisterhood: The Beecher Sisters on Women's Rights and Woman's Sphere.* Chapel Hill: University of North Carolina Press, 1988.

Breault, Judith Colussi. *The World of Emily Howland: Odyssey of a Humanitarian.* Millbrae, Calif.: Les Femmes, 1976.

Campbell, Stanley W. *The Slave Catchers: Enforcement of the Fugitive Slave Law, 1850–1860.* Chapel Hill: University of North Carolina Press, 1968.

Cazden, Elizabeth. *Antoinette Brown Blackwell: A Biography.* Old Westbury, N.Y.: Feminist Press, 1983.

Centennial Memorial of the First Baptist Church of Hartford, Connecticut. Hartford: Privately printed, 1890.

Chambers-Schiller, Lee Virginia. *Liberty, A Better Husband: Single Women in America, The Generations of 1780–1840.* New Haven: Yale University Press, 1984.

Chester, Giraud. *Embattled Maiden: The Life of Anna Dickinson.* New York: Putnam, 1951.

Cott, Nancy F. *The Bonds of Womanhood: "Woman's Sphere" in New England.* New Haven: Yale University Press, 1977.

Cromwell, Otelia. *Lucretia Mott.* Cambridge: Harvard University Press, 1958.

Degler, Carl N. *At Odds: Women and the Family in America from the Revolution to the Present.* New York: Oxford University Press, 1980.

Dillon, Merton L. *Benjamin Lundy and the Struggle for Negro Freedom.* Urbana: University of Illinois Press, 1966.

DuBois, Ellen Carol. *Feminism and Suffrage: The Emergence of an Independent Women's Movement in America, 1848–1869.* Ithaca: Cornell University Press, 1978.

Dumond, Dwight Lowell. *Antislavery: The Crusade for Freedom in America.* Ann Arbor: University of Michigan Press, 1961.

Evans, Sara M. *Born for Liberty: A History of Women in America.* New York: Free Press, 1989.

Fladeland, Betty. *Men and Brothers: Anglo-American Antislavery Cooperation.* Urbana: University of Illinois Press, 1972.

Flexner, Eleanor. *Century of Struggle: The Woman's Rights Movement in the United States.* Cambridge: Harvard University Press, Belknap Press, 1959.

Foner, Eric. *Reconstruction: America's Unfinished Revolution, 1863–1877.* New York: Harper & Row, 1988.

Franklin, John Hope. *The Emancipation Proclamation.* Garden City, N.Y.: Doubleday, 1963.

Friedman, Lawrence J. *Gregarious Saints: Self and Community in American Abolitionism, 1830–1870.* New York: Cambridge University Press, 1982.

Gara, Larry. *Liberty Line: The Legend of the Underground Railroad.* Lexington: University of Kentucky Press, 1961.

Garrison, Francis Jackson. *Ann Phillips, Wife of Wendell Phillips: A Memorial Sketch.* Boston: Privately printed, 1886.

Geary, Sister M. Theophane. *A History of Third Parties in Pennsylvania, 1840–1860.* Washington, D.C.: Catholic University of America, 1938.

Gillette, William. *The Right to Vote: Politics and the Passage of the Fifteenth Amendment.* Baltimore: Johns Hopkins University Press, 1965.

Griffith, Elisabeth. *In Her Own Right: The Life of Elizabeth Cady Stanton.* New York: Oxford University Press, 1984.

Hallowell, Anna Davis. *James and Lucretia Mott: Life and Letters.* Boston: Houghton, Mifflin and Co., 1884.

Harveson, Mae Elizabeth. *Catharine Esther Beecher: Pioneer Educator.* Philadelphia: Privately printed, 1932.

Hays, Elinor Rice. *Morning Star: A Biography of Lucy Stone, 1818–1893.* New York: Harcourt, Brace and World, 1961.

Hensel, William U. *The Christiana Riot and the Treason Trials of 1851.* Lancaster, Pa.: New Era Printing Co., 1911.

Hersh, Blanche Glassman. *The Slavery of Sex: Feminist-Abolitionists in America.* Urbana: University of Illinois Press, 1978.

James, Edward T., Janet Wilson James, and Paul S. Boyer, eds. *Notable American Women, 1607–1950: A Biographical Dictionary.* 3 vols. Cambridge: Harvard University Press, Belknap Press, 1971.

James, Joseph B. *The Framing of the Fourteenth Amendment.* Urbana: University of Illinois Press, 1956.

Kraditor, Aileen S. *Means and Ends in American Abolitionism: Garrison and His Critics on Strategy and Tactics, 1834–1850.* New York: Vintage Books, 1970.

Kugler, Israel. *From Ladies to Women: The Organized Struggle for Woman's Rights in the Reconstruction Era.* Westport, Conn.: Greenwood Press, 1987.

Lerner, Gerda. *The Grimké Sisters from South Carolina: Rebels against Slavery.* Boston: Houghton Mifflin Co., 1967.

———. *The Majority Finds Its Past: Placing Women in History.* New York: Oxford University Press, 1979.

Lutz, Alma. *Crusade for Freedom: Women of the Antislavery Movement.* Boston: Beacon Press, 1968.

McLoughlin, William G. *New England Dissent, 1630–1833: The Baptists and the Separation of Church and State.* 2 vols. Cambridge: Harvard University Press, 1971.

McPherson, James M. *The Abolitionist Legacy, from Reconstruction to the NAACP.* Princeton: Princeton University Press, 1975.

———. *Battle Cry of Freedom: The Civil War Era.* New York: Oxford University Press, 1988.

———. *Ordeal by Fire: The Civil War and Reconstruction.* New York: Alfred A. Knopf, 1982.

———. *The Struggle for Equality: Abolitionists and the Negro in the Civil War and Reconstruction.* Princeton, N.J.: Princeton University Press, 1964.

Melder, Keith E. *Beginnings of Sisterhood: The Amerian Woman's Rights Movement, 1800–1850.* New York: Schocken Books, 1977.

Merrill, Walter M. *Against Wind and Tide: A Biography of William Lloyd Garrison.* Cambridge: Harvard University Press, 1963.

Morris, Thomas D. *Free Men All: The Personal Liberty Laws of the North, 1780–1861.* Baltimore: The Johns Hopkins University Press, 1974.

Nevins, Allan. *Ordeal of the Union.* 2 vols. New York: Charles Scribner's Sons, 1947.

Nuermberger, Ruth K. *The Free Produce Movement: A Quaker Protest against Slavery.* Durham, N.C.: Duke University Press, 1942.

O'Connor, Lillian. *Pioneer Woman Orators: Rhetoric in the Ante-Bellum Reform Movement.* New York: Columbia University Press, 1954.

Paludan, Phillip Shaw. *"A People's Contest": The Union and Civil War, 1861–1865.* New York: Harper and Row, 1988.

Pease, Jane H., and William H. Pease. *Bound with Them in Chains: A Biographical History of the Antislavery Movement.* Westport, Conn.: Greenwood Press, 1972.

Perry, Lewis. *Radical Abolitionism: Anarchy and the Government of God in Antislavery Thought.* Ithaca: Cornell University Press, 1973.

Perry, Lewis, and Michael Fellman, eds. *Antislavery Reconsidered: New Perspectives on the Abolitionists.* Baton Rouge: Louisiana State University Press, 1979.

Persons, Stow. *Free Religion: An American Faith.* New Haven: Yale University Press, 1947.

Potter, David M. *The Impending Crisis, 1848–1861.* New York: Harper and Row, 1976.

Ratner, Lorman. *Powder Keg: Northern Opposition to the Antislavery Movement, 1831–1840.* New York: Basic Books, 1968.

Rose, Willie Lee. *Rehearsal for Reconstruction: The Port Royal Experiment.* Indianapolis, Ind.: Bobbs-Merrill, 1964.

Ryan, Mary P. *Women in Public: Between Banners and Ballots, 1825–1880.* Baltimore: Johns Hopkins University Press, 1990.

Sewell, Richard H. *A House Divided: Sectionalism and Civil War, 1848–1865.* Baltimore: Johns Hopkins University Press, 1988.

Sherwin, Oscar. *Prophet of Liberty: The Life and Times of Wendell Phillips.* New York: Bookman Associates, 1858.

Sklar, Kathryn Kish. *Catharine Beecher: A Study in American Domesticity.* New Haven: Yale University Press, 1973.

Smith-Rosenberg, Carroll. *Disorderly Conduct: Visions of Gender in Victorian America.* New York: Alfred A. Knopf, 1985.

Sorin, Gerald. *Abolitionism: A New Perspective.* New York: Praeger Publishers, 1972.

Stewart, James Brewer. *Holy Warriors: The Abolitionists and American Slavery.* New York: Hill and Wang, 1976.

———. *Wendell Phillips: Liberty's Hero.* Baton Rouge: Louisiana State University Press, 1986.

Temperley, Howard. *British Antislavery, 1833–1870.* Columbia: University of South Carolina Press, 1972.

Thomas, John L. *The Liberator: William Lloyd Garrison.* Boston: Little, Brown and Co., 1963.

Trefousse, Hans L. *Andrew Johnson: A Biography.* New York: W. W. Norton and Co., 1989.

Walters, Ronald G. *The Antislavery Appeal: American Abolitionism after 1830.* Baltimore: Johns Hopkins University Press, 1976.

Welter, Barbara. *Dimity Convictions: The American Woman in the Nineteenth Century.* Athens: Ohio University Press, 1976.

Winch, Julie. *Philadelphia's Black Elite: Activism, Accommodation, and the Struggle for Autonomy, 1787–1848.* Philadelphia: Temple Universityy Press, 1988.

Woloch, Nancy. *Women and the American Experience.* New York: Alfred A. Knopf, 1984.

ARTICLES

Alexander, A. John. "The Ideas of Lysander Spooner." *New England Quarterly* 23 (June 1950): 200–217.

Boromé, Joseph A. "The Vigilant Committee of Philadelphia." *Pennsylvania Magazine of History and Biography* 92 (July 1968): 320–51.

Brown, Ira V. "'Am I Not a Woman and a Sister?': The Anti-Slavery Convention of American Women, 1837–1839." *Pennsylvania History* 50 (January 1983): 1–19.

———. "Cradle of Feminism: The Philadelphia Female Anti-Slavery Society, 1833–1840." *Pennsylvania Magazine of History and Biography* 102 (April 1978): 143–66.

———. "Miller McKim and Pennsylvania Abolitionism." *Pennsylvania History* 30 (January 1963): 56–72.

———. "Pennsylvania and the Rights of the Negro." *Pennsylvania History* 28 (January 1961): 45–57.

———. "Racism and Sexism: The Case of Pennsylvania Hall." *Phylon* 37 (June 1976): 126–36.

———. "William D. Kelley and Radical Reconstruction." *Pennsylvania Magazine of History and Biography* 85 (July 1961): 316–29.

———. "The Woman's Rights Movement in Pennsylvania, 1848–1873." *Pennsylvania History* 32 (April 1965): 153–64.

Dahlinger, Charles W. "The Dawn of the Woman's Movement: An Account of the Origin and History of the Pennsylvania Married Woman's Property Law of 1848." *Western Pennsylvania Historical Magazine* 1 (1918): 66–84.

Eckert, Ralph Lowell. "Antislavery Martyrdom: The Ordeal of Passmore Williamson." *Pennsylvania Magazine of History and Biography* 100 (October 1976): 521–38.

Foner, Philip S. "The Battle to End Discrimination against Negroes on Philadelphia Streetcars." *Pennsylvania History* 40 (July 1973): 261–90, and (October 1973): 355–79.

Gara, Larry. "William Still and the Underground Railroad." *Pennsylvania History* 28 (January 1961): 33–44.

Geffen, Elizabeth M. "William Henry Furness: Philadelphia Antislavery Preacher." *Pennsylvania Magazine of History and Biography* 82 (July 1958): 259–92.

Ginzberg, Lori D. "'Moral Suasion Is Moral Balderdash': Women, Politics, and Social Activism in the 1850s." *Journal of American History* 73 (December 1986): 601–22.

"Grew, Miss Mary." In *A Woman of the Century: Fourteen Hundred-seventy Biographical Sketches Accompanied by Portraits of Leading American Women in All Walks of Life*, edited by Frances E. Willard and Mary A. Livermore, p. 341. Buffalo, Chicago, and New York: Charles Wells Moulton, 1893.

Lasser, Carol. "'Let Us Be Sisters Forever': The Sororal Model of Nineteenth-Century Female Friendship." *Signs: Journal of Women in Culture and Society,* 14 (Autumn 1988): 158–81.

"Mary Grew—Reformer." *Woman's Progress* 1 (April 1893): 1–8.

Maynard, Douglas H. "The World's Anti-Slavery Convention of 1840." *Mississippi Valley Historical Review* 47 (December 1960): 452–71.

Nash, Roderick W. "William Parker and the Christiana Riot." *Journal of Negro History* 46 (January 1961): 24–31.

O'Brien, Charles W. "The Growth in Pennsylvania of the Property Rights of Married Women." *American Law Register* 49 (September 1901): 524–30.

Reede, Arthur H. "Whittier's Pennsylvania Years, 1837–1840." *Pennsylvania History* 25 (October 1958): 384–409.

Riegel, Robert E. "The Split of the Feminist Movement in 1869." *Mississippi Valley Historical Review* 49 (December 1962): 485–96.

Roessing, Jennie B. "The Equal Suffrage Campaign in Pennsylvania." *Annals of the American Academy of Political and Social Sciences* 56 (1914): 153–60.

Rush, N. Orwin. "Lucretia Mott and the Philadelphia Antislavery Fairs." *Bulletin of Friends Historical Association* 35 (Autumn 1946): 69–75.

Smith-Rosenberg, Carroll. "The Female World of Love and Ritual—Relations between Women in Nineteenth-Century America." *Signs: Journal of Women in Culture and Society* 1 (Autumn 1975): 1–29.

Stearns, Bertha M. "A Speculation Concerning Charles Brockden Brown." *Pennsylvania Magazine of History and Biography* 59 (April 1936): 99–105.

Thomas, John L. "Romantic Reform in America, 1815–1865," *American Quarterly* 17 (Winter 1965): 656–81.

Wahl, Albert J. "The Pennsylvania Yearly Meeting of Progressive Friends." *Pennsylvania History* 25 (April 1958): 122–36.

Wilkinson, Norman B. "The Philadelphia Free Produce Attack upon Slavery." *Pennsylvania Magazine of History and Biography* 66 (July 1942): 294–313.

THESES

Cohen, William. "The Pennsylvania Anti-Slavery Society." M.A. thesis, Columbia University, 1960.

———. "James Miller McKim: Pennsylvania Abolitionist." Ph.D. thesis, New York University, 1968.

Hochreiter, Robert Stephen. "The *Pennsylvania Freeman*, 1836–1854." Ph.D. thesis, Pennsylvania State University, 1980.

King, Samuel A. "The Personal Liberty Laws." M.A. thesis, Pennsylvania State University, 1937.

Lloyd, William F. "The Roots of Fear: A History of Pennsylvania Hall." M.A. thesis, Pennsylvania State University, 1963.

Index